AA

Driving Test Theory and Practical

p

Produced by AA Publishing (a trading name of Automobile Association Developments Limited; registered number 1878835). A02806

First published by AA Publishing 2004
This edition produced for Parragon with revised questions 2005

Parragon
Queen Street House
4 Queen Street
Bath
BA1 1HE

ISBN-10: 0-7495-4833-9
ISBN-13: 978-0-7495-4833-9

Colour separation by Keene Group, Andover
Printed by Leo Paper Group, China

While every effort has been made to include the widest possible range of questions available at the time of printing, the Government may from time to time change, add or remove questions, and the publisher cannot be held responsible for questions that may appear on a question paper which were not available for inclusion in this book.

How do I get a free driving lesson?

Contents

Introduction

You want to pass the driving test and take advantage of the freedom and mobility that driving a car can give you. Do the following three things and you will achieve your goal of passing the driving test.

Acquire **knowledge** of the rules through your instructor and by studying *The Highway Code*. A key element is to test and reinforce your knowledge.

Take the right **attitude**. Be careful, courteous and considerate to all other road users.

Learn and understand the **skills** of driving by taking lessons from a trained and fully qualified driving instructor.

We're here to help you become a careful and safe driver and we've designed this book to help you take the first steps towards achieving your goal – preparing for your **Theory Test**.

Six essential steps to getting your licence

1. Get your Provisional licence

Use form D1, available from any Post Office, to apply for your provisional licence. The driving licence is issued in the form of a two-part document: a photo card and paper counterpart. So that you can legally begin learning to drive, at the appropriate date, you must be in possession of the correct licence documents. Take care when completing all the forms. Many licences cannot be issued for the required date because of errors or omissions on the application forms. You will have to provide proof of identity such as a current UK passport; make sure you have all the documents needed.

2. Learn *The Highway Code*

The Highway Code is essential reading for all drivers, not just those learning to drive. It sets out all the rules for good driving, as well as the rules for other road users such as pedestrians and motorcycle riders. When you have learned the rules you will be able to answer most of the questions in the Theory Test and be ready to start learning the driving skills you will need to pass your Practical Test.

3. Apply for and take the Theory Test

The driving test is in two parts: the Theory Test and the Practical Test.

Once you have a valid provisional licence you may take the Theory Test at any time, but you must pass it before you are allowed to apply for the Practical Test. However, it is important that you should not take your Theory Test too early in your course of practical lessons. This is because you need the experience of meeting real hazards while you are learning to drive, to help you pass the Hazard Perception element of the Theory Test.

You can book your Theory Test by post, by phone or online. MasterCard, Visa, Switch, Delta, Solo and Electron are accepted. Application forms are available from test centres, Approved Driving Instructors or by calling the booking number below. Forms need to be sent with a cheque, postal order or credit or debit card details.

By Post DSA (Driving Standards Agency), PO Box 148, Salford, M5 3SY
By Phone 0870 010 1372
Online www.dsa.gov.uk

4. Start to learn to drive

We recommended that you learn with an Approved Driving Instructor (ADI). Only an ADI may legally charge for providing tuition.

Choose an instructor or driving school by asking friends or relatives who they recommend. Price is important, so find out whether the school offers any discounts for blocks or courses of lessons paid in advance; if you decide to pay in advance, make sure the driving school is reputable. If lesson prices are very low, ask yourself 'why?' Check how long the lesson will last. And don't forget to ask about the car you'll be learning to drive in. Is it modern and reliable? Is it insured? Does it have dual controls?

The most efficient and cost-effective way to learn to drive is to accept that there is no short-cut approach to learning the necessary skills. Agree with your instructor on a planned course of tuition suited to your needs, take regular lessons, and don't skip weeks and expect to pick up where you left off. Ensure the full official syllabus is covered and, as your skills develop, get as much practice as possible with a relative or friend – but make sure they are legally able to supervise your practice. They must be over 21 years of age and have held a full driving licence for at least three years.

5. Apply for and take the Practical Test

Once you have passed the Theory Test, and with your instructor's guidance based on your progress, you can plan ahead for a suitable test date for the Practical Test.

You can book your Test by calling 0870 010 1372 between 8am and 6pm Monday to Friday. You can pay for your test using a credit or debit card. The person who books the test must be the cardholder.

Make sure you have the following details to hand when booking your Practical Test.

- Theory Test pass certificate number
- driver number shown on your licence
- driving school code number (if known)
- your preferred date
- unacceptable days or periods
- if you can accept a test at short notice
- disability or any special circumstances
- your credit/debit card details

Saturday and weekday evening tests are available at some driving test centres. The fee is higher than for a driving test during normal working hours on weekdays and evening tests are available during the summer months only.

Telephone bookings and enquiries
0870 010 1372

Facsimile
0870 010 2372

Welsh speakers
0870 010 0372

Minicom
0870 010 7372

6. Apply for your full driver's licence

To obtain a full licence you need to send your Pass Certificate and your provisional licence to the DVLA in Swansea, within two years of passing your Practical Test.

After the Practical Test

The Driving Standards Agency and the insurance industry recognise and seek to reward those drivers who enhance their basic skills and widen their experience by taking further training in the form of a Pass Plus scheme.

This is a six-module syllabus which covers town and rural driving, night driving, driving in adverse weather conditions, and on dual carriageways and motorways. It offers you the opportunity to gain more driving experience with the help of an instructor to hand. An increasing number of insurance companies are prepared to offer discounts to new drivers who have completed the course. There is no test to take at the end of the course.

More information

For more practical information on learning to drive including the Theory Test, Hazard Perception and the Practical Test visit www.theAA.com and www.dsa.gov.uk
For information on the Pass Plus scheme visit www.passplus.org.uk

How to use this book

This book is arranged in seven sections.

Part 1 explains what to expect and how to prepare for each part of the Test: Theory, Hazard Perception and Practical.

This section explains how to take the Theory Test using a touch-screen computer and gives details of the video clips used in the Hazard Perception part of the test. In the Practical section we have included information about the Driver's Record which your instructor will complete after each lesson.

We tell you what to expect on the day you take your test, details of the documents you must have with you, and tell you what the examiner will be looking for in your general driving.

We have also included information on the new Vehicle Safety Check questions which now form part of the Practical Test.

Part 2 contains questions and answers for learner drivers set by the experts at the AA driving school as an aid to help you pass your Practical Test. They are designed to test your knowledge of what is required before you even sit in the driver's seat. Topics include parallel parking, reversing and motorway driving.

Part 3 is designed to help you understand each of the 14 topics in the Theory Test. This section will tell you what type of questions you can expect in each section and we've included lots of helpful tips. Each topic is colour coded to its

Learn to drive in a modern car with a reputable driving school

relevant section in Part 4 of this book, which contains all the official Theory Questions. Experience has taught us that learner drivers find particular questions difficult and are often confused when they see questions which are similar. Reading through the background to each topic, before looking at the questions, will help you to avoid the pitfalls and help you to group questions together as you will often find several questions are asking the same thing but in a slightly different way.

Part 4 contains all the official Theory Test questions for car drivers which appear in the question bank of the DSA. You could be tested on any of these questions when you take your touch-screen Theory Test.

The questions are arranged in topics, such as Safety Margins and Rules of the Road. Each theme has its own colour band to help you find your way around. However, as you start to work through the questions you will soon discover that similar questions on the same topic may appear in different sections. Don't be put off by this, but read each question and the choice of answers very carefully. Similar questions may be asked in a slightly different way to test your knowledge.

Most of the Theory Test questions can be answered if you learn *The Highway Code*. However, you will only find the answers to some questions by talking to your driving instructor and learning about good driving practice on the road.

You'll find all the correct answers to the Theory Test questions in Part 6 at the back of the book, that way, you can easily test yourself to see what you are getting right and what you still need to work on.

Part 5 is a short glossary, which explains some of the more difficult words and terms used in the theory questions and *The Highway Code*. It's in alphabetical order and you can use this to check if you're not sure what a chicane is, for example, or what brake fade means.

Part 6 has all the answers to the 916 Theory Test questions.

Part 7 contains *The Highway Code* with its own index.

Part 1
The Tests: What to Expect

The Tests: What to Expect

You have to pass two driving tests before you can apply for a full driving licence – the Theory Test, including Hazard Perception, and the Practical Test. The Theory Test was introduced in 1996 to check that drivers know more than just how to operate a car, and the Hazard Perception element was introduced in 2001 to test learner drivers on their hazard awareness skills.

You are strongly recommended to prepare for the Theory Test and Hazard Perception at the same time as you develop your skills behind the wheel for the Practical Test. Obviously, there are many similarities between the two tests and you need the experience of meeting real hazards in order to pass the Hazard Perception element of the Theory Test.

It is all about making you a safer driver on today's busy roads. By preparing for both tests at the same time, you will reinforce your knowledge and understanding of all aspects of driving and you will improve your chances of passing both tests first time.

The Practical Test was extended in September 2003 to include Vehicle Safety Check questions that test the driver's ability to carry out basic procedures to ensure that the vehicle is safe to drive. Checks include the tyre tread and oil level.

You have to pass both the Hazard Perception test and the Theory Test questions. At the end of the test they will tell you your scores for both parts. Even if you only failed on one part of the Theory Test, you still have to take both parts again next time.

What to expect in the multiple-choice test

You will have 40 minutes to complete the questions in the test, using a touch-screen to select your answers. The test is a set of 35 questions drawn from a bank of almost a 1,000, all of which have multiple-choice answers. In order to pass the test you must answer a minimum of 30 questions correctly within the given time. The Government may change the pass mark from time to time. Your driving school or the DSA will be able to tell you if there has been a change. The questions appear on the screen one at a time and you can return to any of the questions within the 40 minutes to re-check or alter your answers. The system will prompt you to return to any questions you have not answered fully.

Preparing for the Theory Test

Read and get to know *The Highway Code*. You'll find that many of the theory questions relate directly to it. Look at the list of Theory Test topics, then read through the topic summary. Now turn to the section containing the questions. Read through the questions and tick your choice of answer(s). Now check your answer(s) against those at the back of the book. If you don't understand the answer(s), look up the subject in *The Highway Code* or take a note of the question and discuss it with your instructor.

Questions marked with an NI symbol are those not found in Theory Test papers in Northern Ireland.

Remember

- Don't try too many questions at once.
- Don't try to learn the answers by heart.
- The order of the questions in this book may be different from how they are arranged in the test – so don't try to memorise the order.

How to answer the questions

Each question has four, five or six possible answers. You must mark the boxes with the correct answer(s). Each question tells you how many answers to mark.

Study each question carefully, making sure you understand what it is asking you. Look carefully at any diagram, drawing or photograph. Before you look at the answers given, decide what you think the correct answer(s) might be. You can then select the answer(s) that matches the one you had decided on. If you follow this system, you will avoid being confused by answers that appear to be similar.

What to expect in the Hazard Perception Test

After a break of up to three minutes you will begin the Hazard Perception part of the test.

The Hazard Perception test lasts for about 20 minutes. Before you start you will be given some instructions explaining how the test works; you'll also get a chance to practise with the computer and mouse before you start. Next you will see 14 film or video clips of real street scenes with traffic such as cars, pedestrians, cyclists etc. The scenes are shot from the point of view of a driver in a car. You have to notice potential hazards that are developing on the road ahead – that is, problems that could lead to an accident. As soon as you notice a hazard developing, click the mouse. You will have plenty of time to see

Left: Real road scenes feature in the video clips in the Hazard Perception test
Above: Click the mouse when you spot potential hazards – the pedestrian crossing the side road and the cyclist approaching a parked vehicle (ringed in yellow). Click again as the hazard develops when the cyclist (ringed in red) moves out to overtake the parked vehicle.

the hazard – but the sooner you notice it, the more marks you score.

Each clip has at least one hazard in it – some clips may have more than one hazard. You currently have to score a minimum of 44 out of 75 to pass, but the pass mark may change so check with your instructor or the DSA before sitting your test. (Note that the computer has checks built in to show anyone trying to cheat – for example someone who keeps clicking the mouse all the time.) Be aware that, unlike the Theory Test questions, you will not have an opportunity to go back to an earlier clip and change your response, so you need to concentrate throughout the test.

Preparing for the Hazard Perception Test

Who do you think have the most accidents – new or experienced drivers? New drivers have just had lessons, so they should remember how to drive safely, but in fact new drivers have the most accidents.

Learner drivers need training in how to spot hazards because they are often so busy thinking about the car's controls that they forget to watch the road and traffic – and losing concentration for even a second could prove fatal to you or another road user. Proper training can help you to recognise more of the hazards that you will meet when driving and to spot those hazards earlier so you are less likely to have an accident. Your driving instructor has been trained to help you learn hazard perception skills and can give you plenty of practice in what to look out for when driving, how to anticipate hazards, and what action to take to deal with hazards of all kinds.

You won't be able to practise with the real video clips used in the test, of course, but training books and practice videos and DVDs are available.

What to expect in the Practical Test

Once you have passed both parts of your Theory Test, you can apply for the Practical Test. The Practical Test is all about making sure that those who pass are competent and safe in the basic skills of driving.

The requirements for passing your test are a combination of practical skills and mental understanding. The open road can be a risky environment, and your test result will show whether you're ready to go out there alone or whether you need a little more practice first.

You'll be asked to sign a declaration that the insurance of your car is in order. Without this, the test can't proceed.

The paperwork

You'll need to have with you:

- your signed provisional driving licence (both parts if you've got a photo licence). If your licence doesn't have a photo you'll need additional photographic identity (ID) Acceptable ID, such as a current passport, must have your photograph and signature. See the DSA website for an up-to-date list of acceptable photo ID.
- your Theory Test pass certificate
- your appointment letter
- your completed Driver's Record (if you have one) signed by your instructor

Eyesight test

Your driving test begins with an eyesight test. You have to be able to read a normal number plate at a minimum distance of 20.5 metres (about 67.5 feet). If you fail the eyesight test your driving test will stop at that point and you will have failed.

Vehicle safety checks

You will have to answer two vehicle safety check questions. The questions fall into three categories:

- identify
- tell me how you would check…
- show me how you would check…

These questions are designed to make sure that you know how to check that your vehicle is safe to drive.

If you turn up for your test in an unsuitable vehicle, you will forfeit your test fee.

Although some checks may require you to identify where fluid levels should be checked you will not be asked to touch a hot engine or physically check fluid levels. You may refer to vehicle information systems (if fitted) when answering questions on fluid levels and tyre pressures.

All vehicles differ slightly so it is important that you get to know all the safety systems and engine layout in the vehicle in which you plan to take your practical test.

Don't worry about making a few mistakes. You can still pass your test as long as they are only minor driving faults.

The Driving Test

During the test you will be expected to drive for about 40 minutes along normal roads following the directions of the examiner. The roads are selected so as to provide a range of different conditions and road situations and a varied density of traffic.

Your examiner will select suitable areas for you to carry out the set exercises. He or she will tell you to pull up and stop, and will then explain the exercise to you before you do it:

- you *may* or *may not* be asked to perform an emergency stop
- you *will* be asked to perform two reversing exercises selected by the examiner from:
  reversing round a corner;
  reverse parking (behind a parked car, or into a marked bay);
  turning in the road

Driving test standards are monitored so that whatever examiner you get, or whatever test centre you go to, you should get the same result. You might find a senior officer in the car as well as the examiner; he or she is not watching you, but checking that the examiner is doing his or her job properly.

Throughout the test, the examiner will be assessing:

- whether you are competent at controlling the car
- whether you are making normal progress for the roads you are on
- how you react to any hazards that occur in the course of the test
- whether you are noticing all traffic signs and signals and road markings, and reacting to them in the correct manner.

In order to pass the driving test, you must drive

- without committing any serious fault or...
- without committing more than 15 driving errors of a less serious nature

If, during the test, you do not understand what the examiner says to you, ask him or her to repeat the instruction.

If you are faced with an unusually difficult or hazardous situation in the course of your test that results in you making a driving fault, the examiner will take the circumstances into account when marking you for that part of the test.

How to prepare for the Practical Test

Be sure that you are ready to take the test. This is where choosing a reliable qualified driving instructor is vital.

You should feel confident:

- about driving in all conditions
- that you know *The Highway Code*

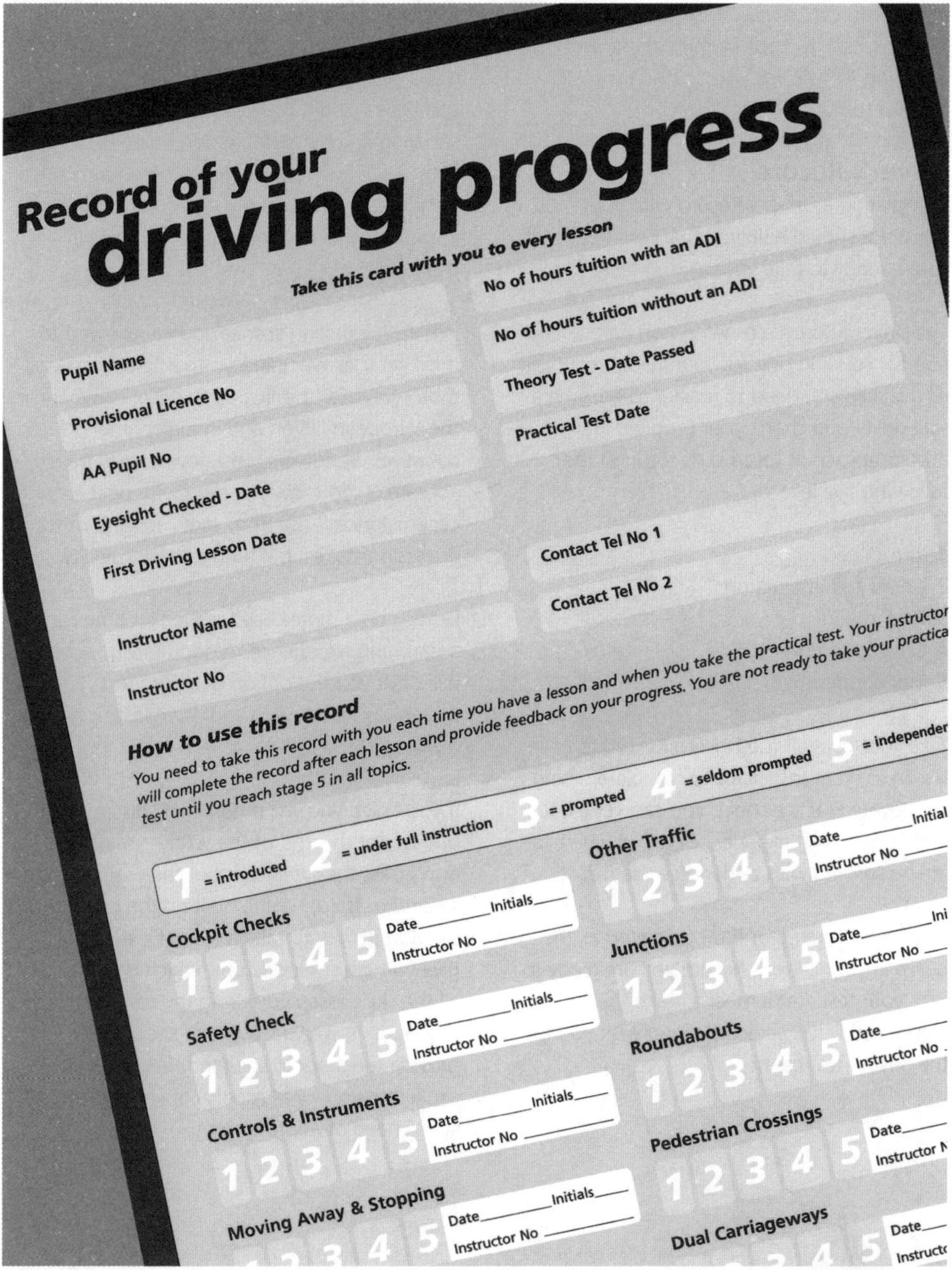

Record of your
driving progress

Take this card with you to every lesson

Pupil Name

Provisional Licence No

AA Pupil No

Eyesight Checked - Date

First Driving Lesson Date

Instructor Name

Instructor No

No of hours tuition with an ADI

No of hours tuition without an ADI

Theory Test - Date Passed

Practical Test Date

Contact Tel No 1

Contact Tel No 2

How to use this record

You need to take this record with you each time you have a lesson and when you take the practical test. Your instructor will complete the record after each lesson and provide feedback on your progress. You are not ready to take your practica test until you reach stage 5 in all topics.

1 = introduced 2 = under full instruction 3 = prompted 4 = seldom prompted 5 = independen

Cockpit Checks 1 2 3 4 5 Date___ Initials___ Instructor No ___

Safety Check 1 2 3 4 5 Date___ Initials___ Instructor No ___

Controls & Instruments 1 2 3 4 5 Date___ Initials___ Instructor No ___

Moving Away & Stopping 3 4 5 Date___ Initials___ Instructor No ___

Other Traffic 1 2 3 4 5 Date___ Initial Instructor No ___

Junctions 1 2 3 4 5 Date___ Ini Instructor No ___

Roundabouts 1 2 3 4 5 Date___ Instructor No

Pedestrian Crossings 1 2 3 4 5 Date___ Instructor N

Dual Carriageways 4 5 Date___ Instructo

- that you can make decisions on your own about how to cope with hazards, without having to wait for your instructor to tell you what to do.

Driver's Record

Completing a Driver's Record with your instructor should help you feel confident that you're ready to take your driving test.

The Driver's Record comes in two parts – one part for you and one for your instructor. It lists all the skills you need to master to become a safe driver and charts your progress in acquiring each of these skills through the following five levels:

1 Introduced
2 Under full instruction
3 Prompted
4 Seldom prompted
5 Independent

Take your copy of the Driver's Record to each lesson for your instructor to complete. Using the Private Practice sheet, you can keep a record of driving experience gained when you are out driving with a friend or relative.

When your instructor has completed all the boxes in your Driver's Record you are ready to take your test. Remember to take the completed Driver's Record along with you to the driving test centre.

After the Test

If you pass your test you'll be given a pass certificate, and a copy of the examiner's report showing any minor faults you made during your test. You'll find it useful to know where your weaknesses lie, so that you can concentrate on improving those aspects of your driving in the future.

With a full driving licence you are allowed to drive vehicles weighing up to 3.5 tonnes, use motorways for the first time, drive anywhere in the European Union and in many other countries worldwide, and tow a small trailer. You are on your own dealing with whatever circumstances arise: fog, snow, ice and other drivers' mistakes. It is a huge responsibility.

Driving on a motorway for the first time can be a daunting experience. A good driving school will offer you the option of a post-test motorway lesson with your own instructor, and it makes sense to take advantage of this.

If you failed you will naturally be disappointed, but it's not the end of the world – many people don't pass their first test, but then sail through a second or third, having built on the experience of what it's like to take a test. The examiner will give you a test report form which is a record of all the skills assessed during the test, identifying any areas of weakness. He or she will also provide feedback in spoken form, and will explain to you what aspects of your driving are still in need of improvement.

Part 2
The Practical Test Questions and Answers

The Practical Test

Good defensive driving depends on adopting the right attitude from the start. These questions will test your knowledge of what is required before you even sit in the driver's seat.

1

What do you need before you can drive on a public road?

Fill in the missing words

P_ _ _ _ _ _ _ _ _ _ _ _ _

_ _ _ _ _ _ _ _

2

The best way to learn is to have regular planned tuition with an ADI (Approved Driving Instructor).

An ADI is someone who has taken and passed all three driving instructor's e_ _ _ _ _ _ _ _ _ _ _ _ _ and is on the official r_ _ _ _ _ _ _ _

Complete the sentence

Answers on page 92

HINTS & TIPS

A fully qualified ADI should display a green certificate on the windscreen of their car. Ask to see it.

3

Anyone supervising a learner must be at least _ _ years old and must have held (and still hold) a full driving licence (motor car) for at least t_ _ _ _ _ years

Complete the sentence

4

Your tuition vehicle must display L-plates. Where should they be placed?

Answer________________________________

____

____

5

Young and inexperienced drivers are more vulnerable. Is this true or false?

Tick the correct box **True** ☐ **False** ☐

6

Showing responsibility to yourself and others is the key to being a safe driver. Ask yourself, would you ...

Tick the correct box

1 Want to drive with someone who has been drinking? **YES** ☐ **NO** ☐

2 Want to drive with someone who takes risks and puts other lives at risk? **YES** ☐ **NO** ☐

3 Want to drive with someone who does not concentrate? **YES** ☐ **NO** ☐

4 Want to drive with someone who drives too fast? **YES** ☐ **NO** ☐

7

Do you want to be a safe and responsible driver?

Tick the correct box **YES** ☐ **NO** ☐

8

You must pass a theory test before you can take the practical test. When would be the best time to sit this test?

Mark two answers

1 Before applying for a provisional licence ☐

2 Just before taking the practical test ☐

3 Some time during the early weeks of your driving lessons ☐

4 After full study of available training materials ☐

9

To use the controls safely you need to adopt a suitable driving position. There are a number of checks you should make.

Fill in the missing words

1 Check the h _ _ _ _ _ _ _ _ is on.

2 Check the d _ _ _ _ are shut.

3 Check your s _ _ _ is in the correct position.

4 Check the h _ _ _ r _ _ _ _ _ _ _ _ is adjusted to give maximum protection.

5 Check the driving m _ _ _ _ _ _ are adjusted to give maximum rear view.

6 Check your s _ _ _ b _ _ _ is securely fastened.

10

Here is a list of functions and a list of controls.

Match each function to its control by placing the appropriate letter in the box

THE FUNCTIONS	THE CONTROLS
A To control the direction in which you want to travel	☐ The handbrake
B To slow or stop the vehicle	☐ The driving mirrors
C To increase or decrease the engine's speed	☐ The gear lever
D To give you a clear view behind	☐ The clutch
E To hold the vehicle still when it is stationary	☐ The steering wheel
F To enable you to change gear	☐ The foot-brake
G To enable you to make or break contact between the engine and the wheels	☐ The accelerator

Fill in the missing word

The accelerator can also be called the g _ _ pedal

Answers on page 92

11

Which foot should you use for each of these controls (in cars with a manual gearbox)?

R = Right foot **L** = Left foot

The foot-brake ☐

The clutch ☐

The accelerator ☐

12

Are the following statements about steering true or false?

Tick the appropriate boxes	**True**	**False**
1 I must keep both hands on the wheel at all times.	☐	☐
2 To keep good control I should feed the wheel through my hands.	☐	☐
3 I can place my hands at any position as long as I am comfortable.	☐	☐
4 When going round corners, it is best to cross my hands (hand over hand).	☐	☐
5 I should never take both hands off the wheel when the vehicle is moving.	☐	☐
6 To straighten up I should feed the wheel back through my hands.	☐	☐

13

Match each of the following functions to its control.

THE FUNCTIONS	**THE CONTROLS**
A To enable you to see the road ahead and other road users to see you without causing dazzle	☐ The direction indicators
B To show other road users which way you intend to turn	☐ Dipped beam
C To use only when visibility is 100 metres/yards or less	☐ Main beam
D To enable you to see further, but not to be used when there is oncoming traffic	☐ Rear fog lamp
E To warn other road users of your presence	☐ Horn
F To warn other road users when you are temporarily obstructing traffic	☐ Hazard lights

Answers on page 92

1

The following is a list of actions involved in moving off from rest. Number the boxes 1 to 9 to show the correct sequence

The first box has been filled in to give you a start

[1] **A** Press the clutch down fully

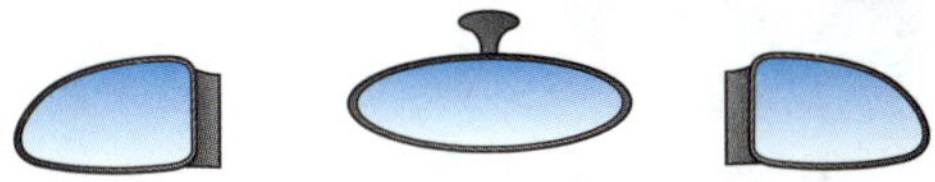

[ ] **B** Check your mirrors

[ ] **C** Set the accelerator pedal

[ ] **D** Move the gear lever into 1st gear

[ ] **E** Decide whether you need to give a signal

[ ] **F** Let the clutch come to biting point and hold it steady

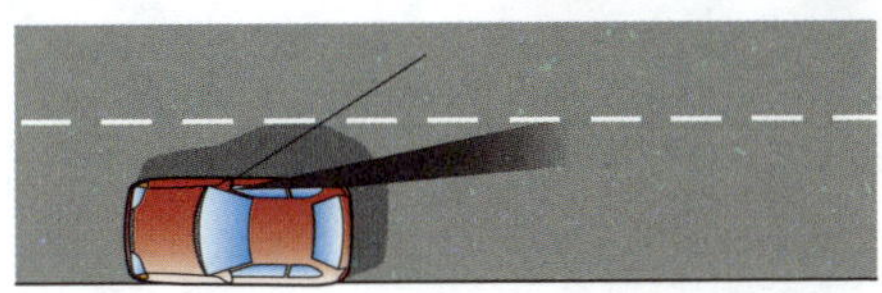

[ ] **G** Check your blind spot

[ ] **H** If safe, release the handbrake and let the clutch up a little more

[ ] **I** Press the accelerator pedal a little more and let the clutch up fully

Answers on page 93

2

The following is a list of actions required for stopping normally.
Number the boxes 1 to 9 to show the correct sequence.

The first box has been filled in to give you a start

[1] **A** Check your mirrors

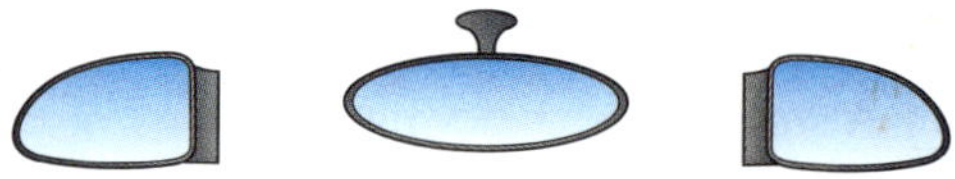

[ ] **B** Take your foot off the accelerator pedal

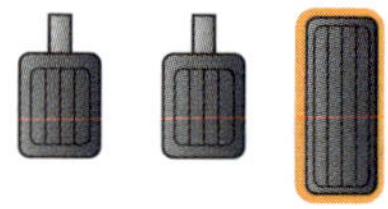

[ ] **C** Decide whether you need to signal and, if necessary, do so

[ ] **D** Press the brake pedal, lightly at first and then more firmly

[ ] **E** As the car stops, ease the pressure off the foot-brake (except when you are on a slope)

[ ] **F** Just before the car stops, press the clutch pedal right down

[ ] **G** Put the gear lever into neutral

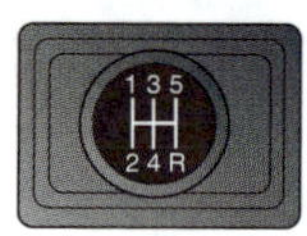

[ ] **H** Apply the handbrake fully

[ ] **I** Take both feet off the pedals

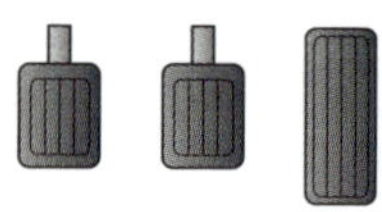

Answers on page 93

Gears enable you to select the power you need from the engine to perform a particular task.

3

Which gear gives you the most power?

Answer ☐

4

If you were travelling at 60mph on a clear road, which gear would you most likely select?

Answer ☐

5

When approaching and turning a corner, as shown in the diagram, which gear would you most likely use?

Answer ☐

6

You need to change gear to match your e_ _ _ _ _ _ speed to the speed at which your v_ _ _ _ _ _ _ is travelling. The s_ _ _ _ _ the engine is making will help you know w_ _ _ _ to change gear.

Complete the sentences

7

Number the boxes to show the correct sequence of actions required when changing up.

The first box has been filled in for you

[1] **A** Place your left hand on the gear lever

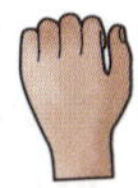

☐ **B** Move the gear lever to the next highest position

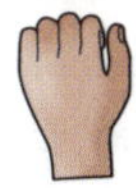

☐ **C** Press the clutch pedal down fully and ease off the accelerator pedal

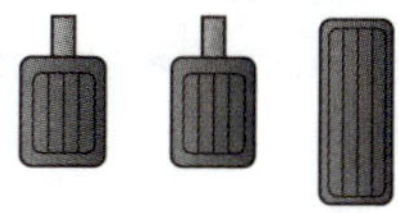

☐ **D** Let the clutch pedal come up fully and, at the same time, press the accelerator pedal

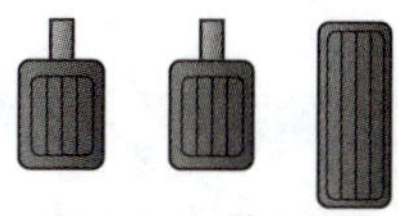

☐ **E** Put your left hand back on the steering wheel

Answers on page 93

8

Are the following statements about changing down true or false?

Tick the appropriate boxes	**True**	**False**
1 I would stay in the highest gear as long as possible, even if my engine started to labour	☐	☐
2 I would change down early so that the engine helps to slow the car down	☐	☐
3 I would avoid using the foot-brake as much as possible	☐	☐
4 I would usually slow the car down by using the foot-brake first. Then, when I am at the required speed, I would change down to the appropriate gear	☐	☐
5 I would always change down through the gears so that I do not miss out any intermediate gears	☐	☐

Answers on page 94

HINTS & TIPS

In your driving test, you will be expected to show that you can control the car smoothly.
If you should stall, put the gears in neutral and the handbrake on, and start again.

9

When changing gear, I should look ...

1 Ahead ☐

2 At the gear lever ☐

3 At my feet ☐

Which is correct?

10

Do's and don'ts

Tick the appropriate boxes	**Do**	**Don't**
1 Force the gear lever if there is any resistance	☐	☐
2 Rush the gear changes	☐	☐
3 Match your speed with the correct gear	☐	☐
4 Use the brakes, where necessary, to reduce speed before changing down	☐	☐
5 Listen to the sound of the engine	☐	☐
6 Take your eyes off the road when changing gear	☐	☐
7 Hold the gear lever longer than necessary	☐	☐
8 Coast with the clutch down or the gear lever in neutral	☐	☐

11

Which wheels turn when you turn the steering wheel?

A The front wheels

B The back wheels

Answer ☐

12

When you turn your steering wheel to the right, which way do your wheels turn?

A To the right

B To the left

Answer ☐

13

The steering lock is ...

A The locking mechanism that stops the steering wheel from moving when the ignition key is removed

B The angle through which the wheels turn when the steering wheel is turned

Answer ☐

14

Which wheels follow the shorter pathway?

A The front wheels

B The back wheels

Answer ☐

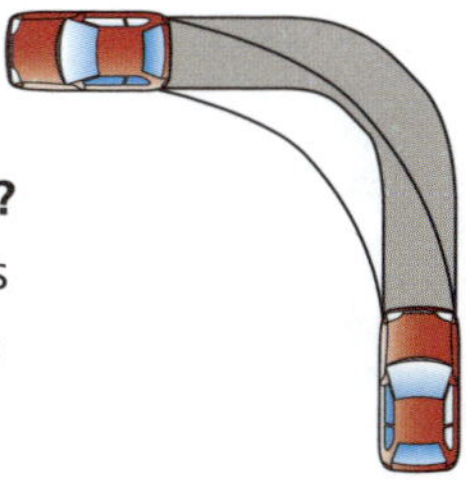

15

Which is the correct position for normal driving?

Put letter A, B or C in the box

Answer ☐

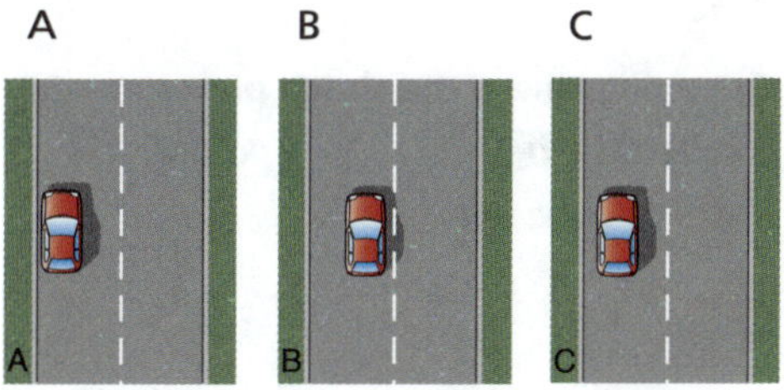

16

Which diagram shows the correct pathway when driving normally?

Put a letter A or B in the box

Answer ☐

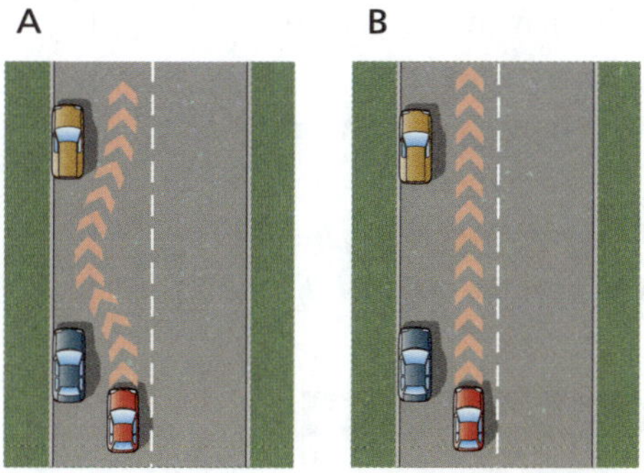

Answers on page 94

17

Pushing the clutch pedal down ...

A Releases the engine from the wheels

B Engages the engine with the wheels

Answer ☐

18

The point where the clutch plates meet is called the b__ __ __ __ __ point.

Fill in the missing word

19

By controlling the amount of contact between the clutch plates, it is possible to control the speed of the car.

Would you use this control ...

Tick the appropriate boxes	**True**	**False**
1 When moving away from rest?	☐	☐
2 When manoeuvring the car in reverse gear?	☐	☐
3 When slowing down to turn a corner?	☐	☐
4 In very slow moving traffic?	☐	☐
5 To slow the car down?	☐	☐

HINTS & TIPS

Remember:
MSM stands for Mirror, Signal, Manoeuvre.
Always use this routine when moving off, turning or overtaking.

Answers on page 94

1

A junction is a point where t __ __ o__ m__ __ __ r__ __ __ __ meet.

Complete the sentence

2

Here are five types of junction.
Name them

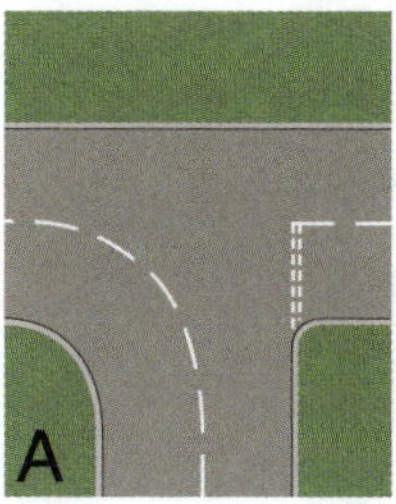

____

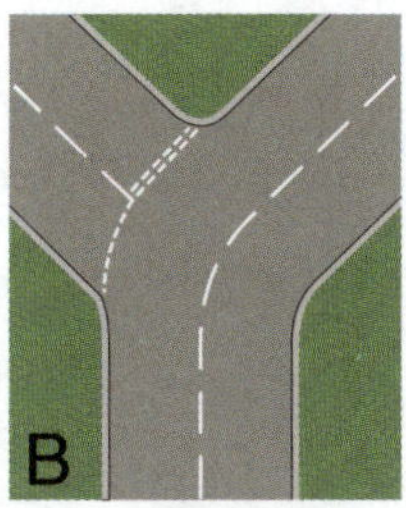

____

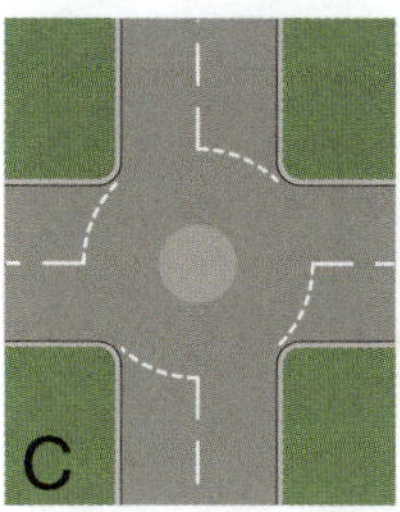

____

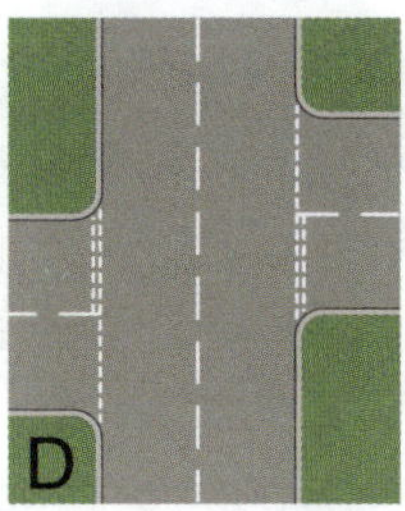

____

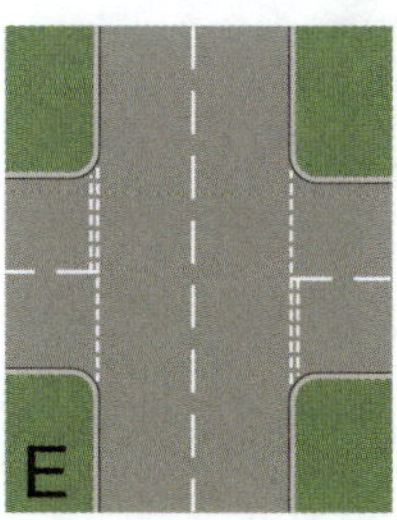

____

Answers on page 95

3

Match these road signs to the junctions shown opposite.

Put letters A, B, C, D and E in the boxes

1 ☐

2 ☐

3 ☐

4 ☐

5 ☐

4

What do these signs mean?

1 Stop and give way
2 Slow down, look, and proceed if safe
3 Give way to traffic on the major road

Put a number in each box

A ☐

B ☐

5

At every junction you should follow a safe routine.

Put the following into the correct order by numbering the boxes 1 to 5

Signal ☐ Speed ☐ Position ☐
Mirrors ☐ Look ☐

6

The diagram below shows a car turning right into a minor road. The boxes are numbered to show the correct sequence of actions.

Complete the sentence

At point 5 you should look and
a _ _ _ _ _ the situation,
d _ _ _ _ _ to go or wait,
and a _ _ accordingly.

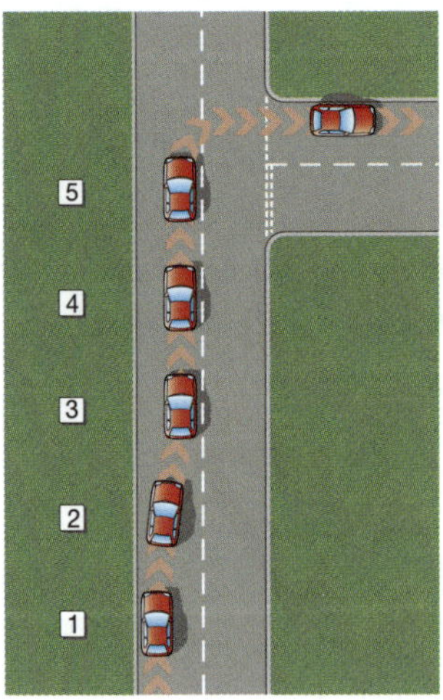

Answers on page 95

7

Turning left into a minor road. Which diagram below shows the best path to follow when driving a motor car A, B, C or D?

Answer ☐

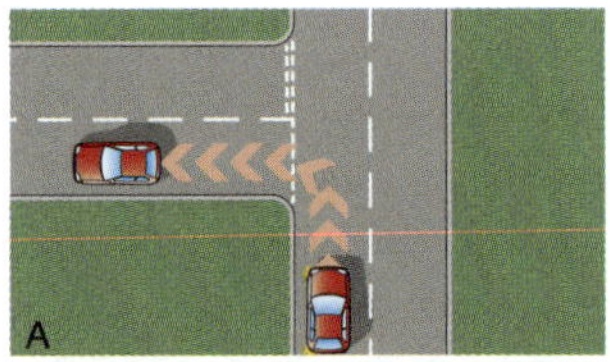

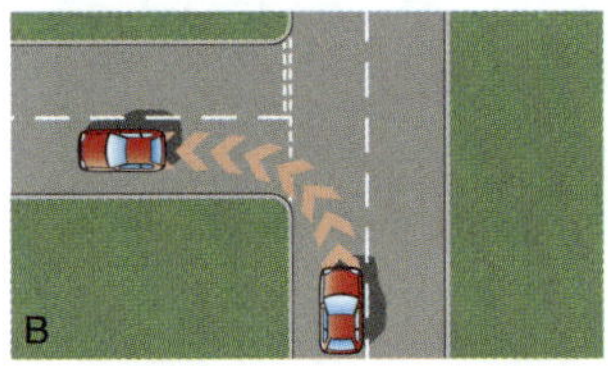

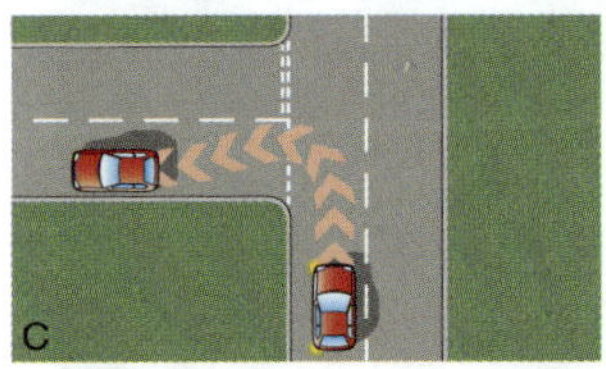

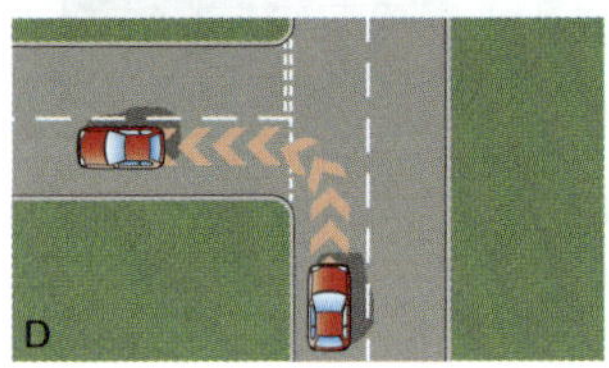

8

You turn into a side road. Pedestrians are already crossing it. Should you ...

Tick the appropriate box

A Sound your horn ☐
B Slow down and give way ☐
C Flash your lights ☐
D Wave them across ☐

9

Turning right into a minor road.
Which diagram shows the best path to follow: A, B, C or D?

Answer ☐

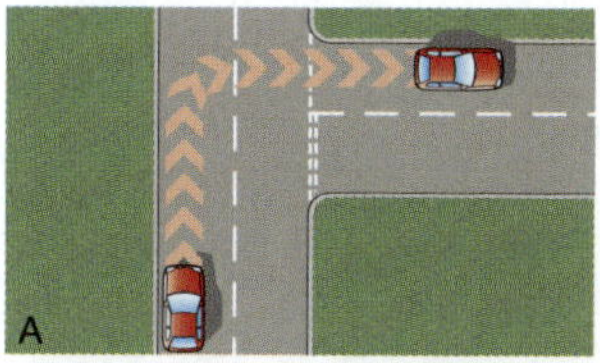

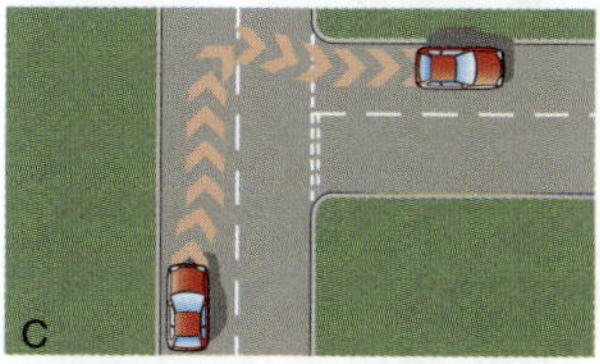

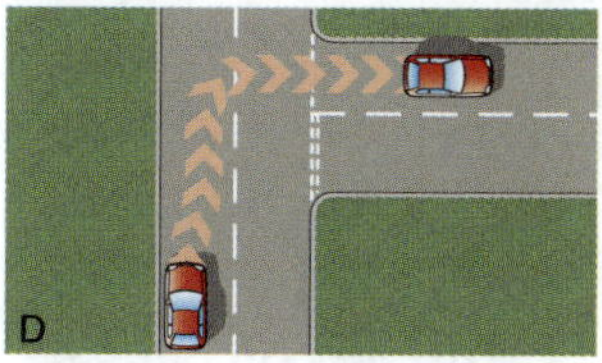

10

These are the golden rules for emerging from junctions.

Complete the sentences

1 Always use your m_ _ _ _ _ _ _ to check the speed and p _ _ _ _ _ _ _ _ of vehicles behind.

2 Always cancel your s_ _ _ _ _ _ .

3 Speed up to a s_ _ _ speed after joining the new road.

4 Keep a s_ _ _ d_ _ _ _ _ _ _ _ between you and the vehicle ahead.

5 Do not attempt to o_ _ _ _ _ _ _ _ until you can assess the new road.

Answers on page 95

11

All crossroads must be approached with caution.

Match actions 1, 2 and 3 listed below with these diagrams

Actions

1 Approach with caution, look well ahead and be prepared to stop. Remember other drivers may assume they have priority.

2 Look well ahead, slow down and be prepared to give way to traffic on the major road.

3 Look well ahead and into the side roads for approaching vehicles. Remember other drivers may not give you priority.

Answer ☐

Answer ☐

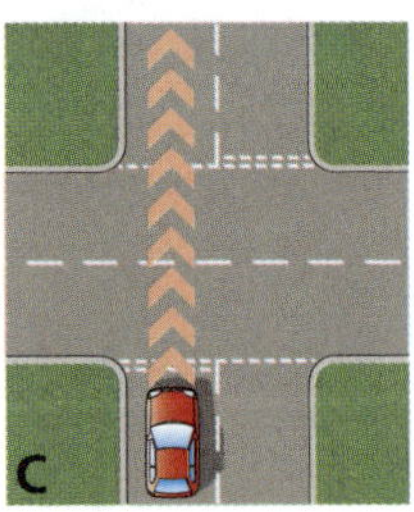

Answer ☐

12

Which of the following statements describes the correct procedure when approaching a roundabout?

Put letter A, B or C in the box

A The broken white line at a roundabout means I must stop and give way to traffic already on the roundabout.

B The broken white line at a roundabout means I must give priority to traffic already on the roundabout.

C The broken white line means I should give way to any traffic approaching from my immediate right.

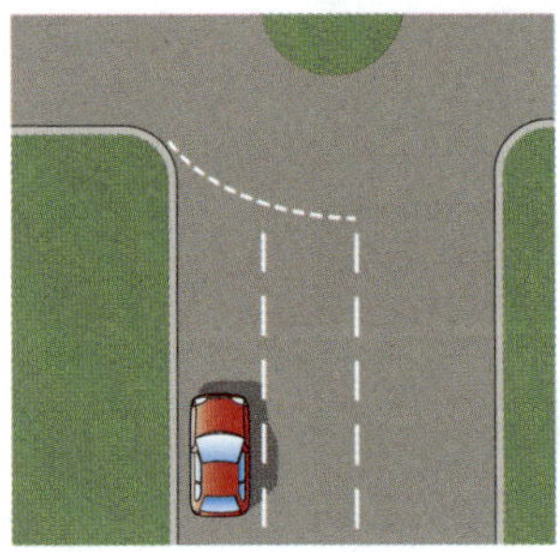

Answer ☐

HINTS & TIPS

At an unmarked crossroads, no one has priority.
Be extra-cautious at these junctions.

Answers on page 95

13

The following sentences give guidance on lane discipline on a roundabout.

Fill in the missing words

1 When turning left at a roundabout, I should stay in the _ _ _ _ hand lane and should stay in that lane throughout.

2 When going ahead at a roundabout, I should be in the _ _ _ _ hand lane, and should stay in that lane throughout, unless conditions dictate otherwise.

3 When turning right at a roundabout, I should approach in the r_ _ _ _ hand lane, or approach as if turning right at a junction, and stay in that lane throughout.

14

The letters A, B and C in the diagram mark places where you should signal.

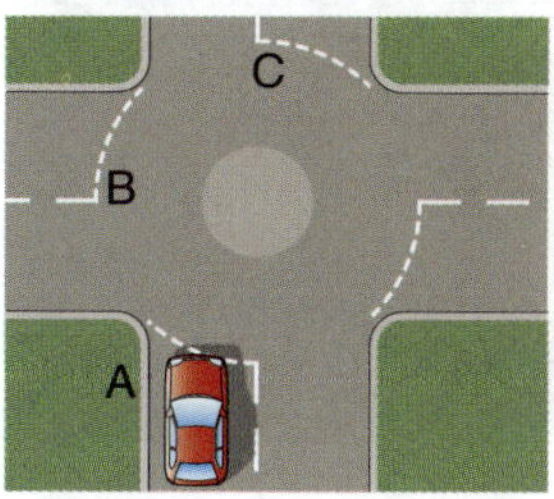

Complete the sentences

1 I would signal at **A** when turning _ _ _ _.

2 I would signal at **B** when g_ _ _ _ _ _ _ _ _.

3 I would signal at **A** and at **C** when turning _ _ _ _ _.

15

At a roundabout you should always use a safe routine.

Fill in the missing words

M_ _ _ _ _ _ _, s_ _ _ _ _ _,
p_ _ _ _ _ _ _ _, s_ _ _ _,
l_ _ _.

16

What does this sign mean?

Write 1, 2 or 3 in the box

1 Roundabout

2 Mini-roundabout

3 Vehicles may pass either side.

Answer ☐

HINTS & TIPS

Be careful at roundabouts where destinations are marked for each lane. Make sure you are in the correct lane for your destination.

Answers on page 95

1

It is safest to park off the road or in a car park whenever possible. If you have to park on the road, think ...

Fill in the missing words

1 Is it s__ __ __ ?

2 Is it c__ __ __ __ __ __ __ __ __ __ __ __ __?

3 Is it l__ __ __ __ ?

2

In this diagram four of the cars are parked illegally or without consideration of others.

Put the numbers of these cars in the boxes

☐ ☐ ☐ ☐

For reverse parallel parking manoeuvres, see pages 52–4.

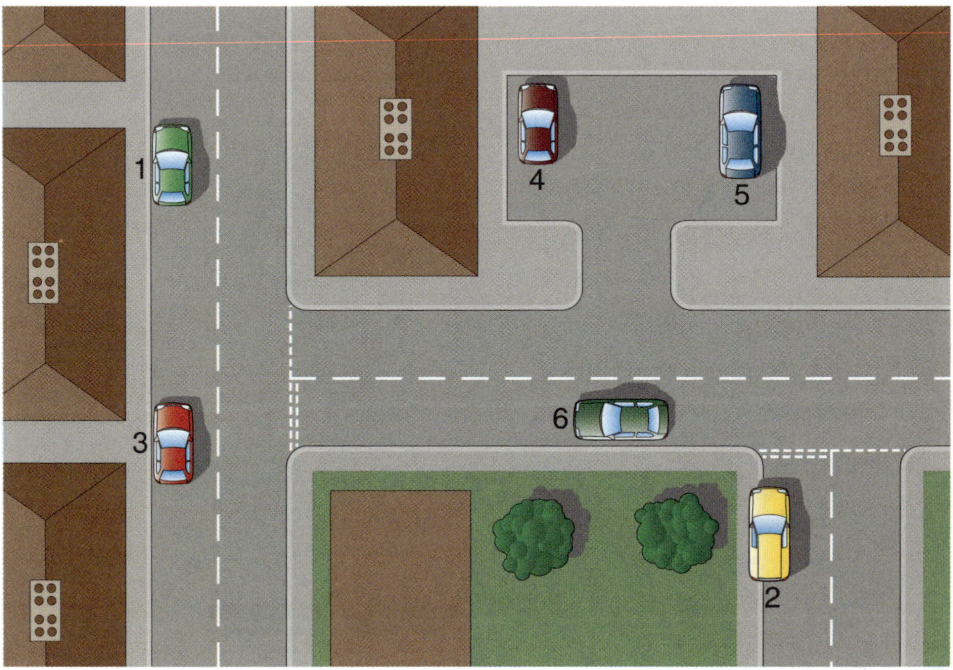

Answers on page 96

3

Check how well you know the rules about where you may and may not park. Are the following statements true or false?

Tick the correct boxes	**True**	**False**
1 In a narrow street, I should park with two wheels up on the pavement to leave more room for other traffic.	☐	☐
2 I am allowed to park in a 'Disabled' space if all other spaces are full.	☐	☐
3 I should not park on the zig-zag lines near a zebra crossing.	☐	☐
4 Red lines painted on the road mean 'No Stopping'.	☐	☐

4

List three places not mentioned in Question 3 where you should *not* park.

1 ______________________________

2 ______________________________

3 ______________________________

HINTS & TIPS

Use your *Highway Code* to find out more about parking regulations

Answers on page 96

1

The diagram shows a stationary vehicle on the left-hand side of the road. Which should have priority, vehicle 1 or vehicle 2?

Answer ☐

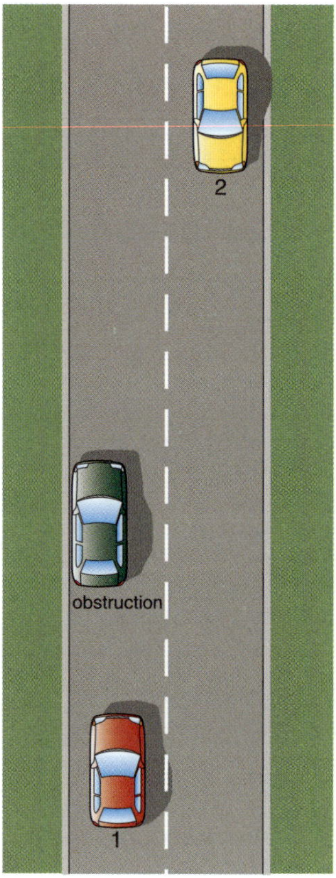

2

This diagram shows a steep downward hill with an obstruction on the right-hand side of the road. Which vehicle should be given priority, vehicle 1 or vehicle 2?

Answer ☐

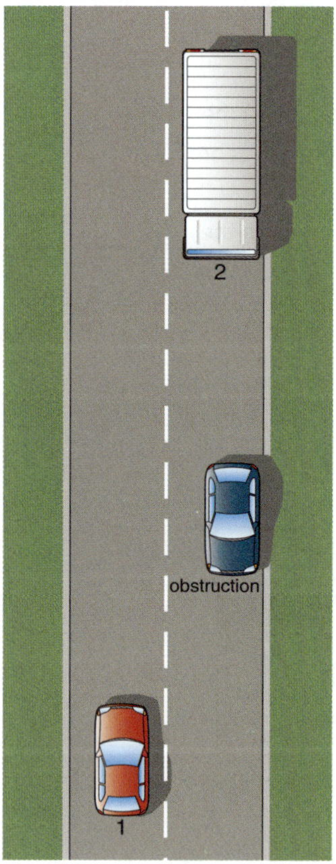

Answers on page 96

3

The diagram shows two vehicles, travelling in opposite directions, turning right at a crossroads.

Are these statements true or false?

Tick the appropriate boxes	**True**	**False**
1 The safest route is to pass each other offside to offside.	☐	☐
2 If the approaching vehicle flashes its headlamps, I should turn as quickly as possible.	☐	☐
3 I should always try to get eye-to-eye contact with the driver of the other vehicle to determine which course to take.	☐	☐

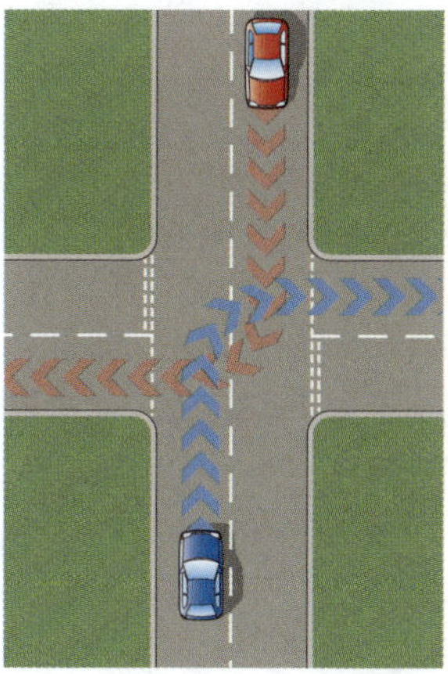

4

Which of the following factors, illustrated in the diagram, should be taken into consideration when turning right into a side road?

Tick the appropriate boxes	**YES**	**NO**
1 The speed of the approaching vehicle (**A**)	☐	☐
2 The roadworks	☐	☐
3 The speed of vehicle **B**	☐	☐
4 The cyclist	☐	☐
5 Your speed (vehicle **C**)	☐	☐
6 The pedestrians	☐	☐
7 The car waiting to turn right (**D**)	☐	☐

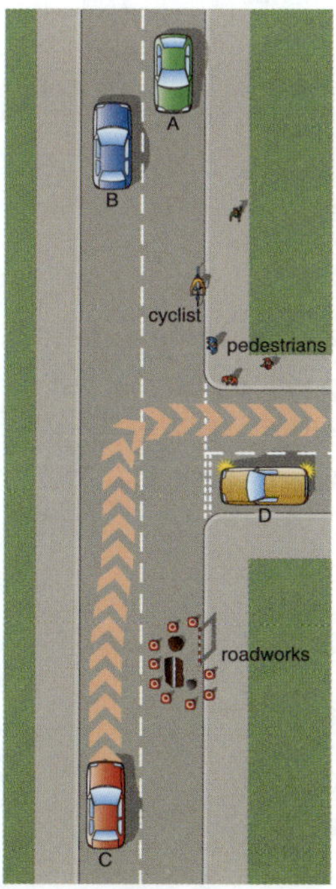

Answers on page 96

1

Are the following statements true or false when stopping in an emergency?

Tick the correct boxes

	True	False
1 Stopping in an emergency increases the risk of skidding.	☐	☐
2 I should push the brake pedal down harder as I slow down.	☐	☐
3 It is important to react quickly.	☐	☐
4 I should always remember to look in my mirrors as I slow down.	☐	☐
5 I should signal left to tell other road users what I am doing.	☐	☐
6 I should keep both hands on the wheel.	☐	☐
7 I should always check my mirrors and look round before moving off.	☐	☐

2

Is the following statement true or false?
An emergency stop will be carried out on every driving test

Tick the correct box **True** ☐ **False** ☐

Answers on page 97

3

Cadence braking is a technique which can be used in very slippery conditions in an emergency.

Fill in the missing words

The technique requires you to p_ _ _ the brake pedal.

The procedure to follow is:

1 Apply m_ _ _ _ _ _ pressure.

2 Release the brake pedal just as the wheels are about to l_ _ _.

3 Then q_ _ _ _ _ _ apply the brakes again. Apply and release the brakes until the vehicle has stopped. This technique should only be used in emergency situations.

4

Anti-lock braking systems (ABS)* work in a similar way to cadence braking.

Fill in the missing words

When braking in an emergency, ABS brakes allow you to s_ _ _ _ and b_ _ _ _ at the same time. You do not have to p_ _ _ the brakes as you would in cadence braking. When using ABS you keep the p_ _ _ _ _ _ _ applied.

HINTS & TIPS

If a vehicle is travelling too close behind you, then increase the gap you have ahead. Always think for the driver behind.

Are these statements about ABS braking true or false?

Tick the correct boxes

	True	False
1 Cars fitted with ABS braking cannot skid.	☐	☐
2 I do not need to leave as much room between me and the car in front if I have ABS brakes because I know I can stop in a shorter distance.	☐	☐

**ABS is a registered trade mark of Bosch (Germany). ABS stands for Anti-Blockiersystem*

The distance taken for a car to reach stopping point divides into thinking distance and braking distance.

5

Could these factors affect thinking distance?

Tick the appropriate boxes

	YES	NO
1 The condition of your tyres	☐	☐
2 Feeling tired or unwell	☐	☐
3 Speed of reaction	☐	☐
4 Going downhill	☐	☐

6

Most drivers' reaction time is well over ...

Tick the appropriate box

½ second ☐

1 second ☐

5 seconds ☐

7

Stopping distance depends partly on the speed at which the car is travelling.

Complete the sentences

1 At 30mph your overall stopping distance will be __ __ metres or __ __ feet.

2 At 50mph your thinking distance will be __ __ metres or __ __ feet.

3 At 70mph your overall stopping distance will be __ __ metres or __ __ __feet.

8

Stopping distance also varies according to road conditions.

Complete the sentences

In wet weather your vehicle will take l __ __ __ __ __ to stop. You should therefore allow m __ __ __ time.

9

Too many accidents are caused by drivers driving too close to the vehicle in front. A safe gap between you and the vehicle in front can be measured by noting a stationary object and counting in seconds the time that lapses between the vehicle in front passing that object and your own vehicle passing that object.

Complete the sentence

Only a fool b __ __ __ __ __ the t __ __ s __ __ __ __ __ rule.

Answers on page 97

1

Are these statements about moving off at an angle true or false?

Tick the correct boxes

	True	False
1 I should check my mirrors as I am pulling out.	☐	☐
2 I should check my mirrors and blindspot before I pull out.	☐	☐
3 I should move out as quickly as possible.	☐	☐
4 The amount of steering required will depend on how close I am to the vehicle in front.	☐	☐
5 I should look for oncoming traffic.	☐	☐
6 As long as I am signalling, people will know what I am doing. I will be able to pull out because somebody will let me in.	☐	☐

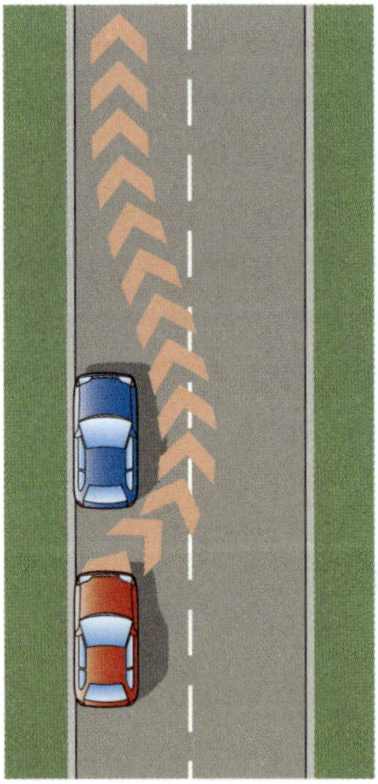

2

Are these statements about moving off uphill true or false?

Tick the correct boxes

	True	False
1 On an uphill gradient the car will tend to roll back.	☐	☐
2 To stop the car rolling back I need to use more acceleration.	☐	☐
3 I do not need to use the handbrake.	☐	☐
4 The biting point may be slightly higher.	☐	☐
5 I need to press the accelerator pedal further down than when moving off on the level.	☐	☐
6 I need to allow more time to pull away.	☐	☐
7 The main controls I use will be the clutch pedal, the accelerator pedal and the handbrake.	☐	☐

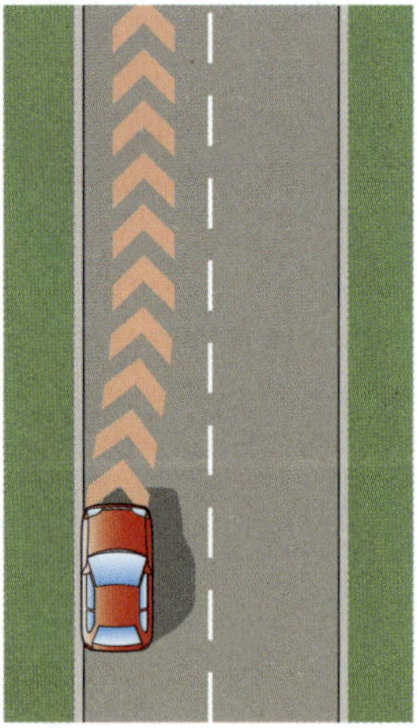

Answers on page 98

3

Are these statements about moving off downhill true or false?

Tick the correct boxes

	True	False
1 The car will tend to roll forwards.	☐	☐
2 The main controls I use will be the handbrake, the clutch pedal and the accelerator pedal.	☐	☐
3 The only gear I can move off in is 1st gear.	☐	☐
4 I should release the handbrake while keeping the foot-brake applied.	☐	☐
5 I should look round just before moving off.	☐	☐
6 I must not have my foot on the foot-brake as I start to release the clutch.	☐	☐

Answers on page 98

4

The following statements are about approaching a junction when going uphill or downhill. With which do you agree?

When going downhill ...	**YES**	**NO**
1 It is more difficult to slow down	☐	☐
2 Putting the clutch down will help slow the car down	☐	☐
3 The higher the gear, the greater the control	☐	☐
4 When changing gear you may need to use the foot-brake at the same time as the clutch	☐	☐

When going uphill ...	**YES**	**NO**
5 Early use of mirrors, signals, brakes, gears and steering will help to position the car correctly	☐	☐
6 You may need to use your handbrake more often	☐	☐
7 When you change gear, the car tends to slow down	☐	☐

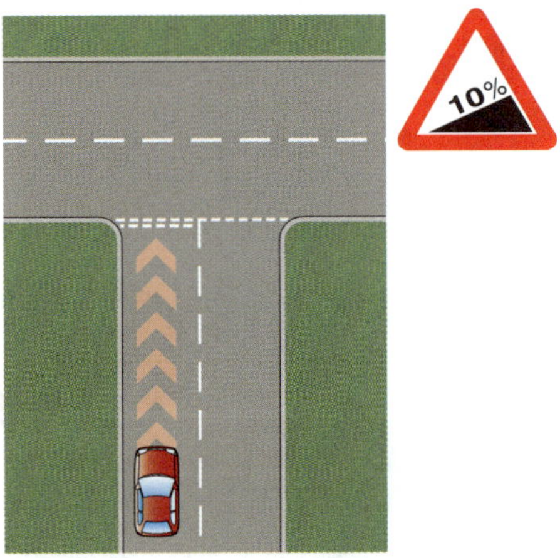

Answers on page 98

1

Before reversing there are three things to consider.

Fill in the missing words

1 Is it s__ __ __?

2 Is it c__ __ __ __ __ __ __ __ __ __ __?

3 Is it within the l__ __?

2

Are the following statements about reversing true or false?

Tick the appropriate boxes

	True	False
1 Other road users should see what I am doing and wait for me.	☐	☐
2 I should wave pedestrians on, so that I can get on with the manoeuvre more quickly.	☐	☐
3 I should avoid being too hesitant.	☐	☐
4 I should avoid making other road users slow down or change course.	☐	☐

3

How should you hold the steering wheel when reversing left?

Which is correct? Answer ☐

A B C

4

These statements are all about reversing.

Tick those which you think are correct

	True	False
1 My car will respond differently in reverse gear.	☐	☐
2 My car will feel no different.	☐	☐
3 Steering is not affected. The car responds the same as when going forward.	☐	☐
4 The steering will feel different. I will have to wait for the steering to take effect.	☐	☐

5

Which way will the rear of the car go when it is reversed? Left or right?

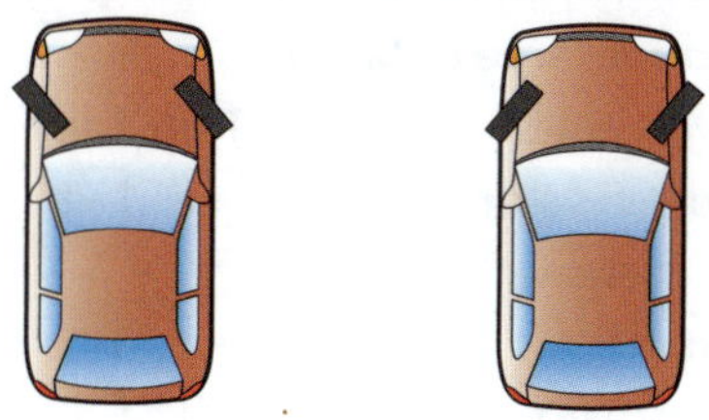

A B

Answer ___________ Answer___________

Answers on page 99

6

It is important to move the vehicle slowly when reversing.

Complete the sentence

Moving the vehicle slowly is safer because I have control and it allows me to carry out good o__ __ __ __ __ __ __ __ __ __ __ checks.

7

When reversing, good observation is vital. Where should you look?

Tick the correct answer

1 At the kerb ☐

2 Ahead ☐

3 Where your car is going ☐

4 Out of the back window ☐

8

Are these statements about reversing round a corner true or false?

Tick the correct boxes

	True	False
1 If the corner is sharp, I need to be further away from the kerb.	☐	☐
2 The distance from the kerb makes no difference.	☐	☐
3 I should try to stay reasonably close to the kerb all the way round.	☐	☐

Answers on page 99

9

Before reversing I should check ...

Tick the correct box

1 Behind me ☐

2 Ahead and to the rear ☐

3 My door mirrors ☐

4 All round ☐

10

Which position is the correct one in which to start steering?

A, B, C or D? Answer ☐

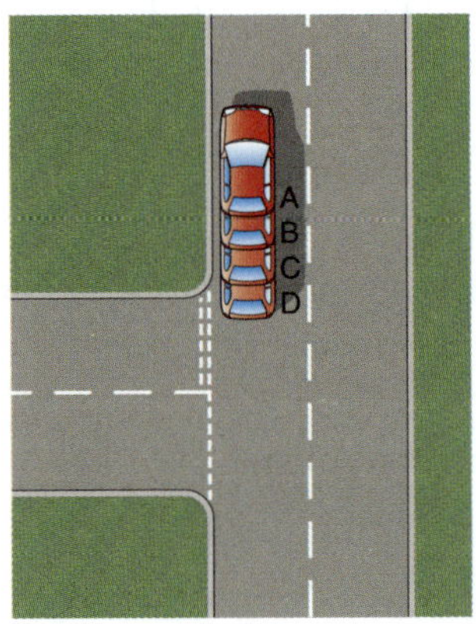

11

Which way should you steer?

Answer________________

12

What will happen to the front of the car?

Answer________________

13

Are these statements about steering when reversing round a corner true or false?

Tick the correct boxes	True	False
1 The more gradual the corner, the less I have to steer.	☐	☐
2 I need to steer the same for every corner.	☐	☐
3 The sharper the corner, the more I have to steer.	☐	☐

14

As I enter the new road, I should continue to keep a look-out for p__ __ __ __ __ __ __ __ __ __ and other r__ __ __ u__ __ __ __.

I should s__ __ __ if necessary.

Complete the sentences

15

True or false? When reversing from a major road into a side road on the right, I have to move to the wrong side of the road.

Tick the correct box **True** ☐ **False** ☐.

16

Which diagram shows the correct path to follow when moving to the right-hand side of the road? A or B?

Answer ☐

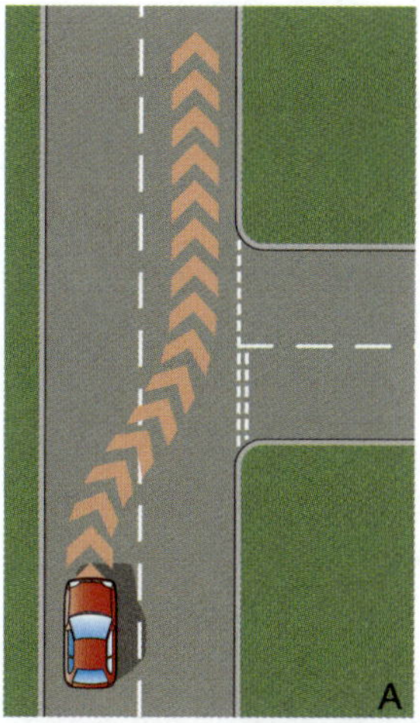

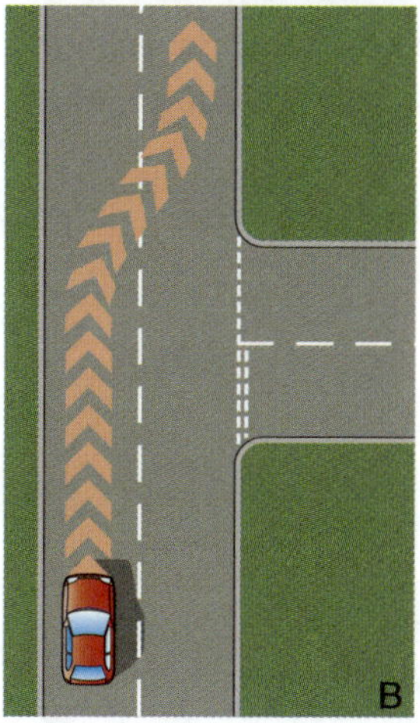

Answers on page 99

17

Which of the following correctly describes your sitting position for reversing to the right?

1 I will need to sit so that I can see over my right shoulder.

2 I will need to sit so that I can see over my right shoulder, ahead and to the left.

3 My position is the same as when reversing to the left.

Which statement is correct? 1, 2 or 3

Answer ☐

18

True or false? I may need to change my hand position on the wheel.

Tick the correct box **True** ☐ **False** ☐

19

True or false? It is easier to judge my position from the kerb when reversing to the right than when reversing to the left.

Tick the correct box **True** ☐ **False** ☐

Answers on page 99

20

Reversing to the right is more dangerous than reversing to the left because ...

1 I cannot see as well

2 I am on the wrong side of the road

3 I might get in the way of vehicles emerging from the side road

Which statement is correct – 1, 2 or 3?

Answer ☐

21

How far down the side road would you reverse before moving over to the left-hand side?

Which diagram is correct? A or B?

Answer ☐

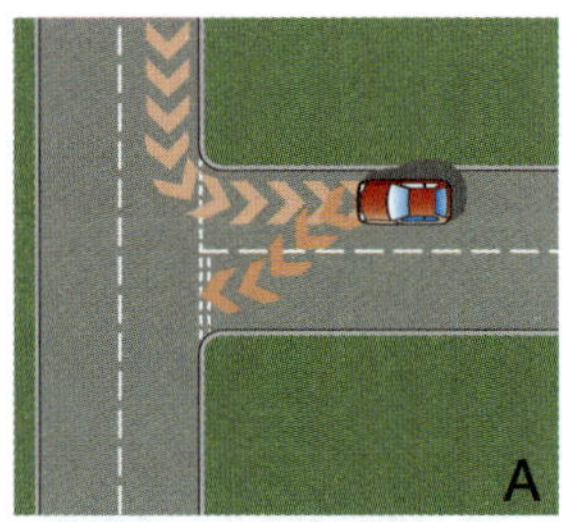

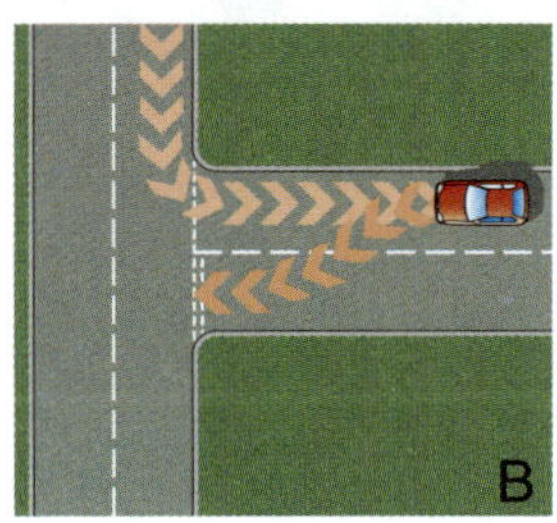

22

Look at the diagrams and decide which is safer.

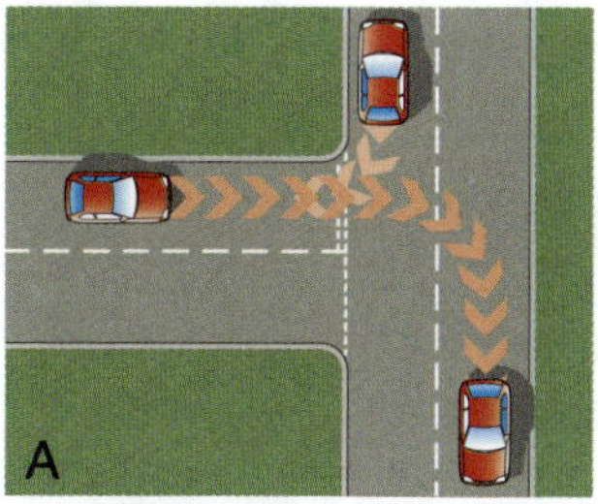

A Reversing into a side road

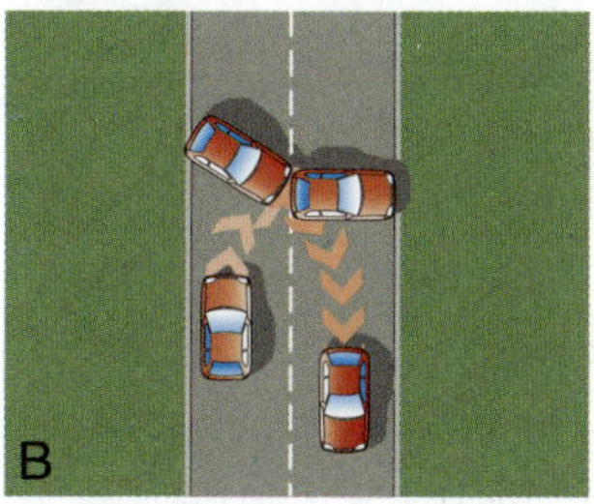

B Turning round in the road

Answer ☐

23

The secret of turning in the road is to move the vehicle s_ _ _ _ _ _ and steer b_ _ _ _ _ _ _.

Complete the sentence

24

I must be able to complete the manoeuvre in three moves: 1 forward, 2 reverse, 3 forward. True or false?

Tick the correct box **True** ☐ **False** ☐

25

Before manoeuvring what should you take into consideration?

Tick the correct boxes

1 The size of your engine ☐

2 The width of the road ☐

3 The road camber ☐

4 The steering circle of your vehicle ☐

5 Parking restrictions ☐

26

Before moving forward, it is important to check a_ _ r_ _ _ _ _ for other road users.

Complete the sentence

HINTS & TIPS

When taking your test, you will be assessed on how well you can control the car; so don't rush your manoeuvres.

Answers on page 100

27

Turning in the road requires proper use of the steering wheel.

Answer the following questions…

1 When going forwards, which way should you steer?

Answer ______________________________

2 Before you reach the kerb ahead, what should you do?

Answer ______________________________

3 When reversing, which way should you steer?

Answer ______________________________

4 Before you reach the kerb behind you, what should you do?

Answer ______________________________

5 As you move forward again, which way should you steer to straighten up?

Answer ______________________________

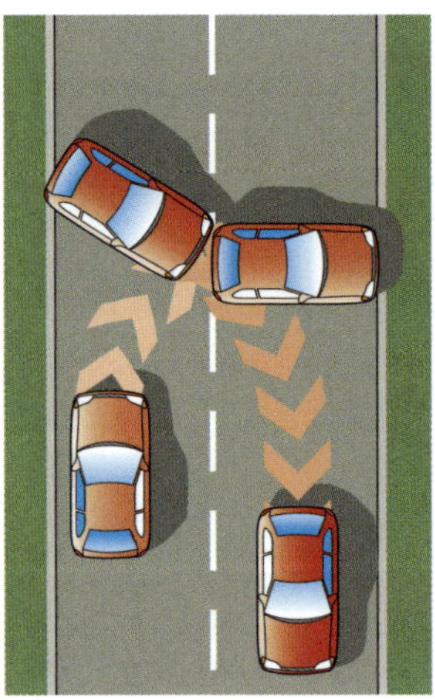

28

Reversing is a potentially dangerous manoeuvre. Good observation is essential.

Answer the following questions

1 If you are steering left when reversing, which shoulder should you look over?

Answer ______________________________

2 As you begin to steer to the right, where should you look?

Answer ______________________________

29

When parking between two cars ...

1 The car is more manoeuvrable when driving forwards

2 The car is more manoeuvrable when reversing

3 There is no difference between going into the space forwards or reversing into it

Which statement is correct? 1, 2 or 3?

Answer ☐

HINTS & TIPS

In your driving test you may be asked to reverse into a parking bay at the test centre, or to park behind another car, using reverse gear. So make sure you practise these manoeuvres.

Answers on page 100

30

The diagram shows a car preparing to reverse into a parking space. Which position is the correct one in which to start steering left, A, B, C or D?

Answer ☐

31

With practice you should be able to park in a gap ...

1 Your own car length

2 1½ times your own car length

3 2 times your own car length

4 2½ times your own car length

Answer ☐

32

Use the diagram to help you answer the following questions.

1 Which way would you steer?

Answer ________________________

2 At this point what would you try to line up with the offside (right-hand side) of your vehicle?

Answer ________________________

3 As you straighten up what do you have to be careful of?

Answer ________________________

4 What do you need to do to straighten up?

Answer ________________________

5 What would you need to do in order to position the vehicle parallel to the kerb?

Answer ________________________

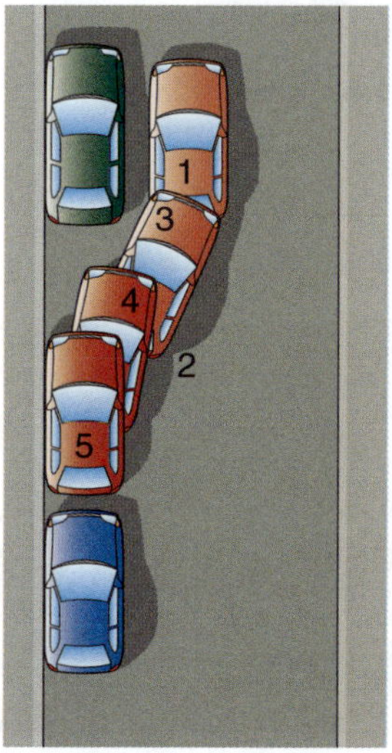

Answers on page 100

33

True or false? During my driving test ...

Tick the correct boxes

	True	False
1 I will certainly be asked to perform the manoeuvre in Question 32	☐	☐
2 I have to be able to park in a tight space between two cars	☐	☐
3 It may be that only the lead car is present	☐	☐

34

When carrying out this manoeuvre, where is it important to look?

Answer ______________________________

35

Look at the diagram and answer the following question.

Which bay should you use and why?

Answer ______________________________

____

____

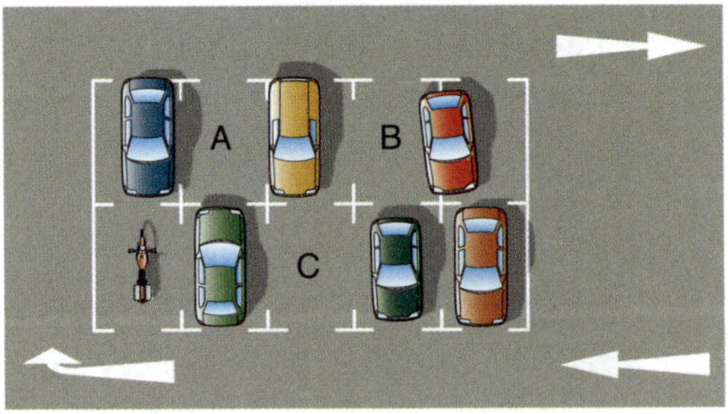

36

Why, wherever possible, should you choose to reverse into a parking bay?

Answer ______________________________

____

____

____

37

As well as being very aware of how c_ _ _ _ _ I am to the parked cars on either side, I should also be alert for cars moving near me from all d_ _ _ _ _ _ _ _ _ _ _, as well as the possibility of p_ _ _ _ _ _ _ _ _ _ _ walking around my car.

Complete the sentence

Answers on page 100

1

Traffic lights have three lights, red, amber, and green, which change from one to the other in a set order. Number the boxes 1 to 5 to show the correct order. The first answer has been filled in to give you a start.

☐ Amber [1] Red ☐ Red and amber
☐ Red ☐ Green

2

What do the colours mean?

Fill in the correct colour for each of the following

1 Go ahead if the way is clear.

Colour ________________

2 Stop and wait.

Colour ________________

3 Stop unless you have crossed the stop line or you are so close to it that stopping might cause an accident.

Colour ________________

4 Stop and wait at the stop line.

Colour ________________

3

Which of the following statements are true?

On approach to traffic lights you should ...

Tick the appropriate boxes

1 Speed up to get through before they change ☐

2 Be ready to stop ☐

3 Look for pedestrians ☐

4 Sound your horn to urge pedestrians to cross quickly ☐

4

Some traffic lights have green filters. Do they mean ...

1 You can filter in the direction of the arrow only when the main light is showing green?

2 You can filter even when the main light is not showing green?

Answer ☐

5

The diagram shows the three lanes at a set of traffic lights.

Which lane would you use for ...

1 Going ahead **Answer** ________________

2 Turning right **Answer** ________________

3 Turning left **Answer** ________________

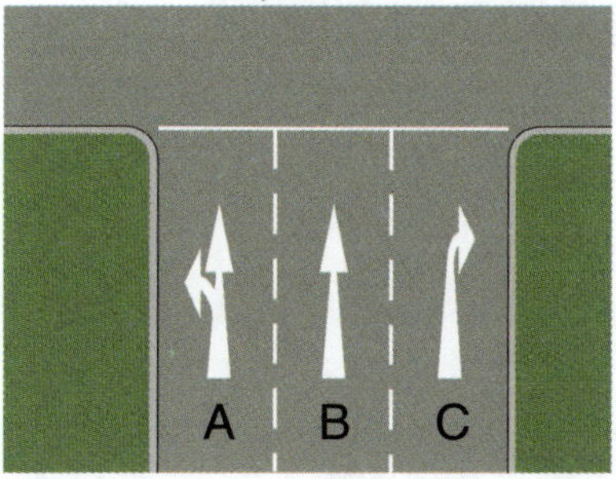

Answers on page 101

6

At some traffic lights and junctions you will see yellow criss-cross lines (box junctions). Can you ...

Tick the correct boxes

	YES	NO
1 Wait within them when going ahead if your exit is not clear?	☐	☐
2 Wait within them when going right if your exit is not clear?	☐	☐
3 Wait within them if there is oncoming traffic stopping you turning right but your exit is clear?	☐	☐

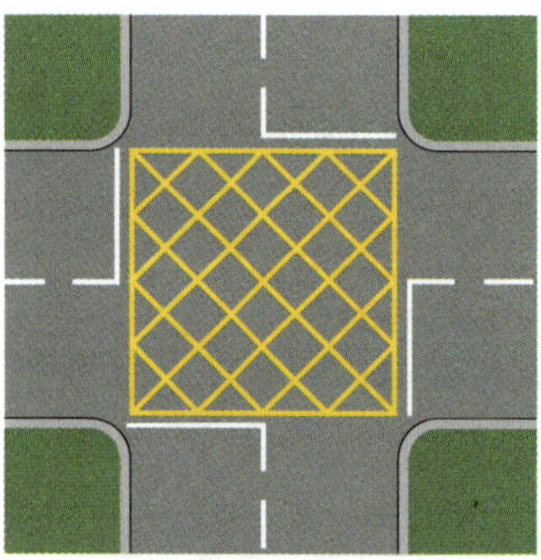

Answers on page 101

Pedestrians have certain rights of way at pedestrian crossings.

7

On approaching a zebra crossing, drivers will notice four features. Name them

1 ______________________________

____

2 ______________________________

____

3 ______________________________

____

4 ______________________________

____

8

Are these statements about pedestrian crossings true or false?

Tick the correct boxes

	True	False
1 I cannot park or wait on the zig-zag lines on the approach to a zebra crossing.	☐	☐
2 I cannot park or wait on the zig-zag lines on either side of the crossing.	☐	☐
3 I can overtake on the zig-zag lines on the approach to a crossing as long as the other vehicle is travelling slowly.	☐	☐
4 I must give way to a pedestrian once he/she has stepped on to the crossing.	☐	☐

5 If, on approach to a crossing, I intend to slow down or stop, I should use a slowing-down arm signal. ☐ ☐

9

On approaching a pelican crossing, drivers will notice three key features. Name them

1 ____________________

____

____

____

2 ____________________

____

____

____

3 ____________________

____

____

____

10

If you see a pedestrian at a zebra crossing or pelican crossing carrying a white stick, do you think ...

Tick the correct box

1 He/she has difficulty walking? ☐

2 He/she is visually handicapped? ☐

11

The traffic lights at a pelican crossing have the same meaning as ordinary traffic lights, but they do not have a red and amber phase.

1 What do they show instead of the red and amber phase?

Answer____________________

____

2 What does the light mean?

Answer____________________

____

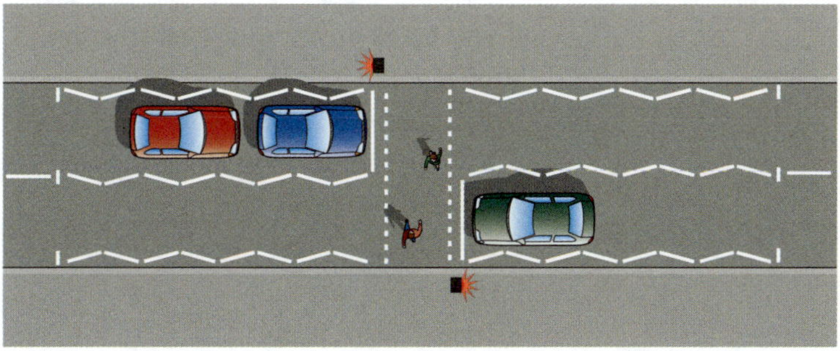

Answers on pages 101–2

12

What sound is usually heard at a pelican crossing when the green man is shown to pedestrians?

Answer________________________________

____

____

____

13

Toucan and puffin crossings are similar to pelican crossings but with one main difference. Name it.

Answer________________________________

____

____

____

14

As well as pedestrians, what other type of road users should you watch for at a toucan crossing?

Answer________________________________

____

____

____

Answers on page 102

A level crossing is where the road crosses at a railway line. It is potentially dangerous and should be approached with caution.

15

Match each traffic sign below with its correct meaning.

1 Level crossing without gates or barriers ☐
2 Level crossing with lights ☐
3 Level crossing with gates or barriers ☐
4 Level crossing without lights ☐

A

B

C

D

16

If you break down on a level crossing, should you ...

Tick the appropriate boxes

1 Tell your passengers to wait in the vehicle while you go to get help? ☐
2 Get everybody out and clear of the crossing? ☐
3 Telephone the police? ☐
4 Telephone the signal operator? ☐
5 If there is still time, push your car clear of the crossing? ☐

One-way systems are where all traffic flows in the same direction.

1

Which of these signs means one-way traffic?

A

B

Answer ☐

2

Are these statements about one-way systems true or false?

Tick the correct boxes

	True	False
1 In one-way streets traffic can pass me on both sides.	☐	☐
2 Roundabouts are one-way systems.	☐	☐
3 For normal driving I should stay on the left.	☐	☐
4 I should look out for road markings and get in lane early.	☐	☐

As a rule, the more paint on the road, the more important the message.

3

Road markings are divided into three categories.

Fill in the missing words

1 Those which give i _ _ _ _ _ _ _ _ _ _ _.

2 Those which give w _ _ _ _ _ _ _.

3 Those which give o _ _ _ _ _.

4

There are two main advantages which road markings have over other traffic signs. Name them.

1 ______________________________

____

2 ______________________________

____

Answers on page 102

5

What do these lines across the road mean?

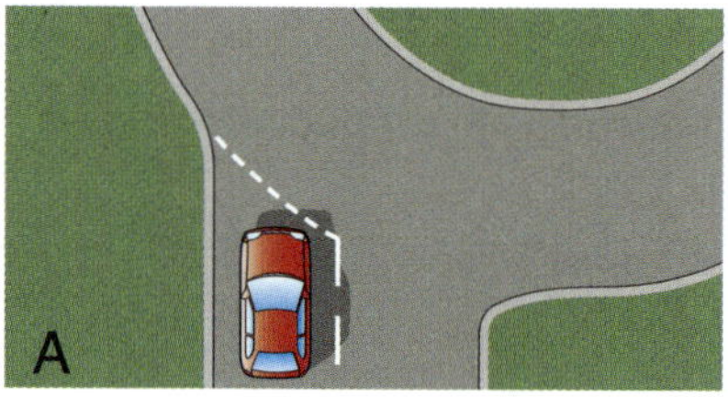

1 Stop and give way

2 Give priority to traffic coming from the immediate right.

3 Give way to traffic coming from the right.

Answer ☐

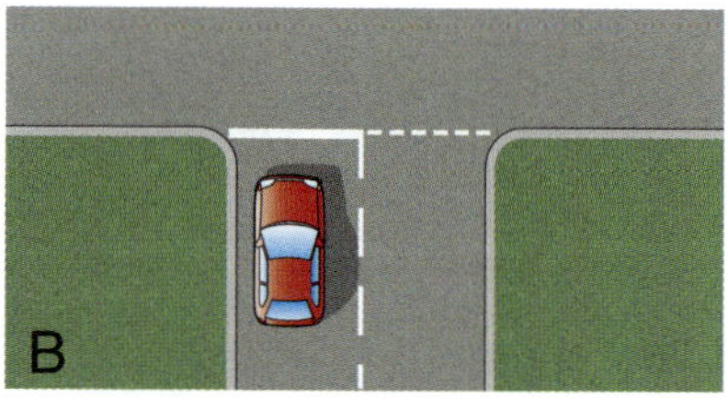

1 Give way to traffic on the major road.

2 Stop at the line and give way to traffic on the major road.

Answer ☐

Answers on page 102

6

Where you see double solid white lines painted along the centre of the road, what does this mean?

Tick any boxes you think are appropriate.

More than one answer may be correct.

1 I must not park or wait on the carriageway. ☐

2 I can park between 7pm and 7am. ☐

3 I must not overtake. ☐

4 I must not cross the white line except to turn right or in circumstances beyond my control. ☐

7

What is the purpose of these hatched markings (chevrons)?

Answer________________________________

____

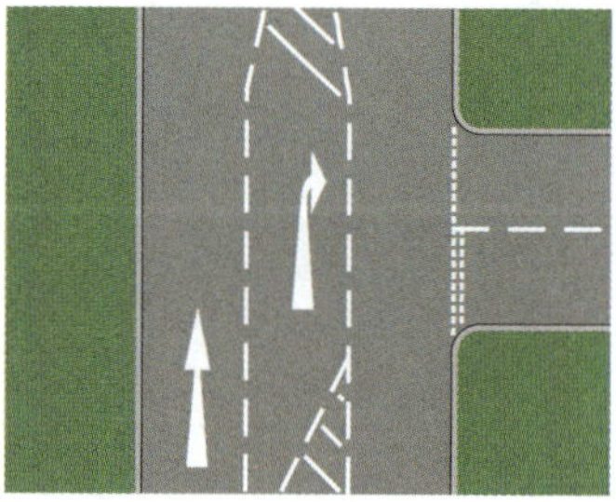

8

What does it mean if the chevrons are edged with a solid white line?

Answer______________________________

____

The shape and colour of a sign will help you understand what it means.

9

Look at the sign shapes below and say whether each gives an order, a warning or information.

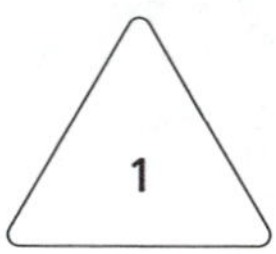

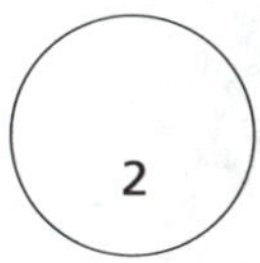

Answer__________ Answer__________

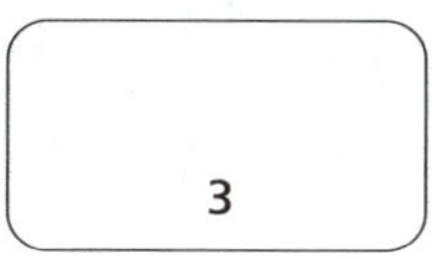

Answer__________

10

Complete the sentences

1 A circular sign with a blue background tells you what you m_ _ _ do.

2 A circular sign with a red border tells you what you m_ _ _ n_ _ do.

Answers on pages 102–3

11

What do these signs mean?

Answer______________________

____

____

____

Answer______________________

____

____

____

12

Some junctions have a stop sign, others have a give way sign. *Complete the sentence*

A stop sign is usually placed at a junction where v_ _ _ _ _ _ is l_ _ _ _ _ _ _.

13

Information signs are colour-coded.

Match each of the following signs to its colouring.

A White letters on a brown background ☐ Motorway signs

B Black letters on a white background ☐ Primary routes

C Black letters on a white background with a blue border ☐ Other routes

D White letters on a blue background with a white border ☐ Local places

E White letters on a green background, yellow route numbers with a white border ☐ Tourist signs

1

Good observation is vital in today's busy traffic.

Complete the sentence

When using my mirrors I should try to make a mental note of the s__ __ __ __,
b__ __ __ __ __ __ __ __ __ and
i__ __ __ __ __ __ __ __ __ __ of the driver behind.

2

Driving in built-up areas is potentially dangerous.

Look at the diagram opposite

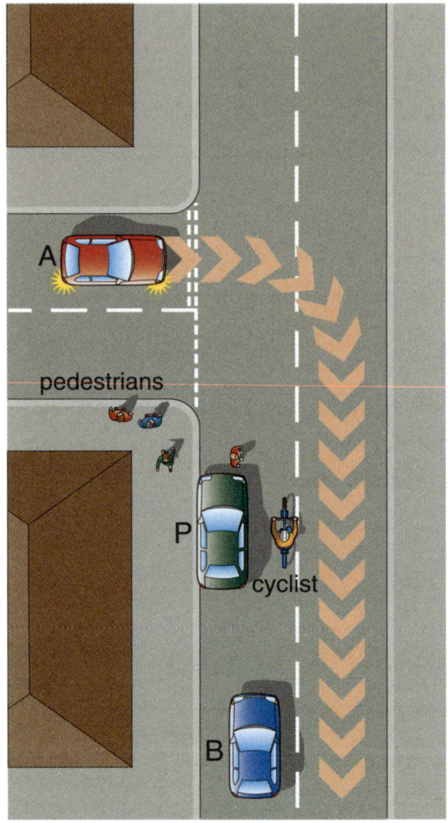

1 What action should the driver of car **A** take?

List four options

A ____________________________
B ____________________________
C ____________________________
D ____________________________

2 What action should the driver of car **B** take?

List four options

A ____________________________
B ____________________________
C ____________________________
D ____________________________

HINTS & TIPS

Observation means looking all around and seeing anything that matters. Don't stare at just one thing – keep your eyes moving.

Answers on pages 102–4

3

Motorcyclists are often less visible than other road users.

Complete this well-known phrase

Think once, think twice, think b__ __ __.

4

When you observe traffic following too close behind you, would you

Tick the correct box

1 Speed up to create a bigger gap? ☐

2 Touch your brake lights to warn the following driver? ☐

3 Keep to a safe speed, and keep checking the behaviour and intentions of the following driver? ☐

5

Some hazards are potential, others are actual and there all the time, such as a bend in the road.

A Name five more actual hazards

1 ______________________

2 ______________________

3 ______________________

4 ______________________

5 ______________________

B Name five potential hazards, such as a dog off its lead

1 ______________________

2 ______________________

3 ______________________

4 ______________________

5 ______________________

6

Modern driving requires full concentration. Are the following statements true or false?

Tick the correct boxes	**True**	**False**
1 Carrying a mobile phone can reduce the stress of a long journey.	☐	☐
2 I must not use a hand-held phone while driving.	☐	☐
3 Conversation on a hands-free phone can still distract my attention.	☐	☐
4 I should pull up in a safe place to make or receive calls.	☐	☐

Answers on page 104

7

When driving, all the following actions have something in common.

What is it?

Reading a map

Eating

Changing a cassette

Listening to loud music

Answer________________________________

____

____

____

One of the features of driving on the open road is taking bends properly.

8

As a rule you should be travelling at the correct s_ _ _ _, using the correct g_ _ _, and be in the correct p_ _ _ _ _ _ _ _.

9

Should you brake ...

Tick the appropriate box

1 Before you enter the bend? ☐

2 As you enter the bend? ☐

3 While negotiating the bend? ☐

Answers on page 104

10

Which way does force push a car on a bend?

A Inwards or **B** Outwards

Answer ☐

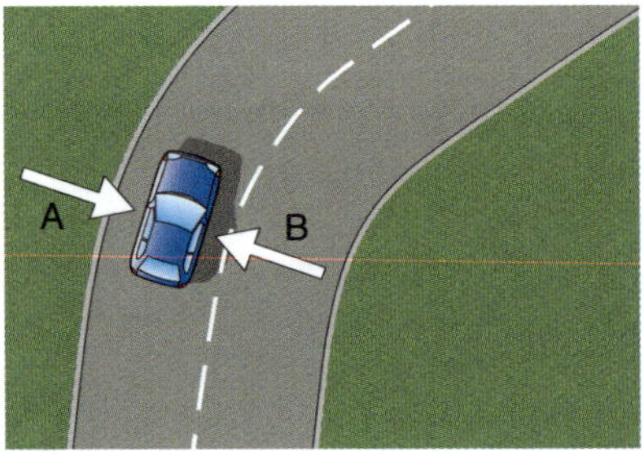

11

What happens to the weight of the car when you use the brakes?

A It is thrown forwards

B It remains even

C It is thrown back

Answer ☐

12

When you approach a bend, what position should you be in?

Complete the sentences

A On a right-hand bend I should keep to the ______________________________

____

B On a left-hand bend I should keep to the______________________________

____

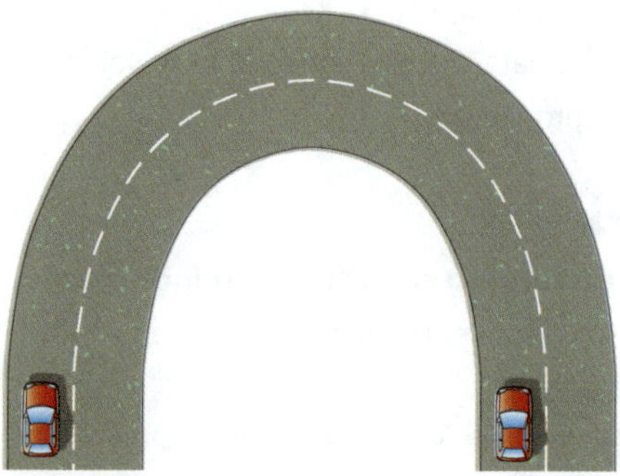

Overtaking is a potentially dangerous manoeuvre.

13

Before overtaking, consider whether it is really n__ __ __ __ __ __ __ __ __.

Fill in the missing word

Always use the safety routine when overtaking.

Put these actions into their correct sequence by putting numbers 1 to 7, as seen in the diagram, in the boxes

☐ Signal ☐ Mirrors ☐ Look
☐ Position ☐ Mirrors ☐ Speed
☐ Manoeuvre

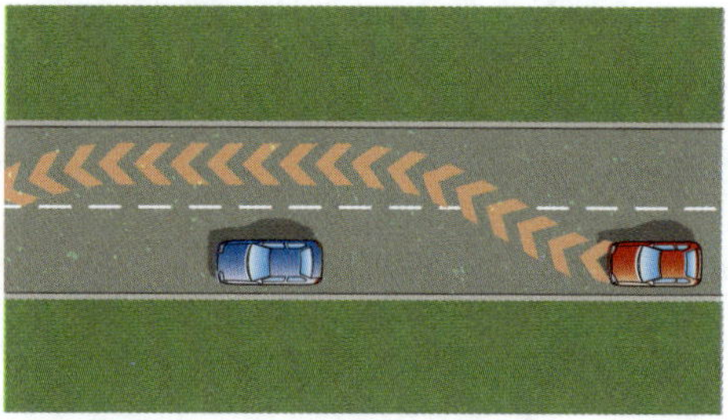

14

What is the minimum amount of clearance you should give a cyclist or motor cyclist?

Answer ______________________________

____

Answers on pages 104–5

15

There are four situations in which you may, with caution, overtake on the left-hand side of the car in front.

Name them

1 ______________________________

2 ______________________________

3 ______________________________

4 ______________________________

16

List four places where it would be dangerous to overtake.

1 ______________________________

2 ______________________________

3 ______________________________

4 ______________________________

17

Dual carriageways can appear similar to motorways, but there are important differences. Which of the following statements apply to dual carriageways?

Tick the relevant boxes

1 Reflective studs are not used ☐.

2 Cyclists are allowed. ☐

3 The speed limit is always 60mph. ☐

4 You cannot turn right to enter or leave a dual carriageway. ☐

5 Milk floats and slow moving farm vehicles are prohibited. ☐

18

When turning right from a minor road on to a dual carriageway, where would you wait …

A When there is a wide central reserve?

Answer______________________________

B When the central reserve is too narrow for your car?

Answer______________________________

19

When travelling at 70mph on a dual carriageway, which lane would you use?

Answer______________________________

Answers on pages 105–6

20

What do these signs mean?

A

Answer________________________________

B

Answer________________________________

C

Answer________________________________

21

Which of the signs in Question 20 (see opposite) would you expect to see on a dual carriageway?

Answer________________________________

22

Why is it important to plan your movements especially early when leaving a dual carriageway to the right (see diagram below)?

Answer________________________________

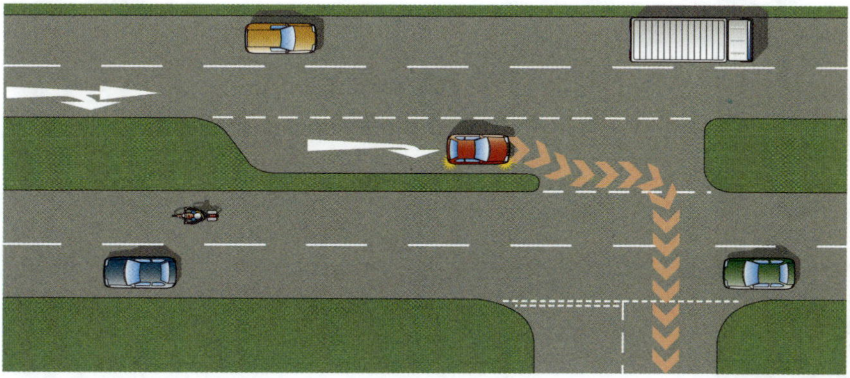

Answers on page 106

1

Cars fitted with automatic transmission select the gear depending on the road speed and the load on the engine. They therefore have no c_ _ _ _ _ pedal.

Fill in the missing word

2

The advantages of an automatic car are ...

1 ______________________________

____

2 ______________________________

____

3

The gear selector has the same function as a manual selector, but what function do each of the following have?

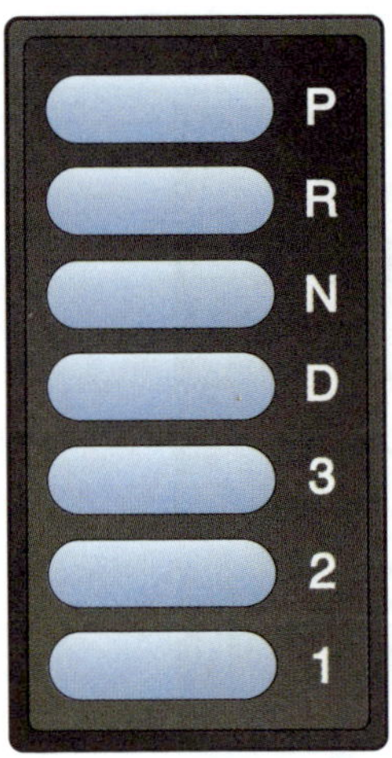

Park______________

____

Reverse______________

____

Neutral______________

____

Drive______________

____

3rd______________

____

2nd______________

____

1st______________

____

4

Automatic cars have a device called a kickdown. Is its function ...

Tick the correct box

1 To select a higher gear? ☐

2 To select a lower gear manually? ☐

3 To provide quick accelerations when needed? ☐

5

When driving an automatic car, would you select a lower gear ...

Tick the correct boxes	**True**	**False**
1 To control speed when going down a steep hill?	☐	☐
2 To slow the car down in normal driving?	☐	☐
3 When going uphill?	☐	☐
4 To overtake, in certain circumstances?	☐	☐
5 When manoeuvring?	☐	☐
6 Before stopping?	☐	☐

6

An automatic car has two foot pedals, the foot-brake and the accelerator.

For normal driving, which foot would you use ...

1 For the brake?

Answer______________________________

2 For the accelerator?

Answer______________________________

Answers on pages 106–7

7

When you are driving an automatic car, using one foot to control both pedals is preferable to using both the left and the right foot. Why?

Answer ______________________________

____

____

____

8

Some cars with automatic transmission have a tendency to 'creep'.

Which gears allow the car to creep?

Answer ______________________________

____

____

____

9

When driving an automatic car, would you use the handbrake ...

Tick the correct box

1 More than in a manual car? ☐

2 The same? ☐

3 Less? ☐

> **HINTS & TIPS**
>
> Remember – if you haven't got your foot on the brake when you select Drive in an automatic car, the vehicle may begin to move forward

10

In which position should the gear selector be when you are starting the engine?

Answer ______________________

or ______________________

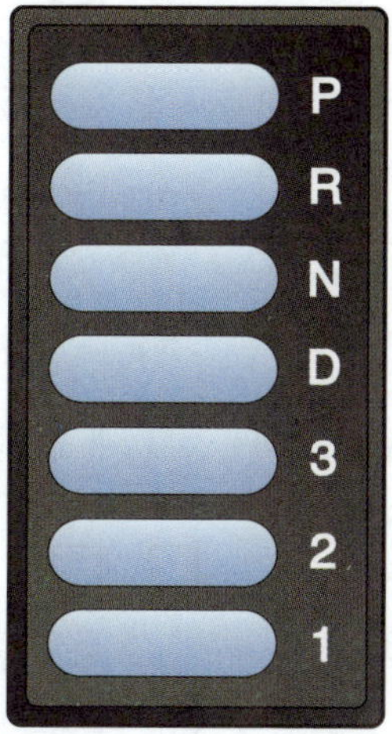

11

As you approach a bend, an automatic car will sometimes change up because there is less pressure on the accelerator. What should you do to prevent this happening?

Tick the correct box

1 Slow down before the bend and accelerate gently as you turn. ☐

2 Brake as you go round the bend. ☐

3 Brake and accelerate at the same time. ☐

Answers on page 107

1

There are many myths and misunderstandings surrounding the driving test.
Are the following true or false?

Tick the correct boxes **True False**

1 The driving test is designed to see whether I can drive around a test route without making any mistakes. ☐ ☐

2 The driving test is designed to see whether I can drive safely under various traffic conditions. ☐ ☐

3 I do not need to know any of *The Highway Code*. ☐ ☐

4 The examiner has a set allocation of passes each week. ☐ ☐

5 I may be expected to drive up to the maximum national speed limit, where appropriate. ☐ ☐

2

The length of the normal driving test is approximately ...

Tick the correct box

1 60 minutes ☐
2 90 minutes ☐
3 40 minutes ☐

3

If, during the test, you do not understand what the examiner says to you, you would take a guess because you must not talk to him or her.

Is this statement true or false?

Tick the correct box **True** ☐ **False** ☐

4

You may have heard people say that it is easier to pass the driving test in certain parts of the country.

Tick the correct box **YES NO**

Do you agree with this statement? ☐ ☐

5

If you fail your test, you can take it again. Which of the following statements is correct?

Tick the correct box(es)

1 If you fail the test, you can apply straight away for another appointment. ☐

2 If you fail the test you have to wait a month before you can apply for another appointment. ☐

3 You can re-take your test, subject to appointment availability, any time. ☐

4 You have to wait 10 working days before you can re-take the test. ☐

Answers on page 107

6

Before the practical part of your test, the examiner will test your eyesight. This is done by asking you to read a number plate at a distance of ...

Tick the correct box

1 30.5 metres (100 feet) ☐
2 20.5 metres (67 feet) ☐
3 40.5 metres (133 feet) ☐

7

What will happen if you fail your eyesight test?

Answer________________________________

____

8

It is essential that you take both sections of your p__ __ __ __ __ __ __ __ __ __ l__ __ __ __ __ __ to the test centre. This document must be s__ __ __ __ __ in ink.

Complete the sentence

9

You will also be required to produce another form of identification; this could be a p__ __ __ __ __ __ __, or a photograph signed and authorised by your i__ __ __ __ __ __ __ __ __ __.

Complete the sentence

10

The examiner will expect you to drive without making any mistakes. Do you think this statement is true or false?

Tick the correct box **True** ☐ **False** ☐

11

Is this statement about what you will be asked to do during the test true or false? I will be asked to perform four set exercises:

Tick the correct boxes	**True**	**False**
1 The emergency stop	☐	☐
2 The turn in the road	☐	☐
3 Reversing into a side road on the right or left	☐	☐
4 Reverse parallel parking or reversing into a parking bay	☐	☐

Answers on page 108

12

When reversing, are you allowed to undo your seat belt?

Tick the correct box **Yes** ☐ **No** ☐

13

If you fail your test, what will the examiner do?

1 ____________________

2 ____________________

14

When you have passed your driving test, what are you entitled to do?

1 ____________________

2 ____________________

3 ____________________

15

I have within the last month passed my test.
Can I supervise a learner driver?

Tick the correct box **YES** ☐ **NO** ☐

16

When you pass your test, where should you send your pass certificate?

Answer____________________

17

While you are waiting for your full licence to be sent to you, can you drive legally?

Tick the correct box **YES** ☐ **NO** ☐

18

It is recommended that you take further tuition once you have passed your test, especially on motorway driving.

Complete the sentence

As a learner driver you will not have experienced the special r__ __ __ __ that apply on the motorway and the h__ __ __ s__ __ __ __ of the other traffic.

19

While taking your driving test, you should drive ...

Tick the correct box

1 Especially carefully, keeping about 5mph below the speed limit ☐

2 As you would normally drive with your instructor ☐

3 With confidence, keeping at or just over the speed limit, to show that you can really drive ☐

20

Can you take a driving test if you are deaf?

Tick the correct box **YES** ☐ **NO** ☐

Answers on page 108

The driving test ensures that all drivers reach a minimum standard.

1

Do you think that learning to drive ends with passing the test?

Tick the correct box **YES** ☐ **NO** ☐

2

What knowledge and skills are not necessarily assessed in the present driving test?

List three

1 ______________________________

2 ______________________________

3 ______________________________

3

Which of these statements do you think best describes advanced driving?

Tick the correct box

1 Advanced driving is learning to handle your car to its maximum performance. ☐

2 Advanced driving is learning to drive defensively with courtesy and consideration to others. ☐

3 Advanced driving is learning to drive fast. ☐

4

Some people have difficulty in driving at night.
Which age group would you expect, in general, to experience most difficulties?

Tick the correct box

1 Older people ☐

2 Younger people ☐

5

Once you have passed your driving test, your licence is usually valid until you reach __ __ years of age.

Complete the sentence

6

There are particular circumstances under which you are required to take a driving test again. Name them

Answer______________________________

HINTS & TIPS

Driving is a skill you can improve for the rest of your life; consider further training after the test.

Answers on page 109

7

Motorways are designed to enable traffic to travel faster in greater safety. Compared to other roads, are they statistically ...

Tick the correct box

1 Safer? ☐

2 Less safe? ☐

3 No different? ☐

8

Are the following groups allowed on the motorway?

Tick the correct boxes

1 Provisional licence holders ☐

2 Motor cycles over 50cc ☐

3 Pedestrians ☐

4 HGV learner drivers ☐

5 Newly qualified drivers with less than three months' experience ☐

6 Motor cycles under 125cc ☐

7 Cyclists ☐

9

There are some routine checks you should carry out on your car before driving on the motorway. Name four of them

1 ____________________

2 ____________________

3 ____________________

4 ____________________

10

On the motorway, if something falls from either your own or another vehicle, should you ...

Tick the correct box

1 Flash your headlights to inform other drivers? ☐

2 Pull over, put your hazard warning lights on and quickly run on to the motorway to collect the object? ☐

3 Pull over on to the hard shoulder, use the emergency telephone to call the police? ☐

4 Flag another motorist down to get help? ☐

Answers on page 109

11

Which colour do you associate with motorway signs?

Tick the correct box

1 Black lettering on a white background ☐

2 White lettering on a green background ☐

3 White lettering on a blue background ☐

12

At night or in poor weather conditions, your headlights will pick out reflective studs. Match the colour of the studs to their function by placing the appropriate letter in the box.

A Amber	Marks the edge of the hard shoulder ☐
B Red	Marks the edge of the central reservation ☐
C Green	Marks the lane lines ☐
D White	Marks exits and entrances ☐

13

Do the broken lines at the end of the acceleration lane mean ...

Tick the correct box

1 The edge of the carriageway? ☐

2 Other traffic should let you in? ☐

3 Give way to traffic already on the carriageway? ☐

14

If you see congestion ahead, is it legal to use your hazard warning lights to warn drivers behind you?

Tick the correct box **YES** ☐ **NO** ☐

15

What is the most common cause of accidents on motorways?

Tick the correct box

1 Vehicles breaking down ☐

2 Drivers falling asleep ☐

3 Drivers travelling too fast, too close to the vehicle in front ☐

4 Fog ☐

16

Are the following statements true or false?

I can use the hard shoulder ...

Tick the correct boxes	**True**	**False**
1 To take a short break	☐	☐
2 To stop and read a map	☐	☐
3 To allow the children to stretch their legs	☐	☐
4 To pull over in an emergency	☐	☐
5 To answer a phone call	☐	☐

Answers on pages 109–10

17

In normal driving on the motorway, you should overtake ...

Tick the correct box

1 On the right ☐

2 On the left ☐

3 On either side ☐

Driving at night can cause problems.

18

Which of these statements do you think is correct?

Tick the correct box

1 Street lighting and my car's headlights mean that I can see just as well as in the daylight. Therefore driving at night is just like driving in the daylight. ☐

2 At night I have to rely on my car's headlights and any additional lighting. Therefore I cannot see as far or drive as fast as in the daylight. ☐

19

At dusk and dawn what action should you take to compensate for driving a dark coloured car?

Answer________________________________

____

20

When driving after dark in a built-up area, should you use ...

Tick the correct box

1 Dipped headlights? ☐

2 Side or dim-dipped lights? ☐

21

***The Highway Code* says you should not use your horn in a built-up area between 11.30pm and 7am.**

What is the exception to that rule?

Answer________________________________

____

22

The diagram below illustrates two vehicles parked at night on a two-way road.

Which one is parked correctly?

Tick the correct box

A ☐ B ☐

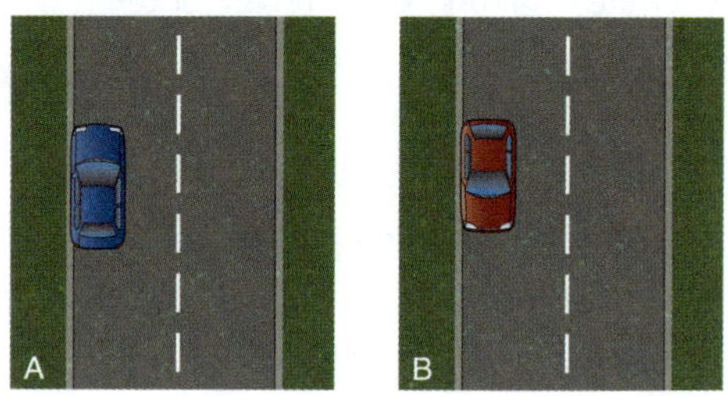

Answers on page 110

23

Certain groups of road users are particularly vulnerable at night. Name two of them

1 ______________________

2 ______________________

24

Under what circumstances would you use dipped headlights during the day?

Answer__________________________

____

and then complete the sentence

S__ __ and b__ s__ __ __.

25

When you are waiting at a junction after dark, your brake lights might d__ __ __ __ __ the driver behind.

It is better to use your h__ __ __ __ __ __ __ __ __.

Complete the sentences

Certain weather conditions can create hazardous driving conditions in the summer as well as in the winter.

26

Which of the following causes greatest danger to drivers?

Tick the correct box

1 Snow ☐

2 Ice ☐

3 Heavy rain ☐

4 Not being able to see properly ☐

27

In wet weather conditions your tyres can lose their grip.

You should allow at least d__ __ __ __ __ the distance between you and the car in front that you allow on a dry road.

Fill in the missing word

28

In very wet conditions there is a danger of a build-up of water between your tyres and the road.

This is called a__ __ __ __ __ __ __ __ __ __ __.

Fill in the missing word

Answers on page 110

29

How can you prevent a build-up of water occurring?

S___ ___ ___ d___ ___ ___ ___.

30

How should you deal with floods?

Tick the correct box

1 Drive through as fast as possible to avoid stopping ☐

2 Drive through slowly in 1st gear, slipping the clutch to keep the engine speed high ☐

3 Drive through in the highest gear possible, slipping the clutch to keep the engine speed high ☐

31

Will less tread on your tyres ...

Tick the correct box

1 Increase your braking distance? ☐

2 Decrease your braking distance? ☐

32

When the tyres lose contact with the road, the steering will feel v___ ___ ___ l___ ___ ___ ___.

Complete the sentence

33

After you have driven through a flood, should you check ...

Tick the correct box

1 Your speedometer? ☐

2 Your brakes? ☐

3 Your oil? ☐

34

There are certain key precautions you should take when driving in fog.

Complete the following sentences

1 S___ ___ ___ d___ ___ ___ ___.

2 Ensure you are able to s___ ___ ___ within the distance you can see to be clear.

3 Use your w___ ___ ___ ___ ___ ___ ___ ___ ___ ___ ___ ___ ___ w___ ___ ___ ___ ___ ___.

4 Use your d___ ___ ___ ___ ___ ___ ___ ___ ___ ___ and your h___ ___ ___ ___ ___ ___ ___ r___ ___ ___ ___ w___ ___ ___ ___ ___ ___ ___ ___ ___ ___ ___ ___ ___.

35

Under what circumstances should you use your rear fog lights?

When visibility is less than __________ metres/yards

Fill in the correct number

Answers on page 110

36

When you are following another vehicle in fog, should you ...

Tick the correct box

1 Follow closely behind because it will help you see where you are going? ☐

2 Leave plenty of room between you and the vehicle in front? ☐

37

When you are following another vehicle in fog, should you use ...

Tick the correct box

1 Main beam headlights? ☐

2 Dipped headlights? ☐

38

Extra precautions are needed when dealing with a junction in fog.

Complete the following sentences

1 Open your w__ __ __ __ __ __ and switch off your a__ __ __ __ s__ __ __ __ __. L__ __ __ __ __ for other vehicles.

2 Signal e__ __ __ __ .

3 Use your b__ __ __ __ __. The light will a__ __ __ __ following vehicles.

4 Use your h__ __ __ if you think it will w__ __ __ other road users.

39

Is the following statement about anti-lock brakes true or false?
Anti-lock brakes will stop me skidding when driving on snow or ice.

Tick the correct box **True** ☐ **False** ☐

40

When driving in snow or ice you should gently test your b__ __ __ __ __ from time to time.

Fill in the missing word

41

In order to slow down when driving on snow or ice you should ...

Fill in the missing words

1 Use your brakes g__ __ __ __ __ .

2 Get into a l__ __ __ g__ __ __ earlier than normal.

3 Allow your speed to d__ __ __ and use b__ __ __ __ __ gently and early.

42

On snow or ice, braking distances can increase by ...

Tick the correct box

1 10 times ☐

2 5 times ☐

3 20 times ☐

4 15 times ☐

Answers on page 111

43

When going downhill in snow, what would you do to help you slow down?

Answer______________________________

44

When cornering in snow or ice, what should you avoid doing?

Answer______________________________

45

How can you reduce the risk of wheel spin?

Answer______________________________

HINTS & TIPS

If you realise that your car is starting to skid, ease off the brake and accelerator, then steer smoothly in the same direction as the skid.

46

Three important factors cause a skid. Name them.

1 ______________________________

2 ______________________________

3 ______________________________

47

Some everyday driving actions, especially in poor weather, can increase the risk of skidding.

Fill in the missing words

1 S__ __ __ __ __ __ __ down.

2 S__ __ __ __ __ __ __ __ up.

3 T__ __ __ __ __ __ __ corners.

4 Driving u__ __ __ __ __ __ and d__ __ __ __ __ __ __ __.

Answers on page 111

All vehicles need routine attention and maintenance to keep them in good working order. Neglecting maintenance can be costly and dangerous.

1

With which of these statements do you agree?

Tick the correct box

1 Allowing the fuel gauge to drop too low is bad for the engine. ☐

2 In modern cars the fuel level makes little difference. ☐

2

What do you put into the engine to lubricate the moving parts?

Answer________________________________

____

____

3

How frequently should you check your oil level?

Tick the correct box

1 Once a month ☐

2 Once a year ☐

3 Every time you fill up with fuel ☐

4

The engine is often cooled by a mixture of w__ __ __ __ and a__ __ __ __ f__ __ __ __ __.

Some engines are a__ __ cooled.

Complete the sentence

5

How frequently should you test your brakes?

Tick the correct box

1 Daily ☐

2 Monthly ☐

3 Weekly ☐

4 When I use them ☐

6

Incorrectly adjusted headlamps can cause d__ __ __ __ __ __ to other road users.

Complete the sentence

7

All headlamps, indicators and brake lights should be kept in good working order. It is also important that they are kept c__ __ __ __ __ .

Fill in the missing word

Answers on page 111

8

Tyres should be checked for u__ __ __ __ __ wear and tyre walls for b__ __ __ __ __ and c__ __ __.

Complete the sentence

9

The legal requirement for tread depth is not less than ...

Tick the correct box

1 1.4mm ☐
2 1.6mm ☐
3 2mm ☐

10

What should you do if your brakes feel slack or spongy?

Answer______________________________

____

____

11

Vehicle breakdowns could result from ...

Fill in the missing words

1 N__ __ __ __ __ __ of the vehicle
2 Lack of r__ __ __ __ __ __ c__ __ __ __ __
3 Little or no p__ __ __ __ __ __ __ __ __ __ __ maintenance
4 A__ __ __ __ of the vehicle

Answers on page 111

12

It is advisable to carry a warning triangle.

1 On a straight road how far back should it be placed?

Tick the correct box

50 metres/yards ☐
200 metres/yards ☐
150 metres/yards ☐

2 On a dual carriageway, how far back should it be placed? At least ...

Tick the correct box

200 metres/yards ☐
150 metres/yards ☐
450 metres/yards ☐

13

If you use a warning triangle, is it worth putting your hazard lights on as well?

Tick the correct box **YES** ☐ **NO** ☐

14

If your vehicle breaks down on a motorway, should you ...

Tick the correct box

1 Gently brake, put your hazard lights on and seek assistance? ☐
2 Pull over to the central reservation as far to the right as possible? ☐
3 Pull over safely on to the hard shoulder as far away from the carriageway as possible? ☐

15

If your vehicle has broken down on the motorway, should you tell your passengers to ...

Tick the correct box

1 Stay in the vehicle while you seek assistance? ☐

2 Wait by the car on the hard shoulder but watch for other vehicles? ☐

3 Get out of the vehicle and wait on the embankment away from the hard shoulder? ☐

16

The marker posts at the side of all motorways have a picture of a telephone handset.

How can you tell which way to walk to reach the nearest telephone?

Answer ______________________________

17

When you use the emergency telephone on a motorway, what will the operator ask you?

1 ______________________________

2 ______________________________

3 ______________________________

4 ______________________________

18

Disabled drivers cannot easily get to an emergency telephone. How can they summon help?

1 ______________________________

2 ______________________________

Answers on page 112

19

If you break down when travelling alone, there are three things you are advised NOT to do.

Complete the sentences

1 Do not ask p__ __ __ __ __ __ m__ __ __ __ __ __ __ __ __ for help.

2 Do not accept help from anyone you d__ n__ __ k__ __ __ (except the emergency services or a breakdown service).

3 Do not l__ __ __ __ you vehicle l__ __ __ __ __ than necessary.

20

If I am first or one of the first to arrive at the scene of an accident, should I ...

Tick the correct boxes	**True**	**False**
1 Always move injured people away from vehicles?	☐	☐
2 Tell the ambulance personnel or paramedics what I think is wrong with those injured?	☐	☐
3 Give casualties something warm to drink?	☐	☐
4 Switch off hazard warning lights?	☐	☐
5 Switch off vehicle engines?	☐	☐
6 Inform the police of the accident?	☐	☐

Answers on page 112

21

If you are involved in an accident, what MUST you do?

Answer ______________________________

____

____

22

If you are involved in an accident and nobody is injured, do you have to call the police?

Tick the correct box **YES** ☐ **NO** ☐

23

What information do you need to exchange if you are involved in an accident?

1 ______________________________

2 ______________________________

3 ______________________________

4 ______________________________

5 ______________________________

24

If you thought you had a fire in your car's engine, what action would you take?

1 ______________________________

____

____

2 ______________________________

____

____

3 ______________________________

____

____

25

There are three items of emergency equipment it is wise to carry in your car.

Fill in the missing words

1 F_ _ _ _ A_ _ kit.

2 F_ _ _
e_ _ _ _ _ _ _ _ _ _.

3 W_ _ _ _ _ _ t_ _ _ _ _ _ _

26

When you rejoin a motorway from the hard shoulder, should you ...

Tick the correct box

1 Signal right and join when there is safe gap? ☐

2 Keep your hazard lights on and drive down the hard shoulder until there is a safe gap? ☐

3 Use the hard shoulder to build up speed and join the carriageway when safe? ☐

27

Fuel combustion causes waste products. One of these is a gas called c_ _ _ _ _ d_ _ _ _ _ _.

This is a major cause of the g_ _ _ _ _ _ _ _ _ effect.

Complete the sentences

28

How much does transport contribute to the production of carbon dioxide in the country (expressed as a percentage of the total production)?

Tick the correct box

1 10 per cent ☐

2 25 per cent ☐

3 50 per cent ☐

4 20 per cent ☐

Answers on page 113

29

The MOT test checks the roadworthiness of a vehicle.

Does it include an exhaust emission test?

Tick the correct box **YES** ☐ **NO** ☐

30

A catalytic convertor stops the emission of carbon dioxide.

Tick the correct box **True** ☐ **False** ☐

31

Which uses up more fuel?

Tick the correct box

1 A car travelling at 50mph ☐

2 A car travelling at 70mph ☐

32

There are some measures car drivers can take to help reduce damage to the environment.

List five

1 ______________________________

2 ______________________________

3 ______________________________

4 ______________________________

5 ______________________________

Before buying a used car it is best to decide what you want the car for and how much you can afford.

33

There are three main sources of supply for used vehicles. You can buy from a d__ __ __ __ __, at an a__ __ __ __ __ __ or p__ __ __ __ __ __ __ __ __.

Complete the sentence

34

When reading a glowing description of a used car, what should you first consider?

Answer______________________________

Answers on page 113

35

Are these statements about buying a used car through a dealer or at an auction true or false?

Tick the correct boxes

	True	False
1 It is often cheaper to buy a car at an auction than through a dealer.	☐	☐
2 I have the same legal rights when I buy at an auction as when I buy from a dealer.	☐	☐
3 I should always read the terms and conditions of trade before I buy a car at an auction.	☐	☐
4 The best way to select a used car dealer is by recommendation.	☐	☐

36

Cars bought through a dealer often have a warranty.

What should you check?

1 ______________________________

2 ______________________________

37

When you test drive a vehicle, you should make sure that it is t_ _ _ _ _, has a current M_ _ certificate (if applicable) and that all i_ _ _ _ _ _ _ _ _ requirements are complied with.

Complete the sentence

38

There are some important items that you should check on before you buy a used car.

List three

1 ______________________________

2 ______________________________

3 ______________________________

39

Do you think the following statement is true or false?

It is advisable to have my vehicle examined by a competent and unbiased expert before I buy.

Tick the correct box **True** ☐ **False** ☐

Answers on page 113

Particular difficulties are encountered when towing a caravan or trailer. There are some very good courses which will help you master the skills required.

1

People can underestimate the length of the total combination of car and caravan or trailer.

Is the overall length usually ...

Tick the correct box

1 Twice the length of a normal car? ☐

2 Three times the length of a normal car? ☐

2

What additional fixtures should you attach to your car to help you see more clearly?

1 ______________________________
____
____

3

When towing you will need more distance than normal to overtake. Is it ...

Tick the correct box

1 Twice the normal distance? ☐

2 Three times the normal distance? ☐

3 Four times the normal distance? ☐

4

A device called a s_ _ _ _ _ _ _ _ _ will make the combination safer to handle.

Fill in the missing word

5

The stability of the caravan will depend on how you load it. Should heavy items be loaded ...

Tick the correct box

1 At the front? ☐

2 At the rear? ☐

3 Over the axle(s)? ☐

6

There are special restrictions for vehicles which are towing.

A What is the speed limit on a dual carriageway?

Tick the correct box

1 50mph ☐

2 60mph ☐

3 70mph ☐

Answers on page 114

B What is the speed on a single carriageway?

Tick the correct box

1 40mph ☐
2 50mph ☐
3 60mph ☐

7

There are some important checks you should make before starting off.

List four

1 ______________________________
____
2 ______________________________
____
3 ______________________________
____
4 ______________________________
____

8

If you decide to stop to take a break, before allowing anyone to enter the caravan you should lower the

j__ __ __ __ __ w__ __ __ __ and

c__ __ __ __ __ __ s__ __ __ __ __ __ __ __ __.

Fill in the missing words

Many people now take their car abroad or hire a vehicle when on holiday.

9

Motoring organisations, such as The Automobile Association, can help you plan and organise your trip.

The AA can provide advice on travel and v__ __ __ __ __ __ __ insurance.

They will also help you organise the d__ __ __ __ __ __ __ __ __ __ __ that you will need.

Fill in the missing words

10

Before travelling to Europe, you should always ...

Complete the sentences

1 Plan the r__ __ __ __ __ you wish to take.

2 Know the local m__ __ __ __ __ __ __ __ r__ __ __ __ __ __ __ __ __ __ __ __.

Answers on page 114

11

It is essential that your vehicle should be checked thoroughly.
List four of the routine checks you should make

1 ______________________________

2 ______________________________

3 ______________________________

4 ______________________________

12

In most European countries you are advised to carry your d_ _ _ _ _ _ _ l_ _ _ _ _ _ _ on you.

Complete the sentence

13

What do the letters IDP stand for?

Answer ______________________________

14

Where might you need an IDP?

Answer ______________________________

15

In most European countries what age do you have to be to drive?

Tick the correct box

1 ☐ 21 **2** ☐ 18 **3** ☐ 16

16

Some European countries can require you to carry additional emergency equipment.
List four of the items you are recommended to carry

1 ______________________________

2 ______________________________

3 ______________________________

4 ______________________________

Answers on page 114

Answers to Questions

Answers to Questions

Section 1

INTRODUCTION TO LEARNING TO DRIVE

Questions on pages 24–5

A1 A current, signed, full or provisional licence for the category of vehicle that you are driving

A2 examinations
register

A3 21 years old
three years

A4 To the front and rear. It is important not to place them in windows where they could restrict good vision.

A5 True

A6 You should have answered No to all the questions.

A7 Yes. This should be the ambition of every driver.

A8 3, 4

ADJUSTING YOUR DRIVING POSITION

Questions on page 25

A9 **1** handbrake
2 doors
3 seat
4 head restraint
5 mirrors
6 seat belt

INTRODUCTION TO VEHICLE CONTROLS

Questions on pages 25–6

A10 The handbrake E
The driving mirrors D
The gear lever F
The clutch G
The steering wheel A
The foot-brake B
The accelerator C

A11 The foot-brake R
The clutch L
The accelerator R

A12 **1** False. You will need one hand to change gear or use other controls.
2 True
3 False. The best position is quarter to three or ten to two.
4 False. It is safest to feed the wheel through your hands.
5 True
6 True

A13 The direction indicators B
Dipped beam A
Main beam D
Rear fog lamp C
Horn E
Hazard lights F

Section 2

MOVING OFF

Questions on page 27

A1 **A** 1
B 5
C 3
D 2
E 6
F 4
G 7
H 8
I 9

STOPPING (NORMALLY)

Questions on page 28

A2 **A** 1
B 3
C 2
D 4
E 6
F 5
G 8
H 7
I 9

GEAR CHANGING

Questions on pages 29–30

A3 1st gear

A4 5th, or 4th if the car has a 4-speed gear box

A5 Usually 2nd gear, but 1st if you need to go very slowly or 3rd if the corner is sweeping and you can take it safely at a higher speed

A6 engine
vehicle
sound
when

A7 **A** 1
B 3
C 2
D 4
E 5

A8 **1** False. This will cause the engine to labour.
2 False. It is good practice to use the brakes to slow the car down. Using the transmission causes wear and tear which can be very costly. Also, the brakes are more effective.
3 False
4 True
5 False. It is good practice to miss out the unwanted gears and select the gear most appropriate to your road speed.

A9 **1**
A10 **1** Don't
2 Don't
3 Do
4 Do
5 Do
6 Don't
7 Don't
8 Don't

STEERING

Questions on page 31

A11 **A**, except in a few cars fitted with four-wheel steering (in which case all four wheels will move)
A12 **A**
A13 **B**
A14 **B**

ROAD POSITIONING

Questions on page 31

A15 **C** well to the left but not too close to the kerb
A16 **B**. Avoid swerving in and out. It is unnecessary and confuses other drivers.

CLUTCH CONTROL

Questions on page 32

A17 **A**
A18 biting
A19 **1** Yes
2 Yes
3 No
4 Yes
5 No

Section 3

JUNCTIONS

Questions on pages 33–5

A1 two or more roads

A2 **A** T-junction
B Y-junction
C Roundabout
D Staggered crossroads
E Crossroads

A3 **1** E
2 C
3 B
4 D
5 A

A4 **A** 1
B 3

A5 **1** Mirrors
2 Signal
3 Position
4 Speed
5 Look

A6 assess
decide
act

A7 **A**

A8 **B**

A9 **D**

A10 **1** mirrors, position
2 signal
3 safe
4 safe distance
5 overtake

CROSSROADS

Questions on page 36

A11 **A 3** Crossroads. Priority for traffic on the major road. Never assume other drivers will give you priority.
B 1 Unmarked crossroads
C 2 Crossroads with give way lines at the end of your road. Give way to traffic on the major road.

ROUNDABOUTS

Questions on pages 36–7

A12 **C**

A13 **1** Left
2 Left
3 Right. Remember to use the MSM routine before signalling left to turn off.

A14 **1** Left
2 Going ahead
3 Right

A15 mirrors
signal
position
speed
look

A16 **2**

Section 4

PARKING (ON THE ROAD)

Questions on pages 38–9

A1 **1** safe
2 considerate
3 legal

A2 Cars 1, 2, 3, 6

A3 **1** False
2 False
3 True
4 True

A4 Any of the following:
at a bus stop
at a school entrance
opposite a junction
on a bend
on the brow of a hill
on a Clearway
on a motorway
at night facing oncoming traffic
in a residents' parking zone.

Section 5

PASSING STATIONARY VEHICLES AND OBSTRUCTIONS

Questions on page 40

A1 Vehicle 2

A2 Vehicle 2, even though the obstruction is on the right. Where safe, when travelling downhill be prepared to give priority to vehicles (especially heavy vehicles) that are coming uphill.

MEETING AND CROSSING THE PATH OF OTHER VEHICLES

Questions on pages 41

A3 **1** True
2 False. Always consider whether it is safe. Are there dangers the other driver cannot see? Remember, flashing headlamps has the same meaning as sounding the horn. It is a warning: 'I am here!' Sometimes it is taken to mean: 'I am here and I am letting you pass.'
3 True

A4 **1** Yes
2 Yes
3 No
4 Yes
5 Yes
6 Yes
7 Yes

Section 6

STOPPING IN AN EMERGENCY

Questions on pages 42–3

A1 **1** True
2 True
3 True
4 False. Looking in the mirror should not be necessary. You should know what is behind you.
5 False
6 True
7 True

A2 False. An emergency stop will be conducted randomly on only some tests. You must always know how to stop safely in an emergency.

A3 pump
1 maximum
2 lock
3 quickly

A4 steer
brake
pump
pressure
1 False. Other elements beyond braking can cause skidding e.g. acceleration or going too fast into a bend.
2 False. Although you may stop in a shorter distance, you still need to leave the correct distance to allow yourself time to react and vehicles behind you time to stop.

STOPPING DISTANCES

Questions on pages 43

A5 **1** No
2 Yes
3 Yes
4 No

A6 ½ second

A7 **1** 23 metres/75 feet
2 15 metres/50 feet
3 96 metres/315 feet

A8 longer
more

A9 breaks
two-second

Section 7

MOVING OFF AT AN ANGLE

Question on page 44

A1 **1** False. You should check your mirrors and blindspot before moving out. Keep alert for other traffic as you pull out and stop if necessary.
2 True
3 False. Move out slowly and carefully.
4 True. The closer you are, the greater the angle.
5 True. As you move out, you are likely to move on to the right-hand side of the road and into conflict with oncoming vehicles.
6 False. You should signal only if it helps or warns other road users. Signalling gives you no right to pull out.

MOVING OFF UPHILL

Question on page 44

A2 **1** True
2 False. Using the accelerator pedal will not move the car forwards.
3 False. As your feet will be using the clutch pedal and the accelerator pedal you need to use the handbrake to stop the car rolling back.
4 True
5 True
6 True
7 True

MOVING OFF DOWNHILL

Question on page 45

A3 **1** True
2 False. Almost certainly you will need to use the foot-brake.
3 False. It is often better to move off in 2nd gear.
4 True. This will stop the car rolling forwards.
5 True
6 False. You will need to have your foot on the foot-brake to stop the car rolling forwards.

APPROACHING JUNCTIONS UPHILL AND DOWNHILL

Question on page 46

A4 The following statements are correct: 1, 4, 5, 6, 7

Section 8

REVERSING

Questions on pages 47–8

A1 safe
convenient
law

A2 **1** False
2 False
3 True
4 True

A3 **A**

A4 **1, 4**

A5 Car A: to the left
Car B: to the right

A6 observation

REVERSING INTO A SIDE ROAD ON THE LEFT

Questions on pages 48–9

A7 **3**

A8 **1** True
2 False
3 True

A9 **4**

A10 **C**

A11 Left

A12 The front of the car will swing out to the right

A13 **1** True
2 False
3 True

A14 pedestrians
road users
stop

REVERSING INTO A SIDE ROAD ON THE RIGHT

Questions on pages 49–50

A15 True

A16 **B**

A17 **2**

A18 True. You may need to place your left hand at 12 o'clock and lower your right hand.

A19 True

A20 **2**

A21 **B**

Answers to Questions

TURNING IN THE ROAD

Questions on pages 51–2

A22 **A**

A23 slowly
briskly

A24 False, but you should try to complete the manoeuvre in as few moves as possible.

A25 **2, 3, 4**

A26 all round

A27 **1** Right
2 Steer briskly left
3 Left
4 Steer briskly right
5 Right

A28 **1** Left
2 Over your right shoulder to where the car is going

REVERSE PARALLEL PARKING

Questions on pages 52–4

A29 **2**

A30 **C**, in line with the rear of the parked vehicle

A31 **2**

A32 **1** To the left
2 The nearside headlamp of the vehicle towards which you are reversing
3 Clipping the rear offside of the lead car
4 Take off the left lock
5 Steer to the right and then take off the right lock as you get straight

A33 **1** False
2 False
3 True. You will be expected to be able to complete the exercise within approximately two car lengths.

A34 All round, particularly for pedestrians and oncoming vehicles

A35 **C**. The other bay widths are reduced by parked vehicles. This may make opening doors a squeeze.

A36 Allows you to make best use of the area in front of the bay. Gives you a better view when driving out of the space

A37 close
directions
pedestrians

Section 9

TRAFFIC LIGHTS AND YELLOW BOX JUNCTIONS

Questions on pages 55–6

A1 **1** red
2 red and amber
3 green
4 amber
5 red

A2 **1** green
2 red and amber
3 amber
4 red

A3 **1** False
2 True
3 True
4 False. Pedestrians who are already crossing have priority.

A4 **2**

A5 **1** Lane A or B
2 Lane C
3 Lane A

A6 **1** No. If your exit is blocked you should not enter a yellow box junction.
2 No. If your exit is blocked you should not enter a yellow box junction.
3 Yes

PEDESTRIAN CROSSINGS

Questions on pages 56–8

A7 **1** Zig-zag lines
2 Flashing yellow beacons on both sides of the road
3 Black and white stripes on the crossing
4 A give way line

A8 **1** True
2 True. You must not park or wait on the zig-zag lines on either side of the crossing.
3 False. You must not overtake on the zig-zag lines on approach to the crossing.
4 True
5 True. A slowing down arm signal should be used. It helps pedestrians understand what you intend to do. They cannot see your brake lights.

A9 **1** Traffic lights
2 Zig-zag lines
3 A white stop line

A10 **2** A white stick means the pedestrian is visually handicapped. A white stick with two reflector bands means the pedestrian may be deaf as well as visually handicapped.

A11 **1** Flashing amber
2 You must give way to pedestrians on the crossing, but if it is clear you may go on.

A12 A bleeping tone. This sounds when the red light shows to drivers and helps visually handicapped pedestrians know when it is safe to cross.

A13 There is no flashing amber light sequence. The light sequence is the same as normal traffic lights.

A14 cyclists

LEVEL CROSSINGS

Questions on page 58

A15 **A** 3
B 1
C 2
D 4

A16 **2**
4
5

Section 10

ONE-WAY SYSTEMS

Questions on page 59

A1 **A** is the correct sign for a one-way street.
B tells you 'Ahead only'.

A2 **1** True
2 True
3 True
4 True

ROAD MARKINGS

Questions on pages 59–61

A3 information
warnings
orders

A4 **1** They can be seen when other signs may be hidden
2 They give a continuing message

A5 **A** 2
B 2

A6 **1, 4**

A7 They are used to separate potentially dangerous streams of traffic.

A8 You must not enter the hatched area.

TRAFFIC SIGNS

Questions on pages 61

A9 **1** Warning
2 Order
3 Information

A10 **1** must
2 must not

A11 **1** You must give way to traffic on the major road. Delay your entry until it is safe to join the major road.
2 You must stop (even if the road is clear). Wait until you can enter the new road safely.

A12 vision is limited

A13 Motorway signs D
Primary routes E
Other routes B
Local places C
Tourist signs A

Section 11

ROAD OBSERVATION

Questions on pages 62–4

A1 speed
behaviour
intentions

A2 **1** Observe that the view into the new road is restricted.
The driver should ...
Move forward slowly, to get a better view.
Note the pedestrian who may walk in front of or behind car **A**.
Note the pedestrian waiting to cross.
Allow the cyclist to pass.
Once in position to see car **B**, stop and give way.
2 Observe that the parked car restricts the view into and out of the side road.
The driver should ...

Slow down on approach to parked car **P**.
Take up position to gain a better view and be more visible to car A and the pedestrian.
Slow down in case the pedestrian walks out from behind the parked car **P**.
Consider signal to pass parked car **P**.
Look carefully into minor road. Note the actions of car **A**. Be prepared to stop.

A3 bike

A4 **3**, but touching the brakes may encourage the driver to drop back

A5 **A**
1 Junctions
2 Hump-back bridges
3 Concealed entrances
4 Dead ground
5 Narrow lanes

B
1 Children playing
2 Horses
3 Pedestrians
4 Especially elderly and young cyclists
5 Other vehicles

A6 **1** True. The ability to advise those at your destination of delays can help to reduce the worry of late arrivals
2 True
3 True
4 True

A7 All are distracting and upset concentration, and should not be carried out while driving.

DEALING WITH BENDS

Questions on pages 64–5

A8 speed
gear
position

A9 **1**

A10 **B**

A11 **A**

A12 **A** On a right-hand bend keep to the left. This will help to improve your view.
B On a left-hand bend keep to the centre of the lane. Do not move to the centre of the road to get a better view. A vehicle travelling in the opposite direction may be taking the bend wide.

OVERTAKING

Questions on pages 65–6

A13 necessary
1 Mirrors
2 Position
3 Speed
4 Look
5 Mirrors
6 Signal
7 Manoeuvre

A14 About the width of a small car, more in windy or poor weather conditions

A15 **1** The vehicle in front is signalling and positioned to turn right
2 You are using the correct lane to turn left at a junction
3 Traffic is moving slowly in queues and the traffic on the right is moving more slowly than you are
4 You are in a one-way street

A16 **1** On approach to a junction
2 The brow of a hill
3 The approach to a bend
4 Where there is dead ground.
NB These are examples. Be guided by *The Highway Code*.

DUAL CARRIAGEWAYS

Questions on pages 66–7

A17 **2** Statements 1, 3, 4 and 5 do not apply:
1 Reflective studs are used on some dual carriageways.
3 The speed limit is subject to local conditions and may vary from 40mph up to the national speed limit.
4 You can turn right on to and off dual carriageways unlike motorways, where all traffic enters and leaves on the left.
5 You may find slow moving vehicles sometimes displaying a flashing amber light.

A18 **A** You would cross over the first carriageway then wait in the gap in the central reservation. Be careful, if you are towing or if your vehicle is long, that you do not cause other road users to change course or slow down.

B You would wait until there is a gap in the traffic long enough for you safely to clear the first carriageway and emerge into the second.

A19 The speed limit applies to all lanes. Use the first lane to travel in and the second for overtaking.

A20 **A** Dual carriageway ends
B Road narrows on both sides
C Two-way traffic straight ahead

A21 **A** and **C**

A22 Traffic is moving much faster, and one or more lanes will have to be crossed.

Section 12

DRIVING AN AUTOMATIC CAR

Questions on pages 68–9

A1 Clutch

A2 **1** Driving is easier
2 There is more time to concentrate on the road

A3 Park – Locks the transmission. This should be selected only when the vehicle is stationary.
Reverse – Enables the car to go backwards, as in a manual car.
Neutral – Has the same function as in a manual car. The engine is not in contact with the driving wheels.
Drive – Is used for driving forwards. It automatically selects the most appropriate gear.
3rd – Has the same function as manual gears
2nd – Has the same function as manual gears
1st – Has the same function as manual gears

A4 **3**

A5 **1** Yes
2 No
3 Yes, if you needed extra control
4 You would probably use kickdown, but possibly in certain circumstances you would manually select a lower gear
5 Yes, maybe using 1st gear
6 No. Use the brakes

A6 **1** The right foot
2 The right foot

A7 It stops you trying to control the brake and accelerator at the same time. It encourages early release of the accelerator and progressive braking.

A8 Drive, reverse, all forward gears.

A9 **1** You should apply the handbrake every time you stop. Otherwise you have to keep your foot on the foot-brake.

A10 Park (P) or Neutral (N)

A11 **1**

Section 13

THE DRIVING TEST

Questions on pages 70–2

A1 **1** False
2 True
3 False
4 False
5 True

A2 **3**

A3 False. If you did not hear clearly or did not understand what the examiner said, you should ask him or her to repeat the instruction. If you have any problem with your hearing, it is advisable to tell the examiner at the start of the test.

A4 No. The standard test does not vary. The test result should be the same wherever it is taken.

A5 **1, 4**

A6 **2**

A7 The test will not proceed. You have failed not only the eyesight section, but the whole test. Remember, if you wear glasses or contact lenses, to wear them for the eyesight test and for the rest of the driving test.

A8 provisional licence
signed

A9 passport
instructor

A10 False. You can make some minor errors and still reach the required standard.

A11 False. Only about one third of test candidates will be asked to complete an emergency stop. You will be asked to do two out of the three reversing manoeuvres.

A12 Yes, but remember to do it up again when you have completed the exercise.

A13 **1** Give you a verbal explanation of the main reasons for failure
2 Write out a form for you to take away showing you your main errors

A14 **1** Drive unsupervised
2 Drive on a motorway
3 Drive without L-plates

A15 No. You must have had at least three years' driving experience (and be over 21 years of age).

A16 To the DVLA, Swansea

A17 Yes. It is a good idea to keep a note of your driver number and the date you passed your test.

A18 rules
high speed

A19 **2** The examiner will expect you to drive normally. You should abide by all speed limits and drive according to road and traffic conditions.

A20 Yes. The examiner will be skilled in giving instructions and directions to deaf candidates.

Section 14

BEYOND THE TEST

Questions on page 73

A1 No

A2 **1** Bad weather driving
2 Night-time driving
3 Motorway driving
4 Skid control ... and more

A3 **2**

A4 **1**, although people of any age can find it difficult to drive at night

A5 70

A6 There are certain serious driving offences which carry the penalty of disqualification. In order to regain a full licence, the disqualified driver has to apply for a provisional licence and take an extended test. If, because of certain illnesses, you have been unable to drive for 10 years, you will be required to take the test again in order to gain a full licence.
For new drivers: the accumulation of six or more penalty points within two years of passing the test will mean reverting to a provisional licence and re-sitting the test.

MOTORWAY DRIVING

Questions on pages 74–6

A7 **1**

A8 **1** No
2 Yes
3 No
4 Yes
5 Yes
6 Yes
7 No

A9 **1** Oil
2 Water
3 Fuel
4 Tyre pressures
These are just some of the checks; for more information, refer to your car's manual.

A10 **3** You should never attempt to retrieve anything from the carriageway.

A11 **3**

A12 **B** Amber
A Red
D Green
C White

A13 **3**

A14 Yes

A15 **3**

A16 **1** False
2 False
3 False
4 True
5 False

A17 **1**, except when traffic is moving slowly in queues and the queue on the right is travelling more slowly

SAFE NIGHT DRIVING

Questions on pages 76–7

A18 **2**

A19 Switch on earlier, switch off later.

A20 **1**. It helps others to see you.

A21 If you are stationary, to avoid danger from a moving vehicle.

A22 **A**. Always park with the flow of traffic. You will show red reflectors to vehicles travelling in your direction.

A23 **1** Pedestrians
2 Cyclists
3 Motor cyclists
} two of these

A24 In poor weather conditions – see and be seen

A25 dazzle
handbrake

ALL-WEATHER DRIVING

Questions on pages 77–80

A26 4

A27 double

A28 aquaplaning

A29 Slow down
Allow time for the tread patterns to disperse the water.

A30 **2**

A31 **1**

A32 very light

A33 **2**

A34 **1** Slow down
2 stop
3 windscreen wipers
4 demister, heated rear windscreen

A35 100 metres/yards

A36 **2**

A37 **2**

A38 **1** windows, audio system.
Listen
2 early
3 brakes, alert
4 horn, warn

A39 False, because your tyres are not in contact with the road

A40 brakes

A41 **1** gently
2 lower gear
3 drop, brakes

A42 **1**

A43 If possible, control your speed before reaching the hill. Select a low gear early.

A44 Using your brakes

A45 Avoid harsh acceleration

A46 **1** The driver
2 The vehicle
3 The road conditions

A47 **1** Slowing
2 Speeding
3 Turning
4 uphill, downhill

Section 15

VEHICLE CARE

Questions on pages 81–2

A1 **1**

A2 Oil

A3 **3**

A4 Water, anti-freeze, air

A5 **1**

A6 dazzle

A7 clean

A8 uneven, bulges, cuts

A9 **2**

A10 Get them checked as quickly as possible

BREAKDOWNS, ACCIDENTS AND EMERGENCIES

Questions on pages 82–5

A11 **1** Neglect
2 routine checks
3 preventative
4 abuse

A12 **1** 50 metres/yards
2 At least 150 metres/yards

A13 Yes. Try to give as much warning as possible.

A14 **3**

A15 **3**

A16 Under the drawing of the handset is an arrow which points to the nearest telephone.

A17 **1** The emergency number (painted on the box)
2 Vehicle details (make, registration mark, colour)
3 Membership details of your motoring organisation
4 Details of the fault

A18 **1** By displaying a Help pennant
2 By using a mobile telephone

A19 **1** passing motorists
2 do not know
3 leave, longer

A20 **1** False. Do not move injured people unless they are in danger.
2 False. Tell them the facts, not what you think is wrong.
3 False. Do not give those injured anything to eat or drink. Keep them warm and reassure them.
4 False. Keep hazard lights on to warn other drivers.
5 True. Switch off engines. Put out cigarettes.
6 True, in the case of injury.

A21 Stop

A22 No

A23 **1** The other driver's name, address and contact number
2 The registration numbers of all vehicles involved
3 The make of the other car
4 The other driver's insurance details
5 If the driver is not the owner, the owner's details.

A24 **1** Pull up quickly
2 Get all passengers out
3 Call assistance

A25 **1** First aid
2 Fire extinguisher
3 Warning triangle

A26 **3**

THE MOTOR CAR AND THE ENVIRONMENT

Questions on pages 85–6

A27 carbon dioxide, greenhouse

A28 **4**

A29 Yes

A30 False. A catalytic convertor reduces the level of carbon monoxide, nitrogen oxide and hydrocarbons by up to 90 per cent. Carbon dioxide is still produced.

A31 **2**

A32 Nine measures are listed here:
1 Make sure your vehicle is in good condition and regularly serviced.
2 Make sure tyres are correctly inflated. Under-inflated tyres waste fuel.
3 Push the choke in as soon as possible when starting from cold.
4 Avoid harsh braking.
5 Buy a fuel-efficient vehicle.
6 Use the most appropriate gear.
7 Use your accelerator sensibly and avoid harsh acceleration.
8 Use unleaded fuel.
9 Dispose of waste oil, old batteries and used tyres sensibly.

BUYING A USED CAR

Questions on pages 86–7

A33 dealer, auction, privately

A34 Why is it being sold?

A35 **1** True
2 False
3 True
4 True

A36 **1** What is covered
2 The length of the agreement

A37 taxed, MOT, insurance

A38 Four items to check are listed here:
1 Mileage
2 Has it been involved in any accidents?
3 Number of owners
4 Is there any hire purchase or finance agreement outstanding?

A39 True. The AA offer a national inspection scheme.

Answers to Questions

Section 16

TOWING A CARAVAN OR TRAILER

Questions on pages 88–9

A1 **1**

A2 Exterior towing mirrors, to give you a good view

A3 **2**

A4 stabilizer

A5 **3**

A6 **A** 2
B 2

A7 Seven checks are listed here:
1 Is the caravan or trailer loaded correctly?
2 Is it correctly hitched up to your vehicle?
3 Are the lights and indicators working properly?
4 Is the braking system working correctly?
5 Is the jockey wheel assembly fully retracted?
6 Are tyre pressures correct?
7 Are all windows, doors and roof lights closed?

A8 jockey wheel, corner steadies

DRIVING IN EUROPE

Questions on pages 89–90

A9 vehicle, documents

A10 **1** route
2 motoring regulations

A11 Here are five routine checks:
1 Tyres, including spare. Always carry a spare tyre.
2 Tool kit and jack.
3 Lamps and brake lights.
4 Fit deflectors to your headlamps to prevent dazzle to other drivers approaching on the left.
5 Check you have an extra exterior mirror on the left.

A12 driving licence

A13 International Driving Permit

A14 Some non-EU countries

A15 **2**

A16 Five items are listed here:
1 Spare lamps and bulbs
2 Warning triangle
3 First aid kit
4 Fire extinguisher
5 Emergency windscreen

Part 3 Understanding the Theory behind the test

Contents Page

Section 1
Alertness

The first section in the Theory Test questions is headed ALERTNESS. Alertness is a short section and is a good place to start.

- Alertness means being wide awake and concentrating on what you are doing – driving – not being distracted by mobile phones or loud music.
- Alertness means looking out for hazards.
- Alertness means noticing all road signs and road markings, and acting on the instructions and information they give.

Are you fit to drive?

'Fit' can mean:

- Did you have any alcoholic drinks before you set out?
- Are you under the influence of illegal substances (drugs)?
- Are you feeling groggy or unwell?
- Are you taking prescription medicine that could affect your ability to control the car?
- Are you too tired to drive?

It's unwise to set out on a journey if you're not well, on the basis of 'I'll see how I go – I'll probably be all right':

- Your reactions are likely to be slower.
- You may be unable to judge distances properly.
- Your actions may be less well co-ordinated than usual and it's not legal.

If you are tired, open the window for a few moments to let in some fresh air. If you drive when you are too tired, you risk falling asleep at the wheel – an all too common cause of serious accidents. Driving for long stretches on a motorway at night can be especially dangerous. If you sense that you are losing your concentration, then take a break at a motorway service station. Plan your journey ahead, giving yourself plenty of time for rest stops – at least every couple of hours.

Tackling the questions

Look at the questions in the Alertness section. You'll see that the Alertness questions are all about these

- anticipation
- observation
- signalling
- reversing
- using your mirrors
- concentration
- getting distracted
- feeling sleepy
- using mobile phones

DID YOU KNOW?

The main causes of distraction are:

- Loud music in the car
- Passengers (usually children)
- Events happening outside (such as accidents)
- Using a mobile phone

Now test yourself on the questions about Alertness

Section 2
Attitude

The government road safety organisations believe that the ATTITUDE of learner drivers is extremely important for road safety.

Attitude means

- Your frame of mind when you get in the car
- How you react when you meet hazards on the road
- How you behave towards other drivers

Attitude is a very important part of being a good driver. Your attitude when you are driving plays a big part in ensuring your safety and that of other road users.

Do you aim to be a careful and safe driver or a fast and skilful driver? If you don't want to end up as another road accident statistic, then carefully and safely is the way to go.

Remember that a car is not an offensive weapon, and often people don't realise what a potentially lethal machine they are in control of when they get behind the wheel. You only have to think about this to understand the importance of your attitude when driving.

You'll see that questions in this section are concerned with encouraging you to be a careful and safe driver, and cover:

- Tailgating
- Consideration for other road users, including pedestrians, buses, slow-moving vehicles and horse riders
- Driving at the right speed for the conditions
- When to flash headlights
- The right place, time and way to overtake

And remembering a few dos and don'ts will help you achieve the right attitude for driving and make passing this section of the test much easier.

Good drivers do

- drive at the right speed and for the road and traffic conditions
- observe speed limits
- overtake only when it is safe to do so
- park in correct and safe places
- wait patiently if the driver in front is a learner or elderly or hesitant
- look out for vulnerable road users such as cyclists, pedestrians and children
- concentrate on their driving at all times
- plan their journey so that they have plenty of time to get to their destination

Good drivers don't

- allow themselves to become involved in road rage
- break speed limits
- drive too fast, particularly in wet, foggy or icy weather
- accelerate or brake too harshly
- overtake and 'cut in', forcing others to brake sharply
- put pressure on other drivers by driving too close behind them (this is called 'tailgating'), flashing headlights or gesturing
- allow their attention to be distracted by passengers, mobile phones or loud music, or what is happening on the road, such as staring at an accident

Tailgating

Driving excessively close behind another vehicle is known as tailgating – and it's dangerous! The car in front may stop suddenly (to avoid hitting a child or animal that has dashed out into the road, for example); when this happens the car following runs the risk of crashing into it.

You should always leave enough space between your vehicle and the one in front, so that you can stop safely if the driver in front suddenly slows down or stops.

Rear-end shunts account for a large percentage of all accidents on the road. In these situations, the driver of the car behind is almost always judged to be the guilty party.

So tailgating is potentially expensive as well as dangerous.

Another time when drivers are tempted to tailgate is when attempting to pass a large, slow-moving vehicle. However, keeping well back will improve your view of the road ahead, so that you're better able to judge when it's safe to overtake and the driver of the large vehicle will also be able to see you.

Useful tip

If you are being followed too closely by another driver you should slow down and increase the distance between your vehicle and the one in front. If you slow down or have to stop suddenly, the driver behind may crash into you, but you will have increased your stopping distance and will not be pushed into the vehicle in front of you.

Always remember

- Expect the unexpected, and make provision for the potential errors of other drivers – everyone makes mistakes sometimes.
- Don't create unnecessary stress for other drivers by showing your frustration in an aggressive manner.

If you are driving at the right speed for the road and weather conditions and a driver behind tries to overtake, you should pull back a bit from the vehicle in front so that if the driver behind insists on overtaking, there is less risk of an accident.

Do not try to stop the car behind from overtaking. Do not move into the middle of the road or move up close to the car in front. These actions could be very dangerous.

You should not give confusing signals such as indicating left or waving the other driver on.

Now test yourself on the questions about Attitude

Section 3

Safety and Your Vehicle

When you go through this section you will notice that the questions are a bit of a mixture. They cover a number of topics about SAFETY, including:

- Understanding the controls of your vehicle
- What the car's warning lights tell you
- Tyres – correct inflation, pressures and tread depths
- When to use hazard warning lights
- Passenger safety
- The environment
- Security and crime prevention

Many of the questions in this section are to do with 'legal requirements' and rules regarding parking your car and using lights. Look up all the sections in *The Highway Code* that deal with parking rules. Find out the rules for red routes, white lines and zigzag lines as well as yellow lines.

Seat belts
If any of your passengers are young people under 14, you are responsible for making sure that they wear seat belts. You are responsible for them by law, even if you are still a learner driver yourself.

Tips for this section

Learn *The Highway Code* and you will be able to answer most of the questions in this section. In particular make sure you know the rules regarding seat belts, tyres, and when to use your lights, including your hazard warning lights.

A confusing question

One of the most confusing questions in this section asks what kind of driving results in high fuel consumption. The answer, of course, is **bad** driving – especially harsh braking and acceleration. This means you will use more fuel than you should and therefore cause more damage to the environment than is necessary.

BUT many people read the word 'high' as meaning 'good' – as in a level of driving skill – and so pick the wrong answer.

Don't let it be you...

Now test yourself on the questions about Safety and Your Vehicle

Section 4
Safety Margins

Experienced drivers are usually better than new or learner drivers at leaving good SAFETY MARGINS. Learner drivers find it harder to keep their vehicle at a safe distance from the one in front. Therefore the questions in this section cover

- safe stopping distances

and

- safe separation distances (these are the same as safety margins)

What is a safety margin?

A safety margin is the space that you need to leave between your vehicle and the one in front so that you will not crash into it if it slows downs or stops suddenly. They are also called 'separation distances' and are an important part of anticipating road and traffic hazards. When you are learning to drive, you can feel pressured to speed up by drivers behind you.

Don't let other drivers make you cut down on your safety margins. Stay a safe distance ehind the vehicle in front. Then you will have time to anticipate and react to hazards.

The two-second rule

In traffic that's moving at normal speed, allow at least a two-second gap between you and the vehicle in front.

Stopping distances

Many people who are taking their Theory Test get confused about this. You will notice that some of the questions ask for your overall stopping distance and others ask for your braking distance. These are different.

Overall stopping distance or stopping distance is not the same as braking distance. Stopping distance is made up of thinking distance + braking distance.

In other words, the time it takes to notice that there's a hazard ahead plus the time it takes to brake to deal with it.

Thinking distance

Thinking distance is sometimes called reaction time or reaction distance. If you are driving at 30mph, your thinking distance will be 30 feet (9 metres). That means your vehicle will travel 30 feet (9 metres) before you start braking.

The link between stopping distance and safety margins

You should always leave enough space between your vehicle and the one in front. If the other driver has to slow down suddenly or stop without warning, you need to be able to stop safely. The space is your safety margin.

Safety margins for other vehicles

Long vehicles and motorcycles need more room to stop – in other words, you must leave a bigger safety margin when following a long vehicle or motorbike. When driving behind a long vehicle, pull back to increase your separation distance and your safety margin so that you get a better view of the road ahead – there could be hazards developing and if you are too close he will be unable to see you in his rear view mirror. Strong winds can blow

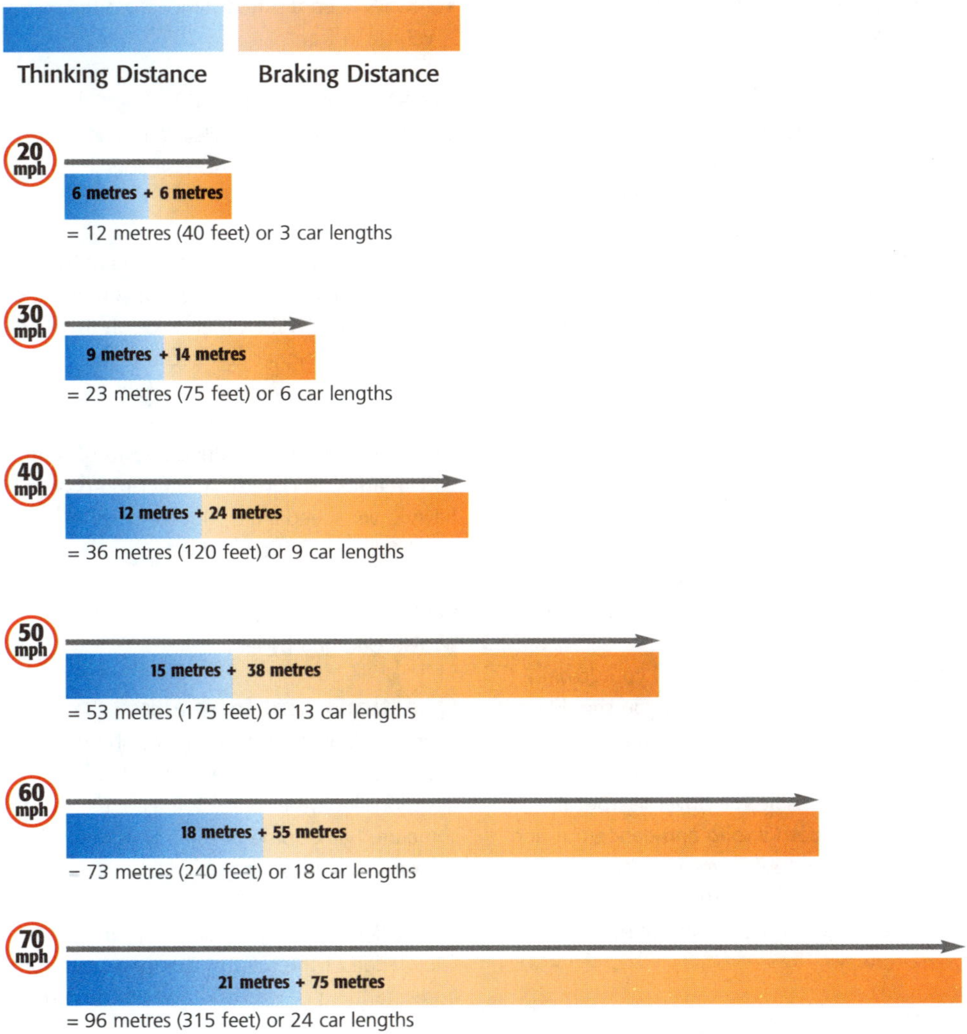
Thinking Distance
Braking Distance
20 mph
6 metres + 6 metres
= 12 metres (40 feet) or 3 car lengths
30 mph
9 metres + 14 metres
= 23 metres (75 feet) or 6 car lengths
40 mph
12 metres + 24 metres
= 36 metres (120 feet) or 9 car lengths
50 mph
15 metres + 38 metres
= 53 metres (175 feet) or 13 car lengths
60 mph
18 metres + 55 metres
= 73 metres (240 feet) or 18 car lengths
70 mph
21 metres + 75 metres
= 96 metres (315 feet) or 24 car lengths

AA

lorries and motorbikes off course. So leave a bigger safety margin.

Different conditions and safety margins

You may find that one or more questions in your Theory Test might be about driving in 'different conditions'. These questions aim to make sure you know what adjustments you should make to your driving when either road conditions are different from normal, for example, when parts of the road are closed off for roadworksor weather conditions affect your driving.

Road works

You should always take extra care when you see a sign warning you that there are road works ahead. Remember, road works are a hazard and you have to anticipate them.

If you see the driver in front of you slowing down, take this as a sign that you should do the same – even if you can't see a hazard ahead. You still need to keep a safe distance from him. Harassing the driver in front by 'tailgating' is both wrong and dangerous and so is overtaking to fill the gap. It's especially important that you know what to do when you see a sign for road works ahead on a motorway.

- There may be a lower speed limit than normal – keep to it.
- Use your mirrors and indicators, and get into the correct lane in plenty of time.
- Don't overtake the queue and then force your way in at the last minute (this is an example of showing an inconsiderate attitude to other road users).
- Always keep a safe distance from the vehicle in front.

Weather conditions

In bad weather (often called 'adverse' weather), you need to increase your safety margins.

When it's raining you need to leave at least twice as much distance between you and the vehicle in front. When there's ice on the road leave an even bigger gap because your stopping distance increases tenfold.

It's amazing how often drivers go too fast in bad weather. In adverse weather motorways have lower speed limits, but some drivers don't take any notice of them.

When it's icy you should multiply your two-second gap by ten.

Questions that look alike

There are a number of questions about anti-lock brakes in this section. Lots of questions look the same. Some are easy and some are hard. Some of them appear to be the same but they are not.

The questions test two things – your knowledge of the rules of the road and your understanding of words to do with driving.

Now test yourself on the questions about Safety Margins

Section 5

Hazard Awareness

How often does a motorist protest that the accident happened before they had time to realise the person they hit was there? Some accidents will inevitably happen, but part of your instructor's job while teaching you to drive is to help you learn to anticipate problems before they happen.

What is the difference between Hazard Awareness and Hazard Perception?

- Hazard Awareness and Hazard Perception mean the same thing.
- Hazard Perception is the name for the part of the Theory Test that uses video clips. This test is about spotting developing hazards. One of the key skills of good driving, this is called anticipation.
- Anticipating hazards means looking out for them in advance and taking action now.
- Hazard Awareness is about being alert whenever you are driving.

That is why some of the questions in the HAZARD AWARENESS section deal with things that might make you less alert.
For example feeling tired, feeling ill, taking medicines prescribed by your doctor or drinking alcohol

Other questions in Hazard Awareness cover noticing road and traffic signs as well as road markings, what to do at traffic lights and when to slow down for hazards ahead.

Why are young male drivers more at risk?

New drivers have a greater than average chance of being involved in accidents. Statistics show that young male drivers have the most accidents.

- Maybe it's because when they first get their licence they want to show off to other drivers.
- Some people think that driving much too fast will earn them 'respect' from their friends.
- Some people think that they are such good drivers that the rules of the road should not apply to them.

Whatever the reason – drivers who don't watch out for hazards are at risk of being involved in an accident. The problem has a lot to do with people's attitude to driving. You'll find more about this aspect of driving in the Attitude part of the Theory Test.

We've already said that young drivers often don't learn to anticipate hazards until they are older and more experienced. The Hazard Perception test aims to 'fill the gap' in hazard perception for young drivers and other new drivers by making sure they have some proper training to make up for their lack of experience.

This should make them safer drivers when they start out on the road alone.

Looking for clues to hazards developing on the road

As you get more driving experience you will start to learn about the times and places where you are most likely to meet hazards. Think about some of these examples.

Rush hour

You know that people take more risks when driving in the rush hour. Maybe they have to drop their children off at school before going to work. Maybe they are late for a business meeting. So you have to be prepared for bad driving, such as other drivers pulling out in front of you.

Dustbin day

Drivers in a hurry may get frustrated if they are held up in traffic because of a hazard such as a dustcart. They may accelerate and pull out to overtake even though they cannot see clearly ahead. You should not blindly follow the lead of another driver. Check for yourself that there are no hazards ahead.

Schoolchildren

Young children are often not very good at judging how far away a car is from them, and may run into the road unexpectedly. Always be on the lookout for hazards near a school entrance.

Parked cars

Imagine you are driving on a quiet one-way street with cars parked down each side of the road. You wouldn't expect to meet any vehicles coming the other way – but what about children playing? They might run out into the road after a football. It would be difficult to see them because of the parked cars, until they were in the road in front of you.

More examples of hazards

So, what kinds of hazards are we talking about? And what should you do about them?

Road markings and road signs sometimes highlight likely hazards for you.

The list below gives some of the hazards you should look out for when driving along a busy street in town.

After each hazard there are some ideas about what you should be looking out for, and what to do next.

- You see a bus which has stopped in a lay-by ahead.

There may be some pedestrians hidden by the bus who are trying to cross the road, or the bus may signal to pull out. Be ready to slow down and stop.

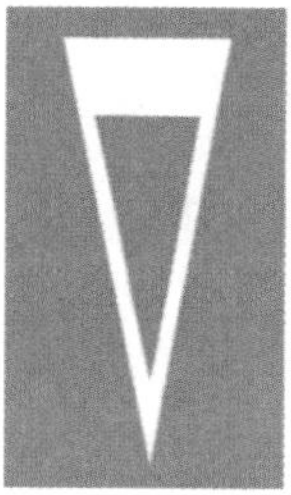

- You see a white triangle painted on the road surface ahead.

This is a hazard warning sign. It tells you that there is a 'Give Way' junction just ahead. Slow down and be ready to stop.

- You see a sign for a roundabout on the road ahead.

Anticipate that other drivers may need to change lane, and be ready to leave them enough room.

- You come to some road works where the traffic is controlled by temporary traffic lights.

Watch out for drivers speeding to get through before the lights change.

- You look in your rear view mirror and see an emergency vehicle with flashing lights coming up behind you.

An emergency vehicle wants to pass, so get ready to pull over when it's safe.

- You see a small child standing with an adult near the edge of the pavement.

Check if the child is safely holding the adult's hand. Be ready to stop safely if the child suddenly steps into the road.

- You notice dustbins or rubbish bags put out on the pavement.

The dustcart could be around the next corner, or the bin men could be crossing the road with bags of rubbish. Be ready to slow down and stop if necessary.

- You hear a siren.

Look all around to find out where the emergency vehicle is. You may have to pull over to let it pass.

You will find out more about the different types of hazards you may encounter, including what to look for when driving on narrow country roads, or in bad (adverse) weather conditions, in the Vehicle Handling section of this book.

Always expect the unexpected
Don't forget that not all hazards can be anticipated. There are bound to be some you haven't expected.

Red flashing warning lights
Level crossings, ambulance stations, fire stations and swing bridges all have red lights that flash on and off to warn you when you must stop.

Observation

Another word for taking in information through our eyes is observation. Observation is one of the three key skills needed in hazard perception. The three skills are

- observation
- anticipation
- planning

An easy way to remember this is **O A P** for

Observe
Anticipate
Plan

Talk to yourself!

It's a good idea to 'talk to yourself' when you're learning to drive – and even after you've passed your test. Talk about all the things you see that could be potential hazards. Your driving instructor might suggest this as a way of making you concentrate and notice hazards ahead.

Even if you don't talk out loud, you can do a 'running commentary' in your head on everything you see around you as you drive.

For example, you might say to yourself – 'I am following a cyclist and the traffic lights ahead are red. *When the lights change I will allow him/her plenty of time and room to move off.*'
or
'The dual carriageway ahead is starting to look very busy. There is a sign showing that the right lane is closing in 800 yards. *I must get ready to check my mirrors and, if safe to do so, drop back to allow other vehicles to move into the left-hand lane ahead of me.*'

Note: Don't forget the mirrors! This way, you will notice more hazards, and you will learn to make more sense of the information that your eyes are taking in.

Learn your road signs!
Notice the information at the bottom of the first page of traffic signs in *The Highway Code*. It explains that you won't find every road sign shown here.

You can buy a copy of *Know Your Traffic Signs* from a bookshop to see some of the extra signs that are not in *The Highway Code*.

Note: In Wales, some road signs include the Welsh spelling as well as the English, and in Scotland, some signs are written using Gaelic spelling. You'll also see some 'old-style' road signs around, which are slightly different too.

Scanning the road

Learner drivers tend to look straight ahead of their car and may not notice all the hazards that might be building up on both sides. You will spot more hazards when driving if you train yourself to scan the road.

- Practise looking up and ahead as far as possible.
- Use all your mirrors to look out for hazards too.
- Don't forget that you have 'blind spots' when driving – work out where they are and find safe ways of checking all round for hazards.
- Ask your driving instructor to help you with all of this.

How is learning to scan the road going to help me pass my Theory Test?

- The idea of the Hazard Perception element of the test is to encourage you to get some real experience of driving before you take the Theory Test.
- If you meet real hazards on the road and learn how to anticipate them, you'll learn how to pass the Hazard Perception element of the test.
- In the video test you may not be able to look all around you as you would when driving a car; but the clips will be as realistic as possible in giving you a wide 'view' of the road ahead.

Observation questions

Study some of the pictures in the Hazard Awareness section.

They include photographs of scenes such as

- a cyclist at traffic lights, seen from the viewpoint of a driver in a car behind the cyclist

- what you see as a driver when you are approaching a level crossing

- what you see when coming up to a 'blind bend'

- a view of the road ahead with traffic building up where one lane is closing.

Look out for situations like these when you are out driving with your instructor, and use the practice to improve your hazard awareness.

As well as photographs, there are pictures of road and traffic signs.

What do these signs mean?

What actions should you take when you see these signs?

- If you are not sure, look them up in *The Highway Code*.

- Think about why the square yellow sign with the two children is in the Vehicle Markings section and not with the rest of the road signs.

Now test yourself on the questions about Hazard Awareness

Section 6
Vulnerable Road Users

Today's new vehicles are becoming safer all the time for the driver inside the car, but sadly this is not always the case for the pedestrian or cyclist outside. Many road users who are not driving cars have nothing to protect them if they are in an accident with a motor vehicle.

The questions in the VULNERABLE ROAD USERS section deal with the following:

- why different types of road users are vulnerable
- what you as a driver must do to keep them safe

Who are vulnerable road users?
The following are all vulnerable road users and you must drive with extra care when you are near vulnerable road users.

- pedestrians
- children
- elderly people
- people with disabilities
- cyclists
- motorcycle riders
- horse riders
- learner drivers and new drivers
- animals being herded along the road

Cyclists

Give cyclists plenty of room. Remember to keep well back from cyclists when you are coming up to a junction or a roundabout because you cannot be sure what they are going to do. On the roundabout they may go in any direction – left, right or straight ahead. They are allowed to stay in the left lane and signal right if they are going to continue round. Leave them enough room to cross in front of you if they need to. Turn to the section headed Vulnerable Road Users in the Theory Test questions to see some pictures of this. You must also give way to cyclists at toucan crossings and in cycle lanes (see the rules for cyclists set out in *The Highway Code*).

Look out for cyclists!

- It can be hard to see cyclists in busy town traffic.
- It can also be hard to see them coming when you are waiting to turn out at a junction. They can be hidden by other vehicles.

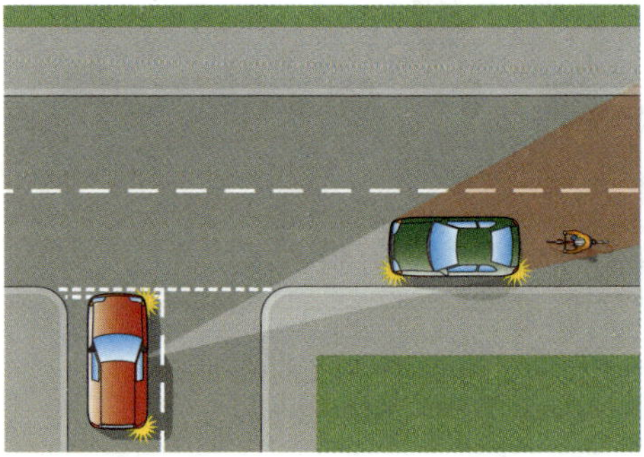

Always be on the lookout for cyclists. Especially, check your mirror to make sure you do not trap a cyclist on your left when you are turning left into a side road. Check your blind spots for cyclists, too.

Controlling your vehicle near cyclists

When you are following a cyclist, you must be able to drive as slowly as they do, and keep your vehicle under control. Only overtake when you can allow them plenty of room, and it is safe to do so.

Cycle lanes

Cycle lanes are reserved for cyclists. Car drivers should not use them.

A cycle lane is marked by a white line on the road. A solid white line means you must not drive or park in the cycle lane during the hours it is in use.

A broken white line means that you should drive or park in it only if there is no alternative. You should not park there at any time when there are waiting restrictions.

When you overtake a cyclist, a motorcyclist or a horse rider, give them at least as much room as you would give a car.

Cyclists and motorcycle riders

Cyclists and motorcycle riders are more at risk than car drivers because

- they are more affected by strong winds, or by turbulence caused by other vehicles
- they are more affected by an uneven road surface, and they may have to move out suddenly to avoid a pot-hole
- car drivers often cannot see them

Pedestrians

Pedestrians most at risk include elderly people and children. Elderly people and others who cannot move easily may be slower to cross roads – you must give them plenty of time. Children don't have a sense of danger on the road; they can't tell how close a car is, or how fast it is going. They may run out into the road without looking. Or they may step out behind you when you are reversing – you may not see them because they are small.

People who are unable to see and/or hear

A blind person will usually carry a white stick to alert you to their presence. If the stick has a red band, this means that the person is also deaf, so will have no warning of an approaching car either visually or from engine noise.

When to give way to pedestrians

At any pedestrian crossing, if a pedestrian has started to cross, wait until they have reached the other side. Do not harass them by revving your engine or edging forward.

At a crossing with lights (pelican, toucan or puffin crossings), pedestrians have priority once they have started to cross even if, when on a pelican crossing, the amber lights start flashing.

Once a pedestrian has stepped on to a zebra crossing, you must stop and wait for them to cross.

Note: It is courteous to stop at a zebra crossing if a pedestrian is waiting to cross.

When you take your Practical Driving Test, you must stop for any pedestrians who are waiting on the pavement at a zebra crossing even if they haven't stepped on to the crossing yet. However, you must not wave to them to cross.

If you want to turn left into a side road and pedestrians have already started to cross the side road on foot, wait for them to finish crossing. People on foot have priority over car drivers.

DID YOU KNOW?
If a car hits a pedestrian at 40mph, the pedestrian will probably be killed.
Even at 30mph, 50% of pedestrians hit by cars will be killed.
At 20mph, pedestrians have a better chance of surviving. This is why you will find 20mph limits and other things to slow traffic in some residential streets and near school entrances.

Other types of vulnerable road users

Be prepared to slow down for animals, learner drivers, and other more unusual hazards such as people walking along the road in organised groups (for example, on a demonstration, or a sponsored walk). There are rules in *The Highway Code* that walkers must follow. But even if they break the rules, make sure you keep to them.

Animals

Drive slowly past horses or other animals. Allow them plenty of space on the road. Don't frighten them by sounding your horn or revving your engine.

If you see a flock of sheep or a herd of cattle blocking the road, you must

- stop
- switch off your engine
- and wait until they have left the road

People riding horses on the road are often children, so you need to take extra care; when you see two riders abreast, it may well be that the one on the outside is shielding a less experienced rider.

Traffic signs

Look up the Traffic Signs and Vehicle Markings sections in *The Highway Code* and find the following signs

- pedestrians walking in the road ahead (no pavement)
- cycle lane and pedestrian route
- advance warning of school crossing patrol ahead
- school crossing patrol
- elderly or disabled people crossing
- sign on back of school bus or coach

Now test yourself on the questions about Vulnerable Road Users

Section 7
Other Types of Vehicle

We have already come across some of the other types of vehicle that share the road with you and your car including motorbikes and bicycles. The questions in this part of the Theory Test are mostly about long vehicles such as lorries. However, you also need to know what to do about

- buses
- caravans
- trams
- tractors and other farm vehicles
- special vehicles for disabled drivers (powered invalid carriages)
- slow vehicles such as road gritters
- motorway repair vehicles

Important points to remember about these types of vehicle

- Many of them can only move very slowly.
- They cannot easily stop or change direction.

The driver's field of vision may be restricted – this means that car drivers have to allow them plenty of room.

Motorcycles

- Motorcycles are easily blown off course by strong winds. If you see a motorcyclist overtaking a high-sided vehicle such as a lorry, keep well back. The lorry may shield the motorcyclist from the wind as it is overtaking, but then a sudden gust could blow the motorcyclist off course.
- It can be hard to see a motorcyclist when you are waiting at a junction. Always look out for them.
- If you see a motorcyclist looking over their shoulder, it could mean that they will soon give a signal to turn right. This applies to cyclists too. Keep back to give them plenty of room.
- Motorcyclists and cyclists sometimes have to swerve to avoid hazards such as bumps in the road, patches of ice and drain covers. As before – give them plenty of room.

Long vehicles

- Like cyclists, long vehicles coming up to roundabouts may stay in the left lane even if they intend to turn right. This is because they need lots of room to manoeuvre. Keep well back so they have room to turn.
- Take great care when overtaking long or high-sided vehicles. Before you pull out to overtake, make sure you have a clear view of the road ahead.
- A long vehicle that needs to turn left off a major road into a minor road may prepare to do so by moving out towards the centre of the road, or by moving across to the other side.

If you're following them

- Give way, and don't try to overtake – on the right or the left.
- You might need to slow down and stop while the driver of the long vehicle makes the turn.

Buses and trams

- Always give way to buses when they signal to pull out.
- Always give way to trams as they cannot steer to avoid you.
- Don't try to overtake a tram.

Trams are **quiet** vehicles – you cannot rely on approaching engine noise to warn you that a tram is coming.

Take extra care when you see this sign, because trams are sometimes allowed to go when car drivers are not.

Tractors and slow-moving vehicles

- Always be patient if you are following a slow vehicle.

Drivers of slow vehicles will usually try to find a safe place to pull in to let the traffic go past. In the meantime you should keep well back, so that you can see the road ahead. Allow a safe distance in case they slow down or stop.

Slow vehicles are not allowed on motorways because they cannot keep up with the fast-moving traffic. Vehicles not allowed on motorways include

- motorcycles under 50cc
- bicycles
- tractors and other farm vehicles
- powered invalid carriages

Now test yourself on the questions about Other Types of Vehicle

Section 8

Vehicle Handling

The questions in this section test how much you know about controlling your vehicle on different road surfaces and in different weather.

Your control is affected by

- the road surface – is it rough or smooth? Are there any holes or bumps? Are there any 'traffic-calming measures', such as humps or chicanes?
- the weather conditions – you have to drive in different ways when there is fog, snow, ice or heavy rain.

Other questions in this section cover driving on country roads – on narrow and one-way roads, humpback bridges, steep hills, fords. Other questions need practical knowledge, for example, on engine braking, brake fade, and coasting your vehicle – use the Glossary.

This section also has some questions on overtaking and parking.

Road surface

The condition of the road surface can affect the way your vehicle handles. Your vehicle handles better on a smooth surface than on a surface that is damaged, bumpy or full of holes. If you have to drive on an uneven surface, keep your speed down so that you have full control of your vehicle, even if your steering wheel is jolted.

Take care also where there are tramlines on the road. The layout of the road affects the way your vehicle handles.

You may have to adjust your driving for traffic calming measures, such as traffic humps (sometimes called 'sleeping policemen') and chicanes. These are double bends that have been put into the road layout to slow the traffic down. The sign before the chicane tells you who has priority.

Traffic calming measures are often used in residential areas or near school entrances to make it safer for pedestrians.

Weather conditions

Bad weather (adverse weather) such as heavy rain, ice or snow affects the way your vehicle handles. If you drive too fast in adverse weather, your tyres may lose their grip on the road when you try to brake. This means the car may skid or 'aquaplane'. Aquaplaning means sliding out of control on a wet surface.

Driving in snow

In snow, the best advice is do not drive at all unless you really have to make a journey. If you have to drive in snowy conditions, leave extra time for your journey and keep to the main roads. You can fit snow chains to your tyres to increase their grip in deep snow.

Driving in fog

In fog your field of vision can be down to a few metres. Your vehicle is fitted with fog lights to help you see and be seen in fog. But you must know how and when to use them. Look up the three rules about fog lights in *The Highway Code*. You'll see that the key points to remember are:

- Don't dazzle other road users with your fog lights.
- Switch them off as soon as you can see better (as soon as the fog starts to clear).

> **Remember the two-second rule**
> You should double the two-second gap to four seconds when driving in rain, and increase the gap by as much as ten times when there is ice on the road.

Country driving

If you have had most of your driving lessons in a town, you need to know how to drive on narrow country roads. Some are only wide enough for one vehicle ('single-track'), and some are on very steep hills.

Your control of the gears, clutch and brakes will be important if you have to follow a tractor very slowly up a hill. On a steep downward slope you have to make sure your vehicle does not 'run away'.

On country roads you might find humpback bridges and fords. The signs below warn you of these hazards.

- Find out what you must do first after you have driven through a ford.

Technical knowledge

We have already mentioned engine braking. Understanding how engine braking works is part of good vehicle handling.

Note: If you press the footbrake constantly on a long hill, you may get brake fade. If you're not sure, check what that means in the Glossary at the back of this book.

Use the gears to control your vehicle on a downhill slope (or 'gradient'). If you put the vehicle in 'neutral', or drive with the clutch down (called coasting), your vehicle will increase speed beyond what is safe and will not be under proper control.

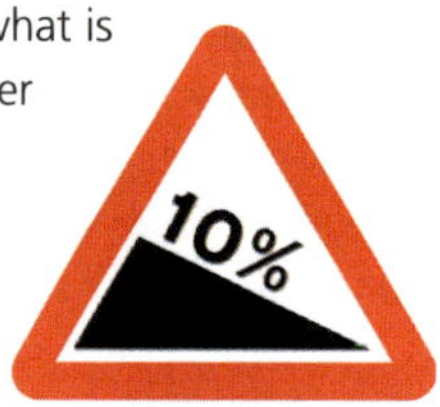

This sign warns you of a steep hill downwards.

- Coasting is wrong and dangerous – you should not be tempted to do it to save fuel.

Remember that if there is sudden heavy rain after a dry hot spell, the road surface can get very slippery.

Now test yourself on the questions about Vehicle Handling

Section 9

Motorway Rules

Learner drivers aren't allowed on motorways, so you can't get experience of what it's like to drive on them until you've passed your test. However, you do need to know all about MOTORWAY RULES before taking your Practical Test, and your Theory Test will most likely include a question about motorways.

As soon as you pass your driving test you will be legally allowed to drive on motorways. You need to know all the motorway rules in advance, so that you are confident and ready to cope with motorway driving when you pass your test.

There are some major roads and dual carriageways that learners can drive on which are very much like motorways. You may drive on some of these fast roads during your driving test, so that your examiner can see how well you cope with hazards at higher speeds.

When driving on these fast roads you will need some of the very same skills that you will need for motorway driving – for example, using lanes properly, knowing when it is safe to overtake, and controlling your vehicle at speed.

If you are learning to drive with a driving school, you will have the chance to book a motorway lesson with your instructor after you have passed your test. It makes sense to take up this offer before you drive on a motorway alone for the first time.

Motorways and other roads

- On a motorway traffic is moving at high speed all the time.
- All lanes are in use.
- No stopping is allowed on a motorway – traffic only slows or comes to a stop because of accidents or other types of hold-up.
- Some road users are not allowed on motorways. These include
- – pedestrians, cyclists and learner drivers
- – horses and other animals
- – motorcycles under 50cc
- – slow-moving vehicles, tractors and farm vehicles and invalid carriages
- You always enter and leave a motorway on the left, via a slip road.
- To the left of the inside lane (left-hand lane) on a motorway is the hard shoulder. You can only drive on this in an emergency.
- Special signs and signals are used on motorways. These include signs above the road on overhead gantries, signs on the central reservation, and amber and red flashing lights.

Checks before your journey

Be extra careful about doing all your regular checks before you set out on a motorway journey. You cannot stop on the motorway to fix small problems, and no one wants to break down in the middle of fast traffic.
Always check

- oil and coolant levels, screen wash container
- tyres and tyre pressures
- fuel gauge
- that all mirrors and windows are free of dirt and grease
- that the horn works

Many of these checks are legally necessary, as well as important for your safety.

How to move on to the motorway

- Join the motorway by building up your speed on the slip road to match the speed of traffic in the left lane of the motorway.
- Use MSM (Mirrors – Signal – Manoeuvre) and move into the flow of traffic when it is safe to do so.

Changing lanes and overtaking

Driving on a motorway needs all the skills you have learned about anticipation and forward planning.

You should

- make good use of all mirrors, and check your blind spots
- signal to move out in plenty of time
- look out for hazards ahead in the lane you want to move to
- not go ahead if it will force another vehicle to brake or swerve
- keep a safe distance from the vehicle in front

Take a break

When you drive on motorways you will sometimes see signs that say 'Tiredness can kill – take a break!' This is very good advice. Motorways are monotonous – boring to drive, with long stretches of road that look the same for miles. A major cause of accidents is drivers falling asleep at the wheel. Plan your journey so that you have time to get out, stretch your legs and have a drink or snack.

The rules you need to know

- Keep to the left-hand lane unless you are overtaking and move back to the left lane as soon as it is safe to do so. Sometimes you need to stay in the centre lane for a time – for example, when a line of lorries is travelling up a hill in the left lane. Stay in the centre lane until you have passed the hazard, then signal left and return to the left lane.
- NEVER
  reverse
  park
  walk
  drive in the wrong direction on the motorway.
- Don't exceed the speed limit. This is normally 70mph, but lower speed limits may be signed when the road is busy, or in bad weather.
- Keep to the correct separation distance (see Safety Margins).
- Don't overtake on the left.
  If traffic is moving slowly in all three lanes you may find that the lane on the left is moving faster than the one to its right for a short time. Or the left lane may be signed for traffic turning off at the next junction only. But these are exceptions to the rule.
- If luggage falls from your vehicle, do not get out to pick it up. Stop at the next emergency phone and tell the police. Posts on the edge of the motorway show the way to the nearest emergency phone. You should use these phones rather than your mobile phone, because the emergency phone connects directly to the police and tells them exactly where you are calling from on the motorway.
- Don't stop on the hard shoulder except in an emergency. The hard shoulder is an extremely dangerous place, as many as one in eight road deaths happen there.

Traffic signs and road markings

Light signals

In *The Highway Code* you'll find the light signals only seen on motorways. Signs above the roadway or on the central reservation are activated as needed to warn of accidents, lane closures or weather conditions. Overhead gantries display arrows or red crosses showing which lanes are open or closed to traffic and which lanes to move to when motorways merge or diverge. They may also show temporary speed limits.

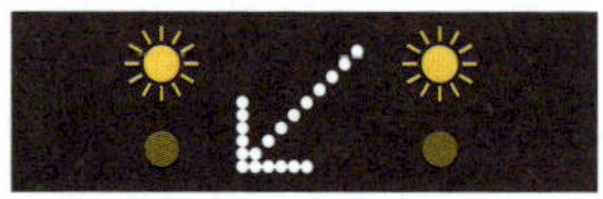

Direction signs

Direction signs on motorways are blue and those on other major roads are green – other direction signs are white with black print.

Reflective studs

It's useful to know the colours of studs on a motorway; this can help in working out which part of the road you're on if it's dark or foggy. White studs mark lanes or the centre of the road and red studs mark the left edge of the carriageway.

Amber studs are used alongside the central reservation and green studs mark the entry to a slip road.
Note: these markings are also found on some dual carriageways.

Using the hard shoulder

- Stop as far to the left as possible and, if you can, near an emergency phone.
- Emergency phones are situated 1 mile apart and have blue and white marker posts every 100 metres. An arrow on the posts points the direction of the nearest phone.

- If you are using a mobile phone you can identify your location from the number on the post.
- Switch on your hazard warning lights.
- Use the left-hand door to get out of the vehicle, and make sure your passengers do too.
- Get everyone away from the road – if possible, behind the barrier or up the bank.
- Leave animals in the vehicle unless they aren't safe there.
- Phone the police with full details of where you are, then go back and wait in a safe place near your vehicle.

Now test yourself on the questions about Motorway Rules

Section 10
Rules of the Road

'Rules of the Road' is a good way to describe what is in *The Highway Code*.

The questions that come under this heading in the Theory Test include several on road signs and road markings. There are many more road sign questions in the section on Road and Traffic Signs. Several of the topics listed in this section have already come up.

Other questions in this section cover
- speed limits
- overtaking
- parking
- lanes and roundabouts
- clearways
- box junctions
- crossroads
- pedestrian crossings
- towing caravans and trailers

Speed limits
Driving too fast for the road, traffic or weather conditions causes accidents. Make sure that you keep below the speed limit shown on the signs for the road that you are on.

30mph in a built-up area

50mph on a long, twisty country road

or as low as 20mph in a residential area with speed humps or traffic calming measures

> The national speed limit for cars on a dual carriageway is 70mph.
> This is also the maximum speed for motorway driving.

National speed limit

When you leave a built-up area you will usually see this sign.

- This sign tells you that the national speed limit for this type of road applies here.
- The national speed limit for cars on a normal road (single carriageway outside a built-up area) is 60mph. So on this road you must drive below 60mph even if it is straight and empty.

Street lights usually mean that a 30mph limit applies, unless there are signs showing other limits.

The right speed for the conditions

If it is raining or there is snow and ice on the road or if you are driving in a high wind you will have to drive more slowly than the maximum speed limit. This will keep you and other road users safe.

- Remember – you have to double the time you allow for stopping and braking in wet weather. Allow even more time in snow and ice.
- You need to be extra careful when driving in fog.

The right speed for your vehicle

Some other vehicles have lower speed limits than cars. You can find out more about speed limits from the table in *The Highway Code*.

Parking rules

There are some general rules about parking that all drivers should know.

- Whenever you can, you should use off-street car parks, or parking bays. These are marked out with white lines on the road.
- Never park where your vehicle could be a danger to other road users.

Look for special signs that tell you that you cannot park there at certain times of the day or that only certain people may park in that place. Examples include signs showing bus lanes, cycle lanes, residents' parking zones and roads edged with red or yellow lines.

Orange or blue badges are given to people with disabilities. Do not park in a space reserved for a disabled driver, even if that is the only place left to park. A disabled driver may need to park there. You will break the law if you park in that space.

Parking at night

- If you park at night on a road that has a speed limit higher than 30mph, you must switch on your parking lights. You must switch on your parking lights even if you have parked in a lay-by on this type of road.
- When parking at night, always park facing in the same direction as the traffic flow.
- If your vehicle has a trailer, you must switch on parking lights, even if the road has a 30mph speed limit.

Where not to park

You are not permitted to park

- on the pavement
- at a bus stop
- in front of someone's drive
- opposite a traffic island
- near a school entrance
- on a pedestrian crossing (or inside the zigzag lines either side of it)
- near a junction
- on a clearway
- on a motorway

Now test yourself on the questions about Rules of the Road

Section 11
Road and Traffic Signs

When you look up the chapter on ROAD AND TRAFFIC SIGNS in the Theory Test questions you will see that it takes up a lot of pages. This is because most of the questions have a picture of a road sign or marking. You will also see that a lot of questions ask 'What does this sign mean?'

But however differently the questions are worded, it all comes down to how well you know *The Highway Code*. You can try to learn as much of *The Highway Code* as possible, but there are other ways you can get to know the road signs.

As you walk or drive around, look at the road signs you see in the street, and the different markings painted on the road surface.

On foot

Look at the signs and signals that all road users must obey, whether they are in a car or walking. For example, when you use a pedestrian crossing, check what kind of crossing it is (such as a pelican, toucan or zebra crossing).

Check whether you know the following

- What are the rules for pedestrians and drivers coming up to the crossing?
- What kinds of crossings are controlled by traffic lights?
- What is different about a zebra crossing?

Road and Traffic Signs

During your driving lessons

If you are having a driving lesson look well ahead so that you see all the signs that tell you what to do next. Obey them in good time.

During your test

When you take your test the examiner will tell you when to move off, when to make a turn and when to carry out one of the set manoeuvres. The examiner will expect you to watch out for lane markings on the road, and signs giving directions, and to decide how to react to these yourself.

Signs

If you see several signs all on the same post, it can be confusing. The general rule is to start at the top and read down the post. The sign at the top tells you about the first hazard you have to look out for.

If you are a passenger in a car on a motorway, look at the motorway signs, because you need to know them, even though you can't drive on a motorway yet yourself.

Check that you can answer the following:
What colour are the signs at the side of the motorway?
What do the light signals above the road tell you?
What signs tell you that you are coming to an exit?

Shapes of signs

Road and traffic signs come in three main shapes. Get to know them. You must learn what the signs mean.

Circles
Signs in circles tell you to do (blue) or not do (red) something – they give orders.

Triangles
Signs in triangles tell you of a hazard ahead – they give warnings.

Rectangles
Signs in rectangles tell you about where you are or where you are going – they give information.

There is only one sign which is octagonal – that is, it has eight sides. This is the sign for STOP. The eight-sided shape makes the sign stand out.

Now test yourself on the questions about Road and Traffic Signs

Section 12
Documents

This is quite a short section in the Theory Test questions. It is also different from the other sections, because it does not deal with either your driving skills or knowledge of *The Highway Code*.

It covers all the paperwork and the laws that you need to know about when you start learning to drive.

In this section there are questions about
- driving licences
- insurance
- MOT certificate
- Vehicle Excise Duty (tax disc)
- Vehicle Registration Document (log book)

This section also covers who can supervise a learner driverand changes you must tell the licensing authority about

Driving licence
If you are learning to drive, you need a provisional licence.
- You must have a valid licence to drive legally.
- All licences now have two parts – a photo card and a paper document.
- Your signature appears on both parts of the licence.
- Take good care of your provisional licence. If you lose it by mistake, you can get another one but you will have to pay a fee, and wait for the new licence to come.
- When you pass your test you can apply for a full licence.

Insurance
You must have a valid insurance certificate that covers you at least for third party liability. If you are learning with a driving school, you are covered by their insurance while you are in the driving school car. When you are in your own or anybody else's car, you must have insurance. Third party insurance cover usually comes as 'Third Party, Fire and Theft'. It is a basic insurance policy that will pay for repairs to another person's car and allows you to claim on the other driver's insurance if you are in an accident that was not your fault. If you have comprehensive insurance, the policy will pay for repairs to your vehicle even when the accident was your fault.

MOT certificate
Cars and motorcycles must have their first MOT test three years after they are new and first registered. After that, they must have an MOT test every year.

The MOT test checks that your vehicle
- is roadworthy – that is, all the parts work properly and the vehicle is safe to drive
- keeps to the legal limits for exhaust emissions – that is, the level of poisons in the gas that comes from the exhaust

If your vehicle is more than three years old you must not drive it without a valid MOT certificate – unless you are on your way to get an MOT and you have booked it in advance.

Vehicle Excise Duty (tax disc)

Your vehicle must have an up-to-date tax disc on the windscreen. The disc shows that you have paid Vehicle Excise Duty up to the date on the disc (you can pay for 6 or 12 months at a time). If you don't renew your tax disc within a month of the old one expiring you will be automatically fined. If you are not going to renew your tax disc (if you don't use your vehicle or keep it on a public road) you must inform the DVLA by completing a Statutory Off Road Vehicle Notification (SORN).

Vehicle Excise Duty is the tax that the government charges you to drive your vehicle on the roads. It is also sometimes called road tax. When you get your tax disc, you must show proof that your vehicle is insured, and that it has a valid MOT if required.

Vehicle Registration Document/Certificate

The Vehicle Registration Document/Certificate has all the important details about you and your vehicle, such as the make and model of the vehicle. It also has your name and address as the registered keeper of the vehicle. It is a record of the vehicle's history and is sometimes called 'the log book'.

DVLA

The Driver and Vehicle Licensing Agency is known as the DVLA. You must tell the DVLA if you are going to keep your car off road and are not renewing your tax disc, when you buy or sell a car and if you change your name or your address.

This is because your details go on to the Vehicle Registration Document/Certificate and you are legally responsible for the vehicle (car tax, parking fines, etc) until you have notified the DVLA that it is off road or you have sold it.

Supervising a learner driver

As a learner driver you cannot drive on your own. If you are not with your driving instructor, you must be supervised by a person who is at least 21 years old, has a full licence for the kind of car you drive and has had that licence for at least three years. Note that if a person has a licence to drive an automatic car only, they cannot supervise a learner in a manual car.

Now test yourself on the questions about Documents

Section 13
Accidents

The questions in this section are about helping anyone who is hurt in a road accident. Some people think they might do more harm than good if they try to help. But if you have a basic knowledge of first aid you won't panic and if you are first on the scene at an accident, you could even save a life. Look up Accidents and First Aid in *The Highway Code*.

The Theory Test questions in this section cover

- what to do when warning lights come on in your vehicle
- what to do if you break down
- safety equipment to carry with you
- when to use hazard warning lights
- what to do – and what not to do – at the scene of an accident
- what to do in tunnels

Basic first aid

What to do at an accident scene

- Check that you are not putting yourself in danger before you go to help somebody else. You may need to warn other drivers of the accident.
- Check all vehicle engines are switched off.
- Make sure no one is smoking.
- Move people who are not injured to a safe place. If the accident has happened on a motorway, if possible get uninjured people away from the hard shoulder, behind the barrier or on to the bank.
- Call the emergency services. You will need to tell them exactly where you are, and how many vehicles are involved in the accident. On motorways, use the emergency phone which connects directly to the police and tells them exactly where you are.
- Do not move injured people – unless there is a risk of fire or of an explosion.
- Give essential first aid to injured people (see below).
- Stay there until the emergency services arrive.

The ABC of first aid

This tells you what three things to check for when you go to help an injured person

A is for Airway
B is for Breathing
C is for Circulation

Airway

If an injured person is breathing, but unconscious, if possible place them in the recovery position. If they are not breathing, first make sure there is nothing in their mouth that might be blocking the airway.

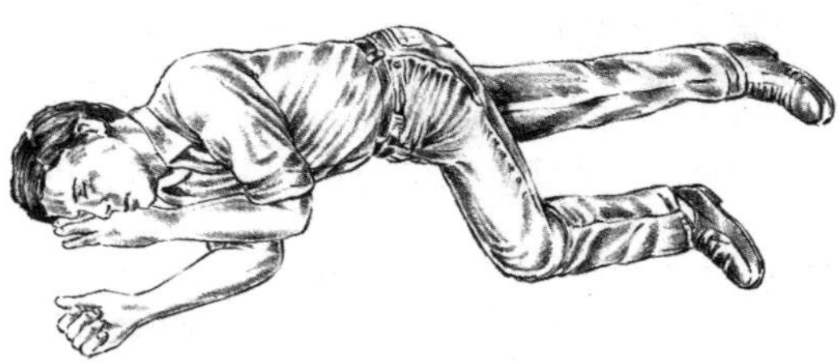

Breathing

If you have checked the airway and they are still not breathing, then give first aid as follows

- lift their chin
- carefully tilt their head back to open their airway

- pinch their nose and blow into their mouth until their chest rises

Repeat this every 4 seconds until the person can breathe alone, or until help arrives.

Circulation

'Circulation' here means 'bleeding'. If a person is bleeding, press firmly on the wound for up to 10 minutes, until the bleeding slows or stops. You can raise an injured arm or leg to reduce the bleeding – as long as the limb is not broken. If you carry a first aid kit use a sterile dressing over the wound.

Other ways to help

- Do speak in a calm way to the injured person.
- Do try to keep them warm and as comfortable as possible.
- Do not give them anything to drink.
- Do not give them a cigarette.
- Don't let injured people wander into the road.

The AA's advice on safety if you break down

If you are on a non-motorway road

- Try to get your vehicle off the main road. At least, get it right to the side of the road or on to the verge.
- If the vehicle is in a place where it might be hit by another vehicle, get any passengers out and to a safer place.
- Switch on the hazard warning lights to warn other drivers.
- If you have a red warning triangle, place it at least 45 metres behind your car to warn other traffic (but don't use it on a motorway).
- If you are a member of a motoring organisation such as the AA, call them and tell them where you are and what has happened. Wait with your vehicle until the patrol arrives.

If you are on a motorway

- If possible, leave the motorway at the next exit. If you can't get that far, drive on to the hard shoulder. Stop far over to the left, and switch on your hazard warning lights.
- Get everyone out of the vehicle, using the nearside doors (but leave pets in the vehicle). Get them to sit on the bank, well away from the traffic.
- Use the nearest orange emergency phone to call the emergency services and tell them where you are and what has happened (for your safety, face the oncoming traffic while you are on the phone).
- Go back to your vehicle and wait on the bank near by until help arrives.
- Do not cross the motorway on foot or try to do repairs yourself – even changing a wheel. This is too dangerous on a motorway.

DID YOU KNOW?
Before driving into a tunnel you should tune into a local radio station and listen to the traffic reports in case there are any accidents or problems in the tunnel.

Now test yourself on the questions about Accidents

Section 14
Vehicle Loading

This last section, called VEHICLE LOADING, is the shortest of all. It covers a mixture of the following

- how to load your vehicle safely
- using a roof rack
- towing caravans and trailers
- child restraints and safety locks

When you have passed your test you can tow a trailer, if the combined weight of the vehicle and trailer is less than 3,500kg. So you need to know the rules about towing.

Towing

When you get your first full driving licence, check it to see how much you are allowed to tow. Do not tow any trailer that comes to more than that weight. The weight of a trailer should be no more than 85% of the weight of the car that is to pull it. But it is best to stay well below that top weight, because towing a trailer will affect the way your vehicle handles. When you are towing, you need to allow more room when overtaking and more time to brake and stop.

When you are turning at a roundabout or junction you will need to think about where you are on the road.

When towing a heavy load, you might need to blow your tyres up to more than the normal pressures. Check your vehicle's handbook for advice. Remember to change back to the normal tyre pressures when you finish your journey.

Roof racks

If you attach a roof rack to your car, it will make a difference to the way in which your vehicle handles. Any load that is carried on a roof rack must be tied down securely.

- The roof rack makes your vehicle taller, so more vulnerable to strong winds.
- You will increase your fuel consumption.
- You need to change the way you drive to allow for the extra weight.

To find out more, look up the parts of *The Highway Code* that deal with Loads and Towing.

Loading a trailer

If the weight of the load is arranged properly, this should cut down the risk of losing control, swerving and snaking.

- Try to spread the weight evenly when you load your trailer. Do not put more weight towards the front, or the back, or to one side.
- It is against the law to have a load that is sticking out in a dangerous way.
- Don't forget that if you park a vehicle with a trailer overnight, it must have lights.

A vehicle towing a trailer

- must not go over a maximum speed limit of 60mph
- must not use the right (outside) lane on a motorway

If you are going to buy a trailer, make sure it fits your car's tow bar. Tow bars must keep to EU regulations, and must have electric sockets to connect to the lights on the trailer.

Snaking

'Snaking' means moving from side to side. A caravan will snake if it is not properly attached or loaded, or if the car pulling it is going too fast.

If you are towing a caravan or trailer and it starts to snake

- slow down – stop pressing the accelerator (do not brake suddenly)
- get back in control of the steering
- then brake gently

You are responsible for passengers in your vehicle

There are also questions in the Vehicle Loading section about the safety of passengers. As the driver, you are responsible for making sure your vehicle is not overloaded – and this applies to people and animals as well as to luggage. Remember that all passengers must wear a seat belt (unless they have a medical certificate saying they should not wear one) and that all children under the age of 14 must wear a seat belt or be strapped into a child seat or other 'restraint' suitable for their age. (See the section on Child Restraints in *The Highway Code*).

Children

Children must not sit in the space behind the back seat of a hatchback car, and no passengers should sit in a caravan while it is being towed.

Pets

Pets should be kept under careful control. You might keep them and you safe with a special harness, or if they are kept behind a screen in a hatchback which would stop them being thrown forward in the event of an accident.

Now test yourself on the questions about Vehicle Loading

Part 4 Theory Test Questions

Contents **Page**

1 Before you make a U-turn in the road, you should

Mark one answer

- A. give an arm signal as well as using your indicators
- B. signal so that other drivers can slow down for you
- C. look over your shoulder for a final check
- D. select a higher gear than normal

2 As you approach this bridge you should

Mark three answers

- A. move into the middle of the road to get a better view
- B. slow down
- C. get over the bridge as quickly as possible
- D. consider using your horn
- E. find another route
- F. beware of pedestrians

3 When following a large vehicle you should keep well back because this

Mark one answer

- A. allows you to corner more quickly
- B. helps the large vehicle to stop more easily
- C. allows the driver to see you in the mirrors
- D. helps you to keep out of the wind

4 In which of these situations should you avoid overtaking?

Mark one answer

- A. Just after a bend
- B. In a one-way street
- C. On a 30mph road
- D. Approaching a dip in the road

5 This road marking warns

Mark one answer

- A. drivers to use the hard shoulder
- B. overtaking drivers there is a bend to the left
- C. overtaking drivers to move back to the left
- D. drivers that it is safe to overtake

6 Your mobile phone rings while you are travelling. You should

Mark one answer

- A. stop immediately
- B. answer it immediately
- C. pull up in a suitable place
- D. pull up at the nearest kerb

7 Why are these yellow lines painted across the road?

Mark one answer

- A. To help you choose the correct lane
- B. To help you keep the correct separation distance
- C. To make you aware of your speed
- D. To tell you the distance to the roundabout

8 You are approaching traffic lights that have been on green for some time. You should

Mark one answer

- A. accelerate hard
- B. maintain your speed
- C. be ready to stop
- D. brake hard

9 Which of the following should you do before stopping?

Mark one answer

- A. Sound the horn
- B. Use the mirrors
- C. Select a higher gear
- D. Flash your headlights

10 What does the term 'blind spot' mean for a driver?

Mark one answer

- A. An area covered by your right-hand mirror
- B. An area not covered by your headlights
- C. An area covered by your left-hand mirror
- D. An area not covered by your mirrors

11 Objects hanging from your interior mirror may

Mark two answers

- A. restrict your view
- B. improve your driving
- C. distract your attention
- D. help your concentration

12 Which of the following may cause loss of concentration on a long journey?

Mark four answers

- A. Loud music
- B. Arguing with a passenger
- C. Using a mobile phone
- D. Putting in a cassette tape
- E. Stopping regularly to rest
- F. Pulling up to tune the radio

13 On a long motorway journey boredom can cause you to feel sleepy. You should

Mark two answers

- A. leave the motorway and find a safe place to stop
- B. keep looking around at the surrounding landscape
- C. drive faster to complete your journey sooner
- D. ensure a supply of fresh air into your vehicle
- E. stop on the hard shoulder for a rest

14 You are driving at dusk. You should switch your lights on

Mark two answers

- [ ] A. even when street lights are not lit
- [ ] B. so others can see you
- [ ] C. only when others have done so
- [ ] D. only when street lights are lit

15 You are most likely to lose concentration when driving if you

Mark two answers

- [ ] A. use a mobile phone
- [ ] B. listen to very loud music
- [ ] C. switch on the heated rear window
- [ ] D. look at the door mirrors

16 Which FOUR are most likely to cause you to lose concentration while you are driving?

Mark four answers

- [ ] A. Using a mobile phone
- [ ] B. Talking into a microphone
- [ ] C. Tuning your car radio
- [ ] D. Looking at a map
- [ ] E. Checking the mirrors
- [ ] F. Using the demisters

17 You should not use a mobile phone while driving

Mark one answer

- [ ] A. until you are satisfied that no other traffic is near
- [ ] B. unless you are able to drive one handed
- [ ] C. because it might distract your attention from the road ahead
- [ ] D. because reception is poor when the engine is running

18 Your vehicle is fitted with a hands-free phone system. Using this equipment whilst driving

Mark one answer

- [ ] A. is quite safe as long as you slow down
- [ ] B. could distract your attention from the road
- [ ] C. is recommended by *The Highway Code*
- [ ] D. could be very good for road safety

19 Using a hands-free phone is likely to

Mark one answer

- [ ] A. improve your safety
- [ ] B. increase your concentration
- [ ] C. reduce your view
- [ ] D. divert your attention

20 You should ONLY use a mobile phone when

Mark one answer

- [ ] A. receiving a call
- [ ] B. suitably parked
- [ ] C. driving at less than 30mph
- [ ] D. driving an automatic vehicle

21 Using a mobile phone while you are driving

Mark one answer

- [ ] A. is acceptable in a vehicle with power steering
- [ ] B. will reduce your field of vision
- [ ] C. could distract your attention from the road
- [ ] D. will affect your vehicle's electronic systems

22 What is the safest way to use a mobile phone in your vehicle?

Mark one answer

- [ ] **A.** Use hands-free equipment
- [ ] **B.** Find a suitable place to stop
- [ ] **C.** Drive slowly on a quiet road
- [ ] **D.** Direct your call through the operator

23 You are driving on a wet road. You have to stop your vehicle in an emergency. You should

Mark one answer

- [ ] **A.** apply the handbrake and footbrake together
- [ ] **B.** keep both hands on the wheel
- [ ] **C.** select reverse gear
- [ ] **D.** give an arm signal

24 When you are moving off from behind a parked car you should

Mark three answers

- [ ] **A.** look round before you move off
- [ ] **B.** use all the mirrors on the vehicle
- [ ] **C.** look round after moving off
- [ ] **D.** use the exterior mirrors only
- [ ] **E.** give a signal if necessary
- [ ] **F.** give a signal after moving off

25 You are travelling along this narrow country road. When passing the cyclist you should go

Mark one answer

- [ ] **A.** slowly, sounding the horn as you pass
- [ ] **B.** quickly, leaving plenty of room
- [ ] **C.** slowly, leaving plenty of room
- [ ] **D.** quickly, sounding the horn as you pass

26 Your vehicle is fitted with a hand-held telephone. To use the telephone you should

Mark one answer

- [ ] **A.** reduce your speed
- [ ] **B.** find a safe place to stop
- [ ] **C.** steer the vehicle with one hand
- [ ] **D.** be particularly careful at junctions

27 To answer a call on your mobile phone while travelling you should

Mark one answer

- [ ] **A.** reduce your speed wherever you are
- [ ] **B.** stop in a proper and convenient place
- [ ] **C.** keep the call time to a minimum
- [ ] **D.** slow down and allow others to overtake

28 **Your mobile phone rings while you are on the motorway. Before answering you should**

Mark one answer

- ☐ **A.** reduce your speed to 30mph
- ☐ **B.** pull up on the hard shoulder
- ☐ **C.** move into the left-hand lane
- ☐ **D.** stop in a safe place

29 **You are turning right on to a dual carriageway. What should you do before emerging?**

Mark one answer

- ☐ **A.** Stop, apply the handbrake and then select a low gear
- ☐ **B.** Position your vehicle well to the left of the side road
- ☐ **C.** Check that the central reservation is wide enough for your vehicle
- ☐ **D.** Make sure that you leave enough room for a vehicle behind

30 **You lose your way on a busy road. What is the best action to take?**

Mark one answer

- ☐ **A.** Stop at traffic lights and ask pedestrians
- ☐ **B.** Shout to other drivers to ask them the way
- ☐ **C.** Turn into a side road, stop and check a map
- ☐ **D.** Check a map, and keep going with the traffic flow

31 **You are waiting to emerge from a junction. The windscreen pillar is restricting your view. What should you be particularly aware of?**

Mark one answer

- ☐ **A.** Lorries
- ☐ **B.** Buses
- ☐ **C.** Motorcyclists
- ☐ **D.** Coaches

32 **When emerging from junctions which is most likely to obstruct your view?**

Mark one answer

- ☐ **A.** Windscreen pillars
- ☐ **B.** Steering wheel
- ☐ **C.** Interior mirror
- ☐ **D.** Windscreen wipers

33 **Windscreen pillars can obstruct your view. You should take particular care when**

Mark one answer

- ☐ **A.** driving on a motorway
- ☐ **B.** driving on a dual carriageway
- ☐ **C.** approaching a one-way street
- ☐ **D.** approaching bends and junctions

34 **You cannot see clearly behind when reversing. What should you do?**

Mark one answer

- ☐ **A.** Open your window to look behind
- ☐ **B.** Open the door and look behind
- ☐ **C.** Look in the nearside mirror
- ☐ **D.** Ask someone to guide you

35 At a pelican crossing the flashing amber light means you MUST

Mark one answer

- [ ] **A.** stop and wait for the green light
- [ ] **B.** stop and wait for the red light
- [ ] **C.** give way to pedestrians waiting to cross
- [ ] **D.** give way to pedestrians already on the crossing

36 You should never wave people across at pedestrian crossings because

Mark one answer

- [ ] **A.** there may be another vehicle coming
- [ ] **B.** they may not be looking
- [ ] **C.** it is safer for you to carry on
- [ ] **D.** they may not be ready to cross

37 At a puffin crossing, which colour follows the green signal?

Mark one answer

- [ ] **A.** Steady red
- [ ] **B.** Flashing amber
- [ ] **C.** Steady amber
- [ ] **D.** Flashing green

38 The conditions are good and dry. You could use the 'two-second rule'

Mark one answer

- [ ] **A.** before restarting the engine after it has stalled
- [ ] **B.** to keep a safe gap from the vehicle in front
- [ ] **C.** before using the 'Mirror-Signal-Manoeuvre' routine
- [ ] **D.** when emerging on wet roads

39 'Tailgating' means

Mark one answer

- [ ] **A.** using the rear door of a hatchback car
- [ ] **B.** reversing into a parking space
- [ ] **C.** following another vehicle too closely
- [ ] **D.** driving with rear fog lights on

40 Following this vehicle too closely is unwise because

Mark one answer

- [ ] **A.** your brakes will overheat
- [ ] **B.** your view ahead is increased
- [ ] **C.** your engine will overheat
- [ ] **D.** your view ahead is reduced

41 You are following a vehicle on a wet road. You should leave a time gap of at least

Mark one answer

- [ ] **A.** one second
- [ ] **B.** two seconds
- [ ] **C.** three seconds
- [ ] **D.** four seconds

42 You are in a line of traffic. The driver behind you is following very closely. What action should you take?

Mark one answer

- [ ] **A.** Ignore the following driver and continue to travel within the speed limit
- [ ] **B.** Slow down, gradually increasing the gap between you and the vehicle in front
- [ ] **C.** Signal left and wave the following driver past
- [ ] **D.** Move over to a position just left of the centre line of the road

43 **A long, heavily laden lorry is taking a long time to overtake you. What should you do?**

Mark one answer

- [ ] A. Speed up
- [ ] B. Slow down
- [ ] C. Hold your speed
- [ ] D. Change direction

44 **Which of the following vehicles will use blue flashing beacons?**

Mark three answers

- [ ] A. Motorway maintenance
- [ ] B. Bomb disposal
- [ ] C. Blood transfusion
- [ ] D. Police patrol
- [ ] E. Breakdown recovery

45 **Which THREE of these emergency services might have blue flashing beacons?**

Mark three answers

- [ ] A. Coastguard
- [ ] B. Bomb disposal
- [ ] C. Gritting lorries
- [ ] D. Animal ambulances
- [ ] E. Mountain rescue
- [ ] F. Doctors' cars

46 **When being followed by an ambulance showing a flashing blue beacon you should**

Mark one answer

- [ ] A. pull over as soon as safely possible to let it pass
- [ ] B. accelerate hard to get away from it
- [ ] C. maintain your speed and course
- [ ] D. brake harshly and immediately stop in the road

47 **What type of emergency vehicle is fitted with a green flashing beacon?**

Mark one answer

- [ ] A. Fire engine
- [ ] B. Road gritter
- [ ] C. Ambulance
- [ ] D. Doctor's car

48 **A flashing green beacon on a vehicle means**

Mark one answer

- [ ] A. police on non-urgent duties
- [ ] B. doctor on an emergency call
- [ ] C. road safety patrol operating
- [ ] D. gritting in progress

49 **A vehicle has a flashing green beacon. What does this mean?**

Mark one answer

- [ ] A. A doctor is answering an emergency call
- [ ] B. The vehicle is slow moving
- [ ] C. It is a motorway police patrol vehicle
- [ ] D. The vehicle is carrying hazardous chemicals

50 **Diamond-shaped signs give instructions to**

Mark one answer

- [ ] A. tram drivers
- [ ] B. bus drivers
- [ ] C. lorry drivers
- [ ] D. taxi drivers

51 On a road where trams operate, which of these vehicles will be most at risk from the tram rails?

Mark one answer

- ☐ **A.** Cars
- ☐ **B.** Cycles
- ☐ **C.** Buses
- ☐ **D.** Lorries

52 What should you use your horn for?

Mark one answer

- ☐ **A.** To alert others to your presence
- ☐ **B.** To allow you right of way
- ☐ **C.** To greet other road users
- ☐ **D.** To signal your annoyance

53 You are in a one-way street and want to turn right. You should position yourself

Mark one answer

- ☐ **A.** in the right-hand lane
- ☐ **B.** in the left-hand lane
- ☐ **C.** in either lane, depending on the traffic
- ☐ **D.** just left of the centre line

54 You wish to turn right ahead. Why should you take up the correct position in good time?

Mark one answer

- ☐ **A.** To allow other drivers to pull out in front of you
- ☐ **B.** To give a better view into the road that you're joining
- ☐ **C.** To help other road users know what you intend to do
- ☐ **D.** To allow drivers to pass you on the right

55 At which type of crossing are cyclists allowed to ride across with pedestrians?

Mark one answer

- ☐ **A.** Toucan
- ☐ **B.** Puffin
- ☐ **C.** Pelican
- ☐ **D.** Zebra

56 A bus has stopped at a bus stop ahead of you. Its right-hand indicator is flashing. You should

Mark one answer

- ☐ **A.** flash your headlights and slow down
- ☐ **B.** slow down and give way if it is safe to do so
- ☐ **C.** sound your horn and keep going
- ☐ **D.** slow down and then sound your horn

57 You are travelling at the legal speed limit. A vehicle comes up quickly behind, flashing its headlights. You should

Mark one answer

- ☐ **A.** accelerate to make a gap behind you
- ☐ **B.** touch the brakes sharply to show your brake lights
- ☐ **C.** maintain your speed to prevent the vehicle from overtaking
- ☐ **D.** allow the vehicle to overtake

58 You should ONLY flash your headlights to other road users

Mark one answer

- ☐ **A.** to show that you are giving way
- ☐ **B.** to show that you are about to turn
- ☐ **C.** to tell them that you have right of way
- ☐ **D.** to let them know that you are there

59 You are approaching unmarked crossroads. How should you deal with this type of junction?

Mark one answer

- ☐ **A.** Accelerate and keep to the middle
- ☐ **B.** Slow down and keep to the right
- ☐ **C.** Accelerate looking to the left
- ☐ **D.** Slow down and look both ways

60 You are approaching a pelican crossing. The amber light is flashing. You must

Mark one answer

- ☐ **A.** give way to pedestrians who are crossing
- ☐ **B.** encourage pedestrians to cross
- ☐ **C.** not move until the green light appears
- ☐ **D.** stop even if the crossing is clear

61 At puffin crossings, which light will not show to a driver?

Mark one answer

- ☐ **A.** Flashing amber
- ☐ **B.** Red
- ☐ **C.** Steady amber
- ☐ **D.** Green

62 You should leave at least a two-second gap between your vehicle and the one in front when conditions are

Mark one answer

- ☐ **A.** wet
- ☐ **B.** good
- ☐ **C.** damp
- ☐ **D.** foggy

63 You are driving on a clear night. There is a steady stream of oncoming traffic. The national speed limit applies. Which lights should you use?

Mark one answer

- ☐ **A.** Full beam headlights
- ☐ **B.** Sidelights
- ☐ **C.** Dipped headlights
- ☐ **D.** Fog lights

64 You are driving behind a large goods vehicle. It signals left but steers to the right. You should

Mark one answer

- ☐ **A.** slow down and let the vehicle turn
- ☐ **B.** drive on, keeping to the left
- ☐ **C.** overtake on the right of it
- ☐ **D.** hold your speed and sound your horn

65 You are driving along this road. The red van cuts in close in front of you. What should you do?

Mark one answer

- ☐ **A.** Accelerate to get closer to the red van
- ☐ **B.** Give a long blast on the horn
- ☐ **C.** Drop back to leave the correct separation distance
- ☐ **D.** Flash your headlights several times

66 You are waiting in a traffic queue at night. To avoid dazzling following drivers you should

Mark one answer

- ☐ **A.** apply the handbrake only
- ☐ **B.** apply the footbrake only
- ☐ **C.** switch off your headlights
- ☐ **D.** use both the handbrake and footbrake

67 You are driving in traffic at the speed limit for the road. The driver behind is trying to overtake. You should

Mark one answer

- ☐ **A.** move closer to the car ahead, so the driver behind has no room to overtake
- ☐ **B.** wave the driver behind to overtake when it is safe
- ☐ **C.** keep a steady course and allow the driver behind to overtake
- ☐ **D.** accelerate to get away from the driver behind

68 You are driving at night on an unlit road behind another vehicle. You should

Mark one answer

- ☐ **A.** flash your headlights
- ☐ **B.** use dipped beam headlights
- ☐ **C.** switch off your headlights
- ☐ **D.** use full beam headlights

69 A bus lane on your left shows no times of operation. This means it is

Mark one answer

- ☐ **A.** not in operation at all
- ☐ **B.** only in operation at peak times
- ☐ **C.** in operation 24 hours a day
- ☐ **D.** only in operation in daylight hours

70 You are driving along a country road. A horse and rider are approaching. What should you do?

Mark two answers

- ☐ **A.** Increase your speed
- ☐ **B.** Sound your horn
- ☐ **C.** Flash your headlights
- ☐ **D.** Drive slowly past
- ☐ **E.** Give plenty of room
- ☐ **F.** Rev your engine

71 A person herding sheep asks you to stop. You should

Mark one answer

- ☐ **A.** ignore them as they have no authority
- ☐ **B.** stop and switch off your engine
- ☐ **C.** continue on but drive slowly
- ☐ **D.** try and get past quickly

72 When overtaking a horse and rider you should

Mark one answer

- ☐ **A.** sound your horn as a warning
- ☐ **B.** go past as quickly as possible
- ☐ **C.** flash your headlights as a warning
- ☐ **D.** go past slowly and carefully

73 You are approaching a zebra crossing. Pedestrians are waiting to cross. You should

Mark one answer

- ☐ **A.** give way to the elderly and infirm only
- ☐ **B.** slow down and prepare to stop
- ☐ **C.** use your headlights to indicate they can cross
- ☐ **D.** wave at them to cross the road

74 You are driving a slow-moving vehicle on a narrow winding road. You should

Mark one answer

- ☐ **A.** keep well out to stop vehicles overtaking dangerously
- ☐ **B.** wave following vehicles past you if you think they can overtake quickly
- ☐ **C.** pull in safely when you can, to let following vehicles overtake
- ☐ **D.** give a left signal when it is safe for vehicles to overtake you

75 You have a loose filler cap on your diesel fuel tank. This will

Mark two answers

- ☐ **A.** waste fuel and money
- ☐ **B.** make roads slippery for other road users
- ☐ **C.** improve your vehicle's fuel consumption
- ☐ **D.** increase the level of exhaust emissions

76 To avoid spillage after refuelling, you should make sure that

Mark one answer

- ☐ **A.** your tank is only three-quarters full
- ☐ **B.** you have used a locking filler cap
- ☐ **C.** you check your fuel gauge is working
- ☐ **D.** your filler cap is securely fastened

77 A vehicle pulls out in front of you at a junction. What should you do?

Mark one answer

- ☐ **A.** Swerve past it and sound your horn
- ☐ **B.** Flash your headlights and drive up close behind
- ☐ **C.** Slow down and be ready to stop
- ☐ **D.** Accelerate past it immediately

78 You stop for pedestrians waiting to cross at a zebra crossing. They do not start to cross. What should you do?

Mark one answer

- ☐ **A.** Be patient and wait
- ☐ **B.** Sound your horn
- ☐ **C.** Carry on
- ☐ **D.** Wave them to cross

79 **You are following this lorry. You should keep well back from it to**

Mark one answer

- ☐ **A.** give you a good view of the road ahead
- ☐ **B.** stop following traffic from rushing through the junction
- ☐ **C.** prevent traffic behind you from overtaking
- ☐ **D.** allow you to hurry through the traffic lights if they change

80 **You are approaching a red light at a puffin crossing. Pedestrians are on the crossing. The red light will stay on until**

Mark one answer

- ☐ **A.** you start to edge forward on to the crossing
- ☐ **B.** the pedestrians have reached a safe position
- ☐ **C.** the pedestrians are clear of the front of your vehicle
- ☐ **D.** a driver from the opposite direction reaches the crossing

81 **Which instrument panel warning light would show that headlights are on full beam?**

Mark one answer

☐ **A.**

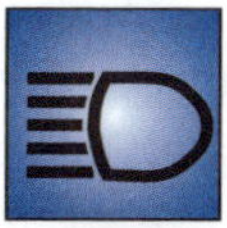

☐ **B.**

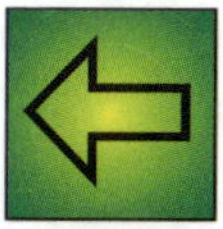

☐ **C.**

☐ **D.**

82 **If your vehicle uses diesel fuel, take extra care when refuelling. Diesel fuel when spilt is**

Mark one answer

- ☐ **A.** sticky
- ☐ **B.** odourless
- ☐ **C.** clear
- ☐ **D.** slippery

83 **Which of these, if allowed to get low, could cause an accident?**

Mark one answer
- [ ] **A.** Anti-freeze level
- [ ] **B.** Brake fluid level
- [ ] **C.** Battery water level
- [ ] **D.** Radiator coolant level

84 **Which TWO are badly affected if the tyres are under-inflated?**

Mark two answers
- [ ] **A.** Braking
- [ ] **B.** Steering
- [ ] **C.** Changing gear
- [ ] **D.** Parking

85 **Motor vehicles can harm the environment. This has resulted in**

Mark three answers
- [ ] **A.** air pollution
- [ ] **B.** damage to buildings
- [ ] **C.** less risk to health
- [ ] **D.** improved public transport
- [ ] **E.** less use of electrical vehicles
- [ ] **F.** using up of natural resources

86 **Excessive or uneven tyre wear can be caused by faults in which THREE of the following?**

Mark three answers
- [ ] **A.** The gearbox
- [ ] **B.** The braking system
- [ ] **C.** The accelerator
- [ ] **D.** The exhaust system
- [ ] **E.** Wheel alignment
- [ ] **F.** The suspension

87 **You must NOT sound your horn**

Mark one answer
- [ ] **A.** between 10pm and 6am in a built-up area
- [ ] **B.** at any time in a built-up area
- [ ] **C.** between 11.30pm and 7am in a built-up area
- [ ] **D.** between 11.30pm and 6am on any road

88 **The pictured vehicle is 'environmentally friendly' because it**

Mark three answers
- [ ] **A.** reduces noise pollution
- [ ] **B.** uses diesel fuel
- [ ] **C.** uses electricity
- [ ] **D.** uses unleaded fuel
- [ ] **E.** reduces parking spaces
- [ ] **F.** reduces town traffic

89 **Supertrams or Light Rapid Transit (LRT) systems are environmentally friendly because**

Mark one answer
- [ ] **A.** they use diesel power
- [ ] **B.** they use quieter roads
- [ ] **C.** they use electric power
- [ ] **D.** they do not operate during rush hour

90 **'Red routes' in major cities have been introduced to**

Mark one answer
- [ ] **A.** raise the speed limits
- [ ] **B.** help the traffic flow
- [ ] **C.** provide better parking
- [ ] **D.** allow lorries to load more freely

91 Road humps, chicanes, and narrowings are

Mark one answer

- A. always at major road works
- B. used to increase traffic speed
- C. at toll-bridge approaches only
- D. traffic calming measures

92 The purpose of a catalytic converter is to reduce

Mark one answer

- A. fuel consumption
- B. the risk of fire
- C. toxic exhaust gases
- D. engine wear

93 Catalytic converters are fitted to make the

Mark one answer

- A. engine produce more power
- B. exhaust system easier to replace
- C. engine run quietly
- D. exhaust fumes cleaner

94 It is essential that tyre pressures are checked regularly. When should this be done?

Mark one answer

- A. After any lengthy journey
- B. After travelling at high speed
- C. When tyres are hot
- D. When tyres are cold

95 When should you NOT use your horn in a built-up area?

Mark one answer

- A. Between 8pm and 8am
- B. Between 9pm and dawn
- C. Between dusk and 8am
- D. Between 11.30pm and 7am

96 You will use more fuel if your tyres are

Mark one answer

- A. under-inflated
- B. of different makes
- C. over-inflated
- D. new and hardly used

97 How should you dispose of a used battery?

Mark two answers

- A. Take it to a local authority site
- B. Put it in the dustbin
- C. Break it up into pieces
- D. Leave it on waste land
- E. Take it to a garage
- F. Burn it on a fire

98 What is most likely to cause high fuel consumption?

Mark one answer

- A. Poor steering control
- B. Accelerating around bends
- C. Staying in high gears
- D. Harsh braking and accelerating

99 The fluid level in your battery is low. What should you top it up with?

Mark one answer

- A. Battery acid
- B. Distilled water
- C. Engine oil
- D. Engine coolant

100 You need to top up your battery. What level should you fill to?

Mark one answer

- A. The top of the battery
- B. Half-way up the battery
- C. Just below the cell plates
- D. Just above the cell plates

101 You have too much oil in your engine. What could this cause?

Mark one answer

- [ ] **A.** Low oil pressure
- [ ] **B.** Engine overheating
- [ ] **C.** Chain wear
- [ ] **D.** Oil leaks

102 You are parking on a two-way road at night. The speed limit is 40mph. You should park on the

Mark one answer

- [ ] **A.** left with parking lights on
- [ ] **B.** left with no lights on
- [ ] **C.** right with parking lights on
- [ ] **D.** right with dipped headlights on

103 You are parked on the road at night. Where must you use parking lights?

Mark one answer

- [ ] **A.** Where there are continuous white lines in the middle of the road
- [ ] **B.** Where the speed limit exceeds 30mph
- [ ] **C.** Where you are facing oncoming traffic
- [ ] **D.** Where you are near a bus stop

104 Which FOUR of these must be in good working order for your car to be roadworthy?

Mark four answers

- [ ] **A.** The temperature gauge
- [ ] **B.** The speedometer
- [ ] **C.** The windscreen washers
- [ ] **D.** The windscreen wipers
- [ ] **E.** The oil warning light
- [ ] **F.** The horn

105 New petrol-engined cars must be fitted with catalytic converters. The reason for this is to

Mark one answer

- [ ] **A.** control exhaust noise levels
- [ ] **B.** prolong the life of the exhaust system
- [ ] **C.** allow the exhaust system to be recycled
- [ ] **D.** reduce harmful exhaust emissions

106 What can cause heavy steering?

Mark one answer

- [ ] **A.** Driving on ice
- [ ] **B.** Badly worn brakes
- [ ] **C.** Over-inflated tyres
- [ ] **D.** Under-inflated tyres

107 Driving with under-inflated tyres can affect

Mark two answers

- [ ] **A.** engine temperature
- [ ] **B.** fuel consumption
- [ ] **C.** braking
- [ ] **D.** oil pressure

108 Excessive or uneven tyre wear can be caused by faults in the

Mark two answers

- [ ] **A.** gearbox
- [ ] **B.** braking system
- [ ] **C.** suspension
- [ ] **D.** exhaust system

109 The main cause of brake fade is

Mark one answer

- [ ] **A.** the brakes overheating
- [ ] **B.** air in the brake fluid
- [ ] **C.** oil on the brakes
- [ ] **D.** the brakes out of adjustment

110 Your anti-lock brakes warning light stays on. You should

Mark one answer

- [ ] **A.** check the brake fluid level
- [ ] **B.** check the footbrake free play
- [ ] **C.** check that the handbrake is released
- [ ] **D.** have the brakes checked immediately

111 While driving, this warning light on your dashboard comes on. It means

Mark one answer

- [ ] **A.** a fault in the braking system
- [ ] **B.** the engine oil is low
- [ ] **C.** a rear light has failed
- [ ] **D.** your seat belt is not fastened

112 It is important to wear suitable shoes when you are driving. Why is this?

Mark one answer

- [ ] **A.** To prevent wear on the pedals
- [ ] **B.** To maintain control of the pedals
- [ ] **C.** To enable you to adjust your seat
- [ ] **D.** To enable you to walk for assistance if you break down

113 The most important reason for having a properly adjusted head restraint is to

Mark one answer

- [ ] **A.** make you more comfortable
- [ ] **B.** help you to avoid neck injury
- [ ] **C.** help you to relax
- [ ] **D.** help you to maintain your driving position

114 What will reduce the risk of neck injury resulting from a collision?

Mark one answer

- [ ] **A.** An air-sprung seat
- [ ] **B.** Anti-lock brakes
- [ ] **C.** A collapsible steering wheel
- [ ] **D.** A properly adjusted head restraint

115 You are driving the children of a friend home from school. They are both under 14 years old. Who is responsible for making sure they wear a seat belt?

Mark one answer

- [ ] **A.** An adult passenger
- [ ] **B.** The children
- [ ] **C.** You, the driver
- [ ] **D.** Your friend

116 Car passengers MUST wear a seat belt if one is available, unless they are

Mark one answer

- [ ] **A.** under 14 years old
- [ ] **B.** under 1.5 metres (5 feet) in height
- [ ] **C.** sitting in the rear seat
- [ ] **D.** exempt for medical reasons

117 You are testing your suspension. You notice that your vehicle keeps bouncing when you press down on the front wing. What does this mean?

Mark one answer

- [ ] **A.** Worn tyres
- [ ] **B.** Tyres under-inflated
- [ ] **C.** Steering wheel not located centrally
- [ ] **D.** Worn shock absorbers

118 A roof rack fitted to your car will

Mark one answer

- [ ] **A.** reduce fuel consumption
- [ ] **B.** improve the road handling
- [ ] **C.** make your car go faster
- [ ] **D.** increase fuel consumption

119 It is illegal to drive with tyres that

Mark one answer

- [ ] **A.** have been bought second-hand
- [ ] **B.** have a large deep cut in the side wall
- [ ] **C.** are of different makes
- [ ] **D.** are of different tread patterns

120 The legal minimum depth of tread for car tyres over three quarters of the breadth is

Mark one answer

- [ ] **A.** 1mm
- [ ] **B.** 1.6mm
- [ ] **C.** 2.5mm
- [ ] **D.** 4mm

121 You are carrying two 13-year-old children and their parents in your car. Who is responsible for seeing that the children wear seat belts?

Mark one answer

- [ ] **A.** The children's parents
- [ ] **B.** You, the driver
- [ ] **C.** The front-seat passenger
- [ ] **D.** The children

122 When a roof rack is not in use it should be removed. Why is this?

Mark one answer

- [ ] **A.** It will affect the suspension
- [ ] **B.** It is illegal
- [ ] **C.** It will affect your braking
- [ ] **D.** It will waste fuel

123 How can you, as a driver, help the environment?

Mark three answers

- [ ] **A.** By reducing your speed
- [ ] **B.** By gentle acceleration
- [ ] **C.** By using leaded fuel
- [ ] **D.** By driving faster
- [ ] **E.** By harsh acceleration
- [ ] **F.** By servicing your vehicle properly

124 To help the environment, you can avoid wasting fuel by

Mark three answers

- [ ] **A.** having your vehicle properly serviced
- [ ] **B.** making sure your tyres are correctly inflated
- [ ] **C.** not over-revving in the lower gears
- [ ] **D.** driving at higher speeds where possible
- [ ] **E.** keeping an empty roof rack properly fitted
- [ ] **F.** servicing your vehicle less regularly

125 To reduce the volume of traffic on the roads you could

Mark three answers

- [ ] **A.** use public transport more often
- [ ] **B.** share a car when possible
- [ ] **C.** walk or cycle on short journeys
- [ ] **D.** travel by car at all times
- [ ] **E.** use a car with a smaller engine
- [ ] **F.** drive in a bus lane

126 Which THREE of the following are most likely to waste fuel?

Mark three answers

- A. Reducing your speed
- B. Carrying unnecessary weight
- C. Using the wrong grade of fuel
- D. Under-inflated tyres
- E. Using different brands of fuel
- F. A fitted, empty roof rack

127 Which THREE things can you, as a road user, do to help the environment?

Mark three answers

- A. Cycle when possible
- B. Drive on under-inflated tyres
- C. Use the choke for as long as possible on a cold engine
- D. Have your vehicle properly tuned and serviced
- E. Watch the traffic and plan ahead
- F. Brake as late as possible without skidding

128 As a driver you can cause more damage to the environment by

Mark two answers

- A. choosing a fuel-efficient vehicle
- B. making a lot of short journeys
- C. driving in as high a gear as possible
- D. accelerating as quickly as possible
- E. having your vehicle regularly serviced

129 To help protect the environment you should NOT

Mark one answer

- A. remove your roof rack when unloaded
- B. use your car for very short journeys
- C. walk, cycle, or use public transport
- D. empty the boot of unnecessary weight

130 Which THREE does the law require you to keep in good condition?

Mark three answers

- A. Gears
- B. Transmission
- C. Headlights
- D. Windscreen
- E. Seat belts

131 Driving at 70mph uses more fuel than driving at 50mph by up to

Mark one answer

- A. 10%
- B. 30%
- C. 75%
- D. 100%

132 Your vehicle pulls to one side when braking. You should

Mark one answer

- A. change the tyres around
- B. consult your garage as soon as possible
- C. pump the pedal when braking
- D. use your handbrake at the same time

133 As a driver, you can help reduce pollution levels in town centres by

Mark one answer

- A. driving more quickly
- B. over-revving in a low gear
- C. walking or cycling
- D. driving short journeys

134 Unbalanced wheels on a car may cause

Mark one answer

- A. the steering to pull to one side
- B. the steering to vibrate
- C. the brakes to fail
- D. the tyres to deflate

135 Turning the steering wheel while your car is stationary can cause damage to the

Mark two answers
- [ ] **A.** gearbox
- [ ] **B.** engine
- [ ] **C.** brakes
- [ ] **D.** steering
- [ ] **E.** tyres

136 How can you reduce the chances of your car being broken into when leaving it unattended?

Mark one answer
- [ ] **A.** Take all valuables with you
- [ ] **B.** Park near a taxi rank
- [ ] **C.** Place any valuables on the floor
- [ ] **D.** Park near a fire station

137 You have to leave valuables in your car. It would be safer to

Mark one answer
- [ ] **A.** put them in a carrier bag
- [ ] **B.** park near a school entrance
- [ ] **C.** lock them out of sight
- [ ] **D.** park near a bus stop

138 How could you deter theft from your car when leaving it unattended?

Mark one answer
- [ ] **A.** Leave valuables in a carrier bag
- [ ] **B.** Lock valuables out of sight
- [ ] **C.** Put valuables on the seats
- [ ] **D.** Leave valuables on the floor

139 Which of the following may help to deter a thief from stealing your car?

Mark one answer
- [ ] **A.** Always keeping the headlights on
- [ ] **B.** Fitting reflective glass windows
- [ ] **C.** Always keeping the interior light on
- [ ] **D.** Etching the car number on the windows

140 How can you help to prevent your car radio being stolen?

Mark one answer
- [ ] **A.** Park in an unlit area
- [ ] **B.** Hide the radio with a blanket
- [ ] **C.** Park near a busy junction
- [ ] **D.** Install a security-coded radio

141 Which of the following should not be kept in your vehicle?

Mark one answer
- [ ] **A.** A first aid kit
- [ ] **B.** A road atlas
- [ ] **C.** The tax disc
- [ ] **D.** The vehicle documents

142 What should you do when leaving your vehicle?

Mark one answer
- [ ] **A.** Put valuable documents under the seats
- [ ] **B.** Remove all valuables
- [ ] **C.** Cover valuables with a blanket
- [ ] **D.** Leave the interior light on

143 You are parking your car. You have some valuables which you are unable to take with you. What should you do?

Mark one answer

- **A.** Park near a police station
- **B.** Put them under the driver's seat
- **C.** Lock them out of sight
- **D.** Park in an unlit side road

144 Which of these is most likely to deter the theft of your vehicle?

Mark one answer

- **A.** An immobiliser
- **B.** Tinted windows
- **C.** Locking wheel nuts
- **D.** A sun screen

145 Wherever possible, which one of the following should you do when parking at night?

Mark one answer

- **A.** Park in a quiet car park
- **B.** Park in a well-lit area
- **C.** Park facing against the flow of traffic
- **D.** Park next to a busy junction

146 When parking and leaving your car you should

Mark one answer

- **A.** park under a shady tree
- **B.** remove the tax disc
- **C.** park in a quiet road
- **D.** engage the steering lock

147 Rear-facing baby seats should NEVER be used on a seat protected with

Mark one answer

- **A.** an airbag
- **B.** seat belts
- **C.** head restraints
- **D.** seat covers

148 When leaving your vehicle parked and unattended you should

Mark one answer

- **A.** park near a busy junction
- **B.** park in a housing estate
- **C.** remove the key and lock it
- **D.** leave the left indicator on

149 How can you lessen the risk of your vehicle being broken into at night?

Mark one answer

- **A.** Leave it in a well-lit area
- **B.** Park in a quiet side road
- **C.** Don't engage the steering lock
- **D.** Park in a poorly-lit area

150 To help keep your car secure you could join a

Mark one answer

- **A.** vehicle breakdown organisation
- **B.** vehicle watch scheme
- **C.** advanced driver's scheme
- **D.** car maintenance class

151 Which TWO of the following will improve fuel consumption?

Mark two answers

- **A.** Reducing your road speed
- **B.** Planning well ahead
- **C.** Late and harsh braking
- **D.** Driving in lower gears
- **E.** Short journeys with a cold engine
- **F.** Rapid acceleration

152 You service your own vehicle. How should you get rid of the old engine oil?

Mark one answer
- [ ] **A.** Take it to a local authority site
- [ ] **B.** Pour it down a drain
- [ ] **C.** Tip it into a hole in the ground
- [ ] **D.** Put it into your dustbin

153 On a vehicle, where would you find a catalytic converter?

Mark one answer
- [ ] **A.** In the fuel tank
- [ ] **B.** In the air filter
- [ ] **C.** On the cooling system
- [ ] **D.** On the exhaust system

154 Why do MOT tests include a strict exhaust emission test?

Mark one answer
- [ ] **A.** To recover the cost of expensive garage equipment
- [ ] **B.** To help protect the environment against pollution
- [ ] **C.** To discover which fuel supplier is used the most
- [ ] **D.** To make sure diesel and petrol engines emit the same fumes

155 To reduce the damage your vehicle causes to the environment you should

Mark three answers
- [ ] **A.** use narrow side streets
- [ ] **B.** avoid harsh acceleration
- [ ] **C.** brake in good time
- [ ] **D.** anticipate well ahead
- [ ] **E.** use busy routes

156 Your vehicle has a catalytic converter. Its purpose is to reduce

Mark one answer
- [ ] **A.** exhaust noise
- [ ] **B.** fuel consumption
- [ ] **C.** exhaust emissions
- [ ] **D.** engine noise

157 A properly serviced vehicle will give

Mark two answers
- [ ] **A.** lower insurance premiums
- [ ] **B.** you a refund on your road tax
- [ ] **C.** better fuel economy
- [ ] **D.** cleaner exhaust emissions

158 You enter a road where there are road humps. What should you do?

Mark one answer
- [ ] **A.** Maintain a reduced speed throughout
- [ ] **B.** Accelerate quickly between each one
- [ ] **C.** Always keep to the maximum legal speed
- [ ] **D.** Drive slowly at school times only

159 When should you especially check the engine oil level?

Mark one answer
- [ ] **A.** Before a long journey
- [ ] **B.** When the engine is hot
- [ ] **C.** Early in the morning
- [ ] **D.** Every 6,000 miles

160 You are having difficulty finding a parking space in a busy town. You can see there is space on the zigzag lines of a zebra crossing. Can you park there?

Mark one answer
- ☐ **A.** No, unless you stay with your car
- ☐ **B.** Yes, in order to drop off a passenger
- ☐ **C.** Yes, if you do not block people from crossing
- ☐ **D.** No, not in any circumstances

161 When leaving your car unattended for a few minutes you should

Mark one answer
- ☐ **A.** leave the engine running
- ☐ **B.** switch the engine off but leave the key in
- ☐ **C.** lock it and remove the key
- ☐ **D.** park near a traffic warden

162 When parking and leaving your car for a few minutes you should

Mark one answer
- ☐ **A.** leave it unlocked
- ☐ **B.** lock it and remove the key
- ☐ **C.** leave the hazard warning lights on
- ☐ **D.** leave the interior light on

163 When leaving your car to help keep it secure you should

Mark one answer
- ☐ **A.** leave the hazard warning lights on
- ☐ **B.** lock it and remove the key
- ☐ **C.** park on a one-way street
- ☐ **D.** park in a residential area

164 When leaving your vehicle where should you park if possible?

Mark one answer
- ☐ **A.** Opposite a traffic island
- ☐ **B.** In a secure car park
- ☐ **C.** On a bend
- ☐ **D.** At or near a taxi rank

165 You are leaving your vehicle parked on a road. When may you leave the engine running?

Mark one answer
- ☐ **A.** If you will be parking for less than 5 minutes
- ☐ **B.** If the battery is flat
- ☐ **C.** When in a 20mph zone
- ☐ **D.** Never on any occasion

166 In which THREE places would parking your vehicle cause danger or obstruction to other road users?

Mark three answers
- ☐ **A.** In front of a property entrance
- ☐ **B.** At or near a bus stop
- ☐ **C.** On your driveway
- ☐ **D.** In a marked parking space
- ☐ **E.** On the approach to a level crossing

167 In which THREE places would parking cause an obstruction to others?

Mark three answers
- ☐ **A.** Near the brow of a hill
- ☐ **B.** In a lay-by
- ☐ **C.** Where the kerb is raised
- ☐ **D.** Where the kerb has been lowered for wheelchairs
- ☐ **E.** At or near a bus stop

168 You are away from home and have to park your vehicle overnight. Where should you leave it?

Mark one answer
- [ ] **A.** Opposite another parked vehicle
- [ ] **B.** In a quiet road
- [ ] **C.** Opposite a traffic island
- [ ] **D.** In a secure car park

169 Before starting a journey it is wise to plan your route. How can you do this?

Mark one answer
- [ ] **A.** Look at a map
- [ ] **B.** Contact your local garage
- [ ] **C.** Look in your vehicle handbook
- [ ] **D.** Check your vehicle registration document

170 It can help to plan your route before starting a journey. You can do this by contacting

Mark one answer **NI**
- [ ] **A.** your local filling station
- [ ] **B.** a motoring organisation
- [ ] **C.** the Driver Vehicle Licensing Agency
- [ ] **D.** your vehicle manufacturer

171 How can you plan your route before starting a long journey?

Mark one answer
- [ ] **A.** Check your vehicle's workshop manual
- [ ] **B.** Ask your local garage
- [ ] **C.** Use a route planner on the internet
- [ ] **D.** Consult your travel agents

172 Planning your route before setting out can be helpful. How can you do this?

Mark one answer
- [ ] **A.** Look in a motoring magazine
- [ ] **B.** Only visit places you know
- [ ] **C.** Try to travel at busy times
- [ ] **D.** Print or write down the route

173 Why is it a good idea to plan your journey to avoid busy times?

Mark one answer
- [ ] **A.** You will have an easier journey
- [ ] **B.** You will have a more stressful journey
- [ ] **C.** Your journey time will be longer
- [ ] **D.** It will cause more traffic congestion

174 Planning your journey to avoid busy times has a number of advantages. One of these is

Mark one answer
- [ ] **A.** your journey will take longer
- [ ] **B.** you will have a more pleasant journey
- [ ] **C.** you will cause more pollution
- [ ] **D.** your stress level will be greater

175 It is a good idea to plan your journey to avoid busy times. This is because

Mark one answer
- [ ] **A.** your vehicle will use more fuel
- [ ] **B.** you will see less road works
- [ ] **C.** it will help to ease congestion
- [ ] **D.** you will travel a much shorter distance

176 By avoiding busy times when travelling

Mark one answer
- [ ] **A.** you are more likely to be held up
- [ ] **B.** your journey time will be longer
- [ ] **C.** you will travel a much shorter distance
- [ ] **D.** you are less likely to be delayed

177 It can help to plan your route before starting a journey. Why should you also plan an alternative route?

Mark one answer

- [ ] **A.** Your original route may be blocked
- [ ] **B.** Your maps may have different scales
- [ ] **C.** You may find you have to pay a congestion charge
- [ ] **D.** Because you may get held up by a tractor

178 You will find that driving smoothly can

Mark one answer

- [ ] **A.** reduce journey times by 15%
- [ ] **B.** increase fuel consumption by about 15%
- [ ] **C.** reduce fuel consumption by about 15%
- [ ] **D.** increase journey times by about 15%

179 You can save fuel when conditions allow by

Mark one answer

- [ ] **A.** using lower gears as often as possible
- [ ] **B.** accelerating sharply in each gear
- [ ] **C.** using each gear in turn
- [ ] **D.** missing out some gears

180 As well as planning your route before starting a journey, you should also plan an alternative route. Why is this?

Mark one answer

- [ ] **A.** To let another driver overtake
- [ ] **B.** Your first route may be blocked
- [ ] **C.** To avoid a railway level crossing
- [ ] **D.** In case you have to avoid emergency vehicles

181 Who of these will not have to pay Congestion Charges in London?

Mark one answer

- [ ] **A.** A van driver making deliveries
- [ ] **B.** A rider of a two-wheeled vehicle
- [ ] **C.** A car driver whose vehicle is more than 1000 cc
- [ ] **D.** A driver who just wants to park in the area

182 Congestion Charges apply in the London area. Who of these will NOT have to pay?

Mark one answer

- [ ] **A.** A person who lives in the area
- [ ] **B.** A driver making deliveries
- [ ] **C.** A person who is just driving through the area
- [ ] **D.** A driver with no other passengers in the vehicle

183 You are making an appointment and will have to travel a long distance. You should

Mark one answer

- [ ] **A.** allow plenty of time for your journey
- [ ] **B.** plan to go at busy times
- [ ] **C.** avoid all national speed limit roads
- [ ] **D.** prevent other drivers from overtaking

184 Braking distances on ice can be

Mark one answer

- [ ] **A.** twice the normal distance
- [ ] **B.** five times the normal distance
- [ ] **C.** seven times the normal distance
- [ ] **D.** ten times the normal distance

185 Freezing conditions will affect the distance it takes you to come to a stop. You should expect stopping distances to increase by up to

Mark one answer

- [ ] **A.** two times
- [ ] **B.** three times
- [ ] **C.** five times
- [ ] **D.** ten times

186 In very hot weather the road surface can become soft. Which TWO of the following will be most affected?

Mark two answers

- [ ] **A.** The suspension
- [ ] **B.** The grip of the tyres
- [ ] **C.** The braking
- [ ] **D.** The exhaust

187 Where are you most likely to be affected by a side wind?

Mark one answer

- [ ] **A.** On a narrow country lane
- [ ] **B.** On an open stretch of road
- [ ] **C.** On a busy stretch of road
- [ ] **D.** On a long, straight road

188 In windy conditions you need to take extra care when

Mark one answer

- [ ] **A.** using the brakes
- [ ] **B.** making a hill start
- [ ] **C.** turning into a narrow road
- [ ] **D.** passing pedal cyclists

189 In good conditions, what is the typical stopping distance at 70mph?

Mark one answer

- [ ] **A.** 53 metres (175 feet)
- [ ] **B.** 60 metres (197 feet)
- [ ] **C.** 73 metres (240 feet)
- [ ] **D.** 96 metres (315 feet)

190 What is the shortest overall stopping distance on a dry road at 60mph?

Mark one answer

- [ ] **A.** 53 metres (175 feet)
- [ ] **B.** 58 metres (190 feet)
- [ ] **C.** 73 metres (240 feet)
- [ ] **D.** 96 metres (315 feet)

191 Your indicators may be difficult to see in bright sunlight. What should you do?

Mark one answer

- [ ] **A.** Put your indicator on earlier
- [ ] **B.** Give an arm signal as well as using your indicator
- [ ] **C.** Touch the brake several times to show the stop lights
- [ ] **D.** Turn as quickly as you can

192 You are following a vehicle at a safe distance on a wet road. Another driver overtakes you and pulls into the gap you have left. What should you do?

Mark one answer

- [ ] **A.** Flash your headlights as a warning
- [ ] **B.** Try to overtake safely as soon as you can
- [ ] **C.** Drop back to regain a safe distance
- [ ] **D.** Stay close to the other vehicle until it moves on

193 When approaching a right-hand bend you should keep well to the left. Why is this?

Mark one answer

- [ ] **A.** To improve your view of the road
- [ ] **B.** To overcome the effect of the road's slope
- [ ] **C.** To let faster traffic from behind overtake
- [ ] **D.** To be positioned safely if you skid

194 You should not overtake when

Mark three answers

- [ ] **A.** intending to turn left shortly afterwards
- [ ] **B.** in a one-way street
- [ ] **C.** approaching a junction
- [ ] **D.** going up a long hill
- [ ] **E.** the view ahead is blocked

195 You have just gone through deep water. To dry off the brakes you should

Mark one answer

- [ ] **A.** accelerate and keep to a high speed for a short time
- [ ] **B.** go slowly while gently applying the brakes
- [ ] **C.** avoid using the brakes at all for a few miles
- [ ] **D.** stop for at least an hour to allow them time to dry

196 You are on a fast, open road in good conditions. For safety, the distance between you and the vehicle in front should be

Mark one answer

- [ ] **A.** a two-second time gap
- [ ] **B.** one car length
- [ ] **C.** 2 metres (6 feet 6 inches)
- [ ] **D.** two car lengths

197 What is the most common cause of skidding?

Mark one answer

- [ ] **A.** Worn tyres
- [ ] **B.** Driver error
- [ ] **C.** Other vehicles
- [ ] **D.** Pedestrians

198 You are driving on an icy road. How can you avoid wheelspin?

Mark one answer

- [ ] **A.** Drive at a slow speed in as high a gear as possible
- [ ] **B.** Use the handbrake if the wheels start to slip
- [ ] **C.** Brake gently and repeatedly
- [ ] **D.** Drive in a low gear at all times

199 Skidding is mainly caused by

Mark one answer
- [ ] A. the weather
- [ ] B. the driver
- [ ] C. the vehicle
- [ ] D. the road

200 You are driving in freezing conditions. What should you do when approaching a sharp bend?

Mark two answers
- [ ] A. Slow down before you reach the bend
- [ ] B. Gently apply your handbrake
- [ ] C. Firmly use your footbrake
- [ ] D. Coast into the bend
- [ ] E. Avoid sudden steering movements

201 You are turning left on a slippery road. The back of your vehicle slides to the right. You should

Mark one answer
- [ ] A. brake firmly and not turn the steering wheel
- [ ] B. steer carefully to the left
- [ ] C. steer carefully to the right
- [ ] D. brake firmly and steer to the left

202 You are braking on a wet road. Your vehicle begins to skid. It does not have anti-lock brakes. What is the FIRST thing you should do?

Mark one answer
- [ ] A. Quickly pull up the handbrake
- [ ] B. Release the footbrake fully
- [ ] C. Push harder on the brake pedal
- [ ] D. Gently use the accelerator

203 Coasting the vehicle

Mark one answer
- [ ] A. improves the driver's control
- [ ] B. makes steering easier
- [ ] C. reduces the driver's control
- [ ] D. uses more fuel

204 Before starting a journey in freezing weather you should clear ice and snow from your vehicle's

Mark four answers
- [ ] A. aerial
- [ ] B. windows
- [ ] C. bumper
- [ ] D. lights
- [ ] E. mirrors
- [ ] F. number plates

205 You are trying to move off on snow. You should use

Mark one answer
- [ ] A. the lowest gear you can
- [ ] B. the highest gear you can
- [ ] C. a high engine speed
- [ ] D. the handbrake and footbrake together

206 When driving in falling snow you should

Mark one answer
- [ ] A. brake firmly and quickly
- [ ] B. be ready to steer sharply
- [ ] C. use sidelights only
- [ ] D. brake gently in plenty of time

207 The main benefit of having four-wheel drive is to improve

Mark one answer

- ☐ **A.** road holding
- ☐ **B.** fuel consumption
- ☐ **C.** stopping distances
- ☐ **D.** passenger comfort

208 You are about to go down a steep hill. To control the speed of your vehicle you should

Mark one answer

- ☐ **A.** select a high gear and use the brakes carefully
- ☐ **B.** select a high gear and use the brakes firmly
- ☐ **C.** select a low gear and use the brakes carefully
- ☐ **D.** select a low gear and avoid using the brakes

209 How can you use your vehicle's engine as a brake?

Mark one answer

- ☐ **A.** By changing to a lower gear
- ☐ **B.** By selecting reverse gear
- ☐ **C.** By changing to a higher gear
- ☐ **D.** By selecting neutral gear

210 You wish to park facing DOWNHILL. Which TWO of the following should you do?

Mark two answers

- ☐ **A.** Turn the steering wheel towards the kerb
- ☐ **B.** Park close to the bumper of another car
- ☐ **C.** Park with two wheels on the kerb
- ☐ **D.** Put the handbrake on firmly
- ☐ **E.** Turn the steering wheel away from the kerb

211 You are driving in a built-up area. You approach a speed hump. You should

Mark one answer

- ☐ **A.** move across to the left-hand side of the road
- ☐ **B.** wait for any pedestrians to cross
- ☐ **C.** slow your vehicle right down
- ☐ **D.** stop and check both pavements

212 You are on a long, downhill slope. What should you do to help control the speed of your vehicle?

Mark one answer

- ☐ **A.** Select neutral
- ☐ **B.** Select a lower gear
- ☐ **C.** Grip the handbrake firmly
- ☐ **D.** Apply the parking brake gently

213 Your vehicle is fitted with anti-lock brakes. To stop quickly in an emergency you should

Mark one answer

- ☐ **A.** brake firmly and pump the brake pedal on and off
- ☐ **B.** brake rapidly and firmly without releasing the brake pedal
- ☐ **C.** brake gently and pump the brake pedal on and off
- ☐ **D.** brake rapidly once, and immediately release the brake pedal

214 **Anti-lock brakes prevent wheels from locking. This means the tyres are less likely to**

Mark one answer

- [ ] **A.** aquaplane
- [ ] **B.** skid
- [ ] **C.** puncture
- [ ] **D.** wear

215 **Anti-lock brakes reduce the chances of a skid occurring particularly when**

Mark one answer

- [ ] **A.** driving down steep hills
- [ ] **B.** braking during normal driving
- [ ] **C.** braking in an emergency
- [ ] **D.** driving on good road surfaces

216 **Anti-lock brakes are most effective when you**

Mark one answer

- [ ] **A.** keep pumping the footbrake to prevent skidding
- [ ] **B.** brake normally, but grip the steering wheel tightly
- [ ] **C.** brake promptly and firmly until you have slowed down
- [ ] **D.** apply the handbrake to reduce the stopping distance

217 **Your car is fitted with anti-lock brakes. You need to stop in an emergency. You should**

Mark one answer

- [ ] **A.** brake normally and avoid turning the steering wheel
- [ ] **B.** press the brake pedal promptly and firmly until you have stopped
- [ ] **C.** keep pushing and releasing the footbrake quickly to prevent skidding
- [ ] **D.** apply the handbrake to reduce the stopping distance

218 **Vehicles fitted with anti-lock brakes**

Mark one answer

- [ ] **A.** are impossible to skid
- [ ] **B.** can be steered while you are braking
- [ ] **C.** accelerate much faster
- [ ] **D.** are not fitted with a handbrake

219 **Anti-lock brakes may not work as effectively if the road surface is**

Mark two answers

- [ ] **A.** dry
- [ ] **B.** loose
- [ ] **C.** wet
- [ ] **D.** good
- [ ] **E.** firm

220 **Anti-lock brakes are of most use when you are**

Mark one answer

- [ ] **A.** braking gently
- [ ] **B.** driving on worn tyres
- [ ] **C.** braking excessively
- [ ] **D.** driving normally

221 Driving a vehicle fitted with anti-lock brakes allows you to

Mark one answer

- A. brake harder because it is impossible to skid
- B. drive at higher speeds
- C. steer and brake at the same time
- D. pay less attention to the road ahead

222 Anti-lock brakes can greatly assist with

Mark one answer

- A. a higher cruising speed
- B. steering control when braking
- C. control when accelerating
- D. motorway driving

223 When would an anti-lock braking system start to work?

Mark one answer

- A. After the parking brake has been applied
- B. Whenever pressure on the brake pedal is applied
- C. Just as the wheels are about to lock
- D. When the normal braking system fails to operate

224 You are driving a vehicle fitted with anti-lock brakes. You need to stop in an emergency. You should apply the footbrake

Mark one answer

- A. slowly and gently
- B. slowly but firmly
- C. rapidly and gently
- D. rapidly and firmly

225 Your vehicle has anti-lock brakes, but they may not always prevent skidding. This is most likely to happen when driving

Mark two answers

- A. in foggy conditions
- B. on surface water
- C. on loose road surfaces
- D. on dry tarmac
- E. at night on unlit roads

226 Anti-lock brakes will take effect when

Mark one answer

- A. you do not brake quickly enough
- B. maximum brake pressure has been applied
- C. you have not seen a hazard ahead
- D. speeding on slippery road surfaces

227 When driving in fog, which of the following are correct?

Mark three answers

- A. Use dipped headlights
- B. Use headlights on full beam
- C. Allow more time for your journey
- D. Keep close to the car in front
- E. Slow down
- F. Use sidelights only

228 You are driving along a country road. You see this sign. AFTER dealing safely with the hazard you should always

Mark one answer

- [ ] **A.** check your tyre pressures
- [ ] **B.** switch on your hazard warning lights
- [ ] **C.** accelerate briskly
- [ ] **D.** test your brakes

229 You are driving in heavy rain. Your steering suddenly becomes very light. You should

Mark one answer

- [ ] **A.** steer towards the side of the road
- [ ] **B.** apply gentle acceleration
- [ ] **C.** brake firmly to reduce speed
- [ ] **D.** ease off the accelerator

230 How can you tell when you are driving over black ice?

Mark one answer

- [ ] **A.** It is easier to brake
- [ ] **B.** The noise from your tyres sounds louder
- [ ] **C.** You see black ice on the road
- [ ] **D.** Your steering feels light

231 The roads are icy. You should drive slowly

Mark one answer

- [ ] **A.** in the highest gear possible
- [ ] **B.** in the lowest gear possible
- [ ] **C.** with the handbrake partly on
- [ ] **D.** with your left foot on the brake

232 You are driving along a wet road. How can you tell if your vehicle is aquaplaning?

Mark one answer

- [ ] **A.** The engine will stall
- [ ] **B.** The engine noise will increase
- [ ] **C.** The steering will feel very heavy
- [ ] **D.** The steering will feel very light

233 How can you tell if you are driving on ice?

Mark two answers

- [ ] **A.** The tyres make a rumbling noise
- [ ] **B.** The tyres make hardly any noise
- [ ] **C.** The steering becomes heavier
- [ ] **D.** The steering becomes lighter

234 You are driving along a wet road. How can you tell if your vehicle's tyres are losing their grip on the surface?

Mark one answer

- [ ] **A.** The engine will stall
- [ ] **B.** The steering will feel very heavy
- [ ] **C.** The engine noise will increase
- [ ] **D.** The steering will feel very light

235 You are travelling at 50mph on a good, dry road. What is your shortest overall stopping distance?

Mark one answer

- ☐ **A.** 36 metres (120 feet)
- ☐ **B.** 53 metres (175 feet)
- ☐ **C.** 75 metres (245 feet)
- ☐ **D.** 96 metres (315 feet)

236 Your overall stopping distance will be much longer when driving

Mark one answer

- ☐ **A.** in the rain
- ☐ **B.** in fog
- ☐ **C.** at night
- ☐ **D.** in strong winds

237 You have driven through a flood. What is the first thing you should do?

Mark one answer

- ☐ **A.** Stop and check the tyres
- ☐ **B.** Stop and dry the brakes
- ☐ **C.** Check your exhaust
- ☐ **D.** Test your brakes

238 You are on a good, dry road surface. Your vehicle has good brakes and tyres. What is the BRAKING distance at 50mph?

Mark one answer

- ☐ **A.** 38 metres (125 feet)
- ☐ **B.** 14 metres (46 feet)
- ☐ **C.** 24 metres (79 feet)
- ☐ **D.** 55 metres (180 feet)

239 You are on a good, dry road surface and your vehicle has good brakes and tyres. What is the typical overall STOPPING distance at 40mph?

Mark one answer

- ☐ **A.** 23 metres (75 feet)
- ☐ **B.** 36 metres (120 feet)
- ☐ **C.** 53 metres (175 feet)
- ☐ **D.** 96 metres (315 feet)

240 You are on a wet motorway with surface spray. You should use

Mark one answer

- ☐ **A.** hazard flashers
- ☐ **B.** dipped headlights
- ☐ **C.** rear fog lights
- ☐ **D.** sidelights

241 You see this sign on the rear of a slow-moving lorry that you want to pass. It is travelling in the middle lane of a three-lane motorway. You should

Mark one answer

- [ ] **A.** cautiously approach the lorry then pass on either side
- [ ] **B.** follow the lorry until you can leave the motorway
- [ ] **C.** wait on the hard shoulder until the lorry has stopped
- [ ] **D.** approach with care and keep to the left of the lorry

242 Where would you expect to see these markers?

Mark two answers

- [ ] **A.** On a motorway sign
- [ ] **B.** At the entrance to a narrow bridge
- [ ] **C.** On a large goods vehicle
- [ ] **D.** On a builder's skip placed on the road

243 What does this signal from a police officer, mean to oncoming traffic?

Mark one answer

- [ ] **A.** Go ahead
- [ ] **B.** Stop
- [ ] **C.** Turn left
- [ ] **D.** Turn right

244 What is the main hazard shown in this picture?

Mark one answer

- [ ] **A.** Vehicles turning right
- [ ] **B.** Vehicles doing U-turns
- [ ] **C.** The cyclist crossing the road
- [ ] **D.** Parked cars around the corner

245 Which road user has caused a hazard?

Mark one answer

- [ ] **A.** The parked car (arrowed A)
- [ ] **B.** The pedestrian waiting to cross (arrowed B)
- [ ] **C.** The moving car (arrowed C)
- [ ] **D.** The car turning (arrowed D)

246 What should the driver of the car approaching the crossing do?

Mark one answer

- [ ] **A.** Continue at the same speed
- [ ] **B.** Sound the horn
- [ ] **C.** Drive through quickly
- [ ] **D.** Slow down and get ready to stop

247 What THREE things should the driver of the grey car (arrowed) be especially aware of?

Mark three answers

- [ ] **A.** Pedestrians stepping out between cars
- [ ] **B.** Other cars behind the grey car
- [ ] **C.** Doors opening on parked cars
- [ ] **D.** The bumpy road surface
- [ ] **E.** Cars leaving parking spaces
- [ ] **F.** Empty parking spaces

248 You think the driver of the vehicle in front has forgotten to cancel their right indicator. You should

Mark one answer

- [ ] **A.** flash your lights to alert the driver
- [ ] **B.** sound your horn before overtaking
- [ ] **C.** overtake on the left if there is room
- [ ] **D.** stay behind and not overtake

249

What is the main hazard the driver of the red car (arrowed) should be aware of?

Mark one answer

- [ ] **A.** Glare from the sun may affect the driver's vision
- [ ] **B.** The black car may stop suddenly
- [ ] **C.** The bus may move out into the road
- [ ] **D.** Oncoming vehicles will assume the driver is turning right

250

In heavy motorway traffic you are being followed closely by the vehicle behind. How can you lower the risk of an accident?

Mark one answer

- [ ] **A.** Increase your distance from the vehicle in front
- [ ] **B.** Tap your foot on the brake pedal sharply
- [ ] **C.** Switch on your hazard lights
- [ ] **D.** Move on to the hard shoulder and stop

251

You see this sign ahead. You should expect the road to

Mark one answer

- [ ] **A.** go steeply uphill
- [ ] **B.** go steeply downhill
- [ ] **C.** bend sharply to the left
- [ ] **D.** bend sharply to the right

252

You are approaching this cyclist. You should

Mark one answer

- [ ] **A.** overtake before the cyclist gets to the junction
- [ ] **B.** flash your headlights at the cyclist
- [ ] **C.** slow down and allow the cyclist to turn
- [ ] **D.** overtake the cyclist on the left-hand side

253 **Why must you take extra care when turning right at this junction?**

Mark one answer
- ☐ **A.** Road surface is poor
- ☐ **B.** Footpaths are narrow
- ☐ **C.** Road markings are faint
- ☐ **D.** There is reduced visibility

254 **This yellow sign on a vehicle indicates this is**

Mark one answer
- ☐ **A.** a broken-down vehicle
- ☐ **B.** a school bus
- ☐ **C.** an ice-cream van
- ☐ **D.** a private ambulance

255 **When approaching this bridge you should give way to**

Mark one answer
- ☐ **A.** bicycles
- ☐ **B.** buses
- ☐ **C.** motorcycles
- ☐ **D.** cars

256 **What type of vehicle could you expect to meet in the middle of the road?**

Mark one answer
- ☐ **A.** Lorry
- ☐ **B.** Bicycle
- ☐ **C.** Car
- ☐ **D.** Motorcycle

257 At this blind junction you must stop

Mark one answer

- [ ] **A.** behind the line, then edge forward to see clearly
- [ ] **B.** beyond the line at a point where you can see clearly
- [ ] **C.** only if there is traffic on the main road
- [ ] **D.** only if you are turning to the right

258 A driver pulls out of a side road in front of you. You have to brake hard. You should

Mark one answer

- [ ] **A.** ignore the error and stay calm
- [ ] **B.** flash your lights to show your annoyance
- [ ] **C.** sound your horn to show your annoyance
- [ ] **D.** overtake as soon as possible

259 An elderly person's driving ability could be affected because they may be unable to

Mark one answer

- [ ] **A.** obtain car insurance
- [ ] **B.** understand road signs
- [ ] **C.** react very quickly
- [ ] **D.** give signals correctly

260 You have just passed these warning lights. What hazard would you expect to see next?

Mark one answer

- [ ] **A.** A level crossing with no barrier
- [ ] **B.** An ambulance station
- [ ] **C.** A school crossing patrol
- [ ] **D.** An opening bridge

261 Why should you be especially cautious when going past this bus?

Mark two answers

- [ ] **A.** There is traffic approaching in the distance
- [ ] **B.** The driver may open the door
- [ ] **C.** It may suddenly move off
- [ ] **D.** People may cross the road in front of it
- [ ] **E.** There are bicycles parked on the pavement

262 In areas where there are 'traffic calming' measures you should

Mark one answer

- [ ] **A.** travel at a reduced speed
- [ ] **B.** always travel at the speed limit
- [ ] **C.** position in the centre of the road
- [ ] **D.** only slow down if pedestrians are near

263 You are planning a long journey. Do you need to plan rest stops?

Mark one answer

- [ ] **A.** Yes, you should plan to stop every half an hour
- [ ] **B.** Yes, regular stops help concentration
- [ ] **C.** No, you will be less tired if you get there as soon as possible
- [ ] **D.** No, only fuel stops will be needed

264 A driver does something that upsets you. You should

Mark one answer

- [ ] **A.** try not to react
- [ ] **B.** let them know how you feel
- [ ] **C.** flash your headlights several times
- [ ] **D.** sound your horn

265 The red lights are flashing. What should you do when approaching this level crossing?

Mark one answer

- [ ] **A.** Go through quickly
- [ ] **B.** Go through carefully
- [ ] **C.** Stop before the barrier
- [ ] **D.** Switch on hazard warning lights

266 What TWO main hazards should you be aware of when going along this street?

Mark two answers

- [ ] **A.** Glare from the sun
- [ ] **B.** Car doors opening suddenly
- [ ] **C.** Lack of road markings
- [ ] **D.** The headlights on parked cars being switched on
- [ ] **E.** Large goods vehicles
- [ ] **F.** Children running out from between vehicles

267 What is the main hazard you should be aware of when following this cyclist?

Mark one answer

- [ ] **A.** The cyclist may move to the left and dismount
- [ ] **B.** The cyclist may swerve out into the road
- [ ] **C.** The contents of the cyclist's carrier may fall on to the road
- [ ] **D.** The cyclist may wish to turn right at the end of the road

268 When approaching this hazard why should you slow down?

Mark two answers

- [ ] **A.** Because of the bend
- [ ] **B.** Because it's hard to see to the right
- [ ] **C.** Because of approaching traffic
- [ ] **D.** Because of animals crossing
- [ ] **E.** Because of the level crossing

269 A driver's behaviour has upset you. It may help if you

Mark one answer

- [ ] **A.** stop and take a break
- [ ] **B.** shout abusive language
- [ ] **C.** gesture to them with your hand
- [ ] **D.** follow their car, flashing your headlights

270 You are on a dual carriageway. Ahead you see a vehicle with an amber flashing light. What will this be?

Mark one answer

- [ ] **A.** An ambulance
- [ ] **B.** A fire engine
- [ ] **C.** A doctor on call
- [ ] **D.** A disabled person's vehicle

271 You are approaching crossroads. The traffic lights have failed. What should you do?

Mark one answer

- [ ] **A.** Brake and stop only for large vehicles
- [ ] **B.** Brake sharply to a stop before looking
- [ ] **C.** Be prepared to brake sharply to a stop
- [ ] **D.** Be prepared to stop for any traffic

272 Why are place names painted on the road surface?

Mark one answer

- [ ] **A.** To restrict the flow of traffic
- [ ] **B.** To warn you of oncoming traffic
- [ ] **C.** To enable you to change lanes early
- [ ] **D.** To prevent you changing lanes

273 What should the driver of the red car (arrowed) do?

Mark one answer

- [ ] **A.** Wave the pedestrians who are waiting to cross
- [ ] **B.** Wait for the pedestrian in the road to cross
- [ ] **C.** Quickly drive behind the pedestrian in the road
- [ ] **D.** Tell the pedestrian in the road she should not have crossed

274 You are following a slower-moving vehicle on a narrow country road. There is a junction just ahead on the right. What should you do?

Mark one answer

- ☐ **A.** Overtake after checking your mirrors and signalling
- ☐ **B.** Stay behind until you are past the junction
- ☐ **C.** Accelerate quickly to pass before the junction
- ☐ **D.** Slow down and prepare to overtake on the left

275 What should you do as you approach this overhead bridge?

Mark one answer

- ☐ **A.** Move out to the centre of the road before going through
- ☐ **B.** Find another route, this is only for high vehicles
- ☐ **C.** Be prepared to give way to large vehicles in the middle of the road
- ☐ **D.** Move across to the right-hand side before going through

276 Why are mirrors often slightly curved (convex)?

Mark one answer

- ☐ **A.** They give a wider field of vision
- ☐ **B.** They totally cover blind spots
- ☐ **C.** They make it easier to judge the speed of following traffic
- ☐ **D.** They make following traffic look bigger

277 What does the solid white line at the side of the road indicate?

Mark one answer

- ☐ **A.** Traffic lights ahead
- ☐ **B.** Edge of the carriageway
- ☐ **C.** Footpath on the left
- ☐ **D.** Cycle path

278 You are driving towards this level crossing. What would be the first warning of an approaching train?

Mark one answer

- ☐ **A.** Both half barriers down
- ☐ **B.** A steady amber light
- ☐ **C.** One half barrier down
- ☐ **D.** Twin flashing red lights

279

You are driving along this motorway. It is raining. When following this lorry you should

Mark two answers

- [ ] **A.** allow at least a two-second gap
- [ ] **B.** move left and drive on the hard shoulder
- [ ] **C.** allow at least a four-second gap
- [ ] **D.** be aware of spray reducing your vision
- [ ] **E.** move right and stay in the right-hand lane

280

You are behind this cyclist. When the traffic lights change, what should you do?

Mark one answer

- [ ] **A.** Try to move off before the cyclist
- [ ] **B.** Allow the cyclist time and room
- [ ] **C.** Turn right but give the cyclist room
- [ ] **D.** Tap your horn and drive through first

281

You are driving towards this left-hand bend. What dangers should you be aware of?

Mark one answer

- [ ] **A.** A vehicle overtaking you
- [ ] **B.** No white lines in the centre of the road
- [ ] **C.** No sign to warn you of the bend
- [ ] **D.** Pedestrians walking towards you

282

While driving, you see this sign ahead. You should

Mark one answer

- [ ] **A.** stop at the sign
- [ ] **B.** slow, but continue around the bend
- [ ] **C.** slow to a crawl and continue
- [ ] **D.** stop and look for open farm gates

283 Why should the junction on the left be kept clear?

Mark one answer

- [ ] **A.** To allow vehicles to enter and emerge
- [ ] **B.** To allow the bus to reverse
- [ ] **C.** To allow vehicles to make a U-turn
- [ ] **D.** To allow vehicles to park

284 When the traffic lights change to green the white car should

Mark one answer

- [ ] **A.** wait for the cyclist to pull away
- [ ] **B.** move off quickly and turn in front of the cyclist
- [ ] **C.** move close up to the cyclist to beat the lights
- [ ] **D.** sound the horn to warn the cyclist

285 You intend to turn left at the traffic lights. Just before turning you should

Mark one answer

- [ ] **A.** check your right mirror
- [ ] **B.** move close up to the white car
- [ ] **C.** straddle the lanes
- [ ] **D.** check for bicycles on your left

286 You should reduce your speed when driving along this road because

Mark one answer

- [ ] **A.** there is a staggered junction ahead
- [ ] **B.** there is a low bridge ahead
- [ ] **C.** there is a change in the road surface
- [ ] **D.** the road ahead narrows

287 You are driving at 60mph. As you approach this hazard you should

Mark one answer

- ☐ **A.** maintain your speed
- ☐ **B.** reduce your speed
- ☐ **C.** take the next right turn
- ☐ **D.** take the next left turn

288 The traffic ahead of you in the left-hand lane is slowing. You should

Mark two answers

- ☐ **A.** be wary of cars on your right cutting in
- ☐ **B.** accelerate past the vehicles in the left-hand lane
- ☐ **C.** pull up on the left-hand verge
- ☐ **D.** move across and continue in the right-hand lane
- ☐ **E.** slow down, keeping a safe separation distance

289 What might you expect to happen in this situation?

Mark one answer

- ☐ **A.** Traffic will move into the right-hand lane
- ☐ **B.** Traffic speed will increase
- ☐ **C.** Traffic will move into the left-hand lane
- ☐ **D.** Traffic will not need to change position

290 You are driving on a road with several lanes. You see these signs above the lanes. What do they mean?

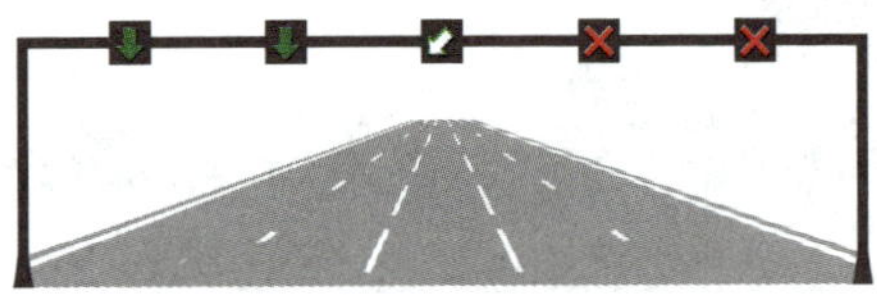

Mark one answer

- ☐ **A.** The two right lanes are open
- ☐ **B.** The two left lanes are open
- ☐ **C.** Traffic in the left lanes should stop
- ☐ **D.** Traffic in the right lanes should stop

291 As a provisional licence holder, you must not drive a motor car

Mark two answers

- [ ] **A.** at more than 40mph
- [ ] **B.** on your own
- [ ] **C.** on the motorway
- [ ] **D.** under the age of 18 years at night
- [ ] **E.** with passengers in the rear seats

292 After passing your driving test, you suffer from ill health. This affects your driving. You MUST

Mark one answer

- [ ] **A.** inform your local police station
- [ ] **B.** get on as best you can
- [ ] **C.** not inform anyone as you hold a full licence
- [ ] **D.** inform the licensing authority

293 You are invited to a pub lunch. You know that you will have to drive in the evening. What is your best course of action?

Mark one answer

- [ ] **A.** Avoid mixing your alcoholic drinks
- [ ] **B.** Not drink any alcohol at all
- [ ] **C.** Have some milk before drinking alcohol
- [ ] **D.** Eat a hot meal with your alcoholic drinks

294 You have been convicted of driving whilst unfit through drink or drugs. You will find this is likely to cause the cost of one of the following to rise considerably. Which one?

Mark one answer

- [ ] **A.** Road fund licence
- [ ] **B.** Insurance premiums
- [ ] **C.** Vehicle test certificate
- [ ] **D.** Driving licence

295 What advice should you give to a driver who has had a few alcoholic drinks at a party?

Mark one answer

- [ ] **A.** Have a strong cup of coffee and then drive home
- [ ] **B.** Drive home carefully and slowly
- [ ] **C.** Go home by public transport
- [ ] **D.** Wait a short while and then drive home

296 You have been taking medicine for a few days which made you feel drowsy. Today you feel better but still need to take the medicine. You should only drive

Mark one answer

- [ ] **A.** if your journey is necessary
- [ ] **B.** at night on quiet roads
- [ ] **C.** if someone goes with you
- [ ] **D.** after checking with your doctor

297 **You are about to return home from holiday when you become ill. A doctor prescribes drugs which are likely to affect your driving. You should**

Mark one answer

- ☐ **A.** drive only if someone is with you
- ☐ **B.** avoid driving on motorways
- ☐ **C.** not drive yourself
- ☐ **D.** never drive at more than 30mph

298 **During periods of illness your ability to drive may be impaired. You MUST**

Mark two answers

- ☐ **A.** see your doctor each time before you drive
- ☐ **B.** only take smaller doses of any medicines
- ☐ **C.** be medically fit to drive
- ☐ **D.** not drive after taking certain medicines
- ☐ **E.** take all your medicines with you when you drive

299 **You feel drowsy when driving. You should**

Mark two answers

- ☐ **A.** stop and rest as soon as possible
- ☐ **B.** turn the heater up to keep you warm and comfortable
- ☐ **C.** make sure you have a good supply of fresh air
- ☐ **D.** continue with your journey but drive more slowly
- ☐ **E.** close the car windows to help you concentrate

300 **You are driving along a motorway and become tired. You should**

Mark two answers

- ☐ **A.** stop at the next service area and rest
- ☐ **B.** leave the motorway at the next exit and rest
- ☐ **C.** increase your speed and turn up the radio volume
- ☐ **D.** close all your windows and set heating to warm
- ☐ **E.** pull up on the hard shoulder and change drivers

301 **You are taking drugs that are likely to affect your driving. What should you do?**

Mark one answer

- ☐ **A.** Seek medical advice before driving
- ☐ **B.** Limit your driving to essential journeys
- ☐ **C.** Only drive if accompanied by a full licence-holder
- ☐ **D.** Drive only for short distances

302 **You are about to drive home. You feel very tired and have a severe headache. You should**

Mark one answer

- ☐ **A.** wait until you are fit and well before driving
- ☐ **B.** drive home, but take a tablet for headaches
- ☐ **C.** drive home if you can stay awake for the journey
- ☐ **D.** wait for a short time, then drive home slowly

303 If you are feeling tired it is best to stop as soon as you can. Until then you should

Mark one answer

☐ **A.** increase your speed to find a stopping place quickly
☐ **B.** ensure a supply of fresh air
☐ **C.** gently tap the steering wheel
☐ **D.** keep changing speed to improve concentration

304 If your motorway journey seems boring and you feel drowsy while driving, you should

Mark one answer

☐ **A.** open a window and drive to the next service area
☐ **B.** stop on the hard shoulder for a sleep
☐ **C.** speed up to arrive at your destination sooner
☐ **D.** slow down and let other drivers overtake

305 Driving long distances can be tiring. You can prevent this by

Mark three answers

☐ **A.** stopping every so often for a walk
☐ **B.** opening a window for some fresh air
☐ **C.** ensuring plenty of refreshment breaks
☐ **D.** completing the journey without stopping
☐ **E.** eating a large meal before driving

306 You go to a social event and need to drive a short time after. What precaution should you take?

Mark one answer

☐ **A.** Avoid drinking alcohol on an empty stomach
☐ **B.** Drink plenty of coffee after drinking alcohol
☐ **C.** Avoid drinking alcohol completely
☐ **D.** Drink plenty of milk before drinking alcohol

307 You take some cough medicine given to you by a friend. What should you do before driving?

Mark one answer

☐ **A.** Ask your friend if taking the medicine affected their driving
☐ **B.** Drink some strong coffee one hour before driving
☐ **C.** Check the label to see if the medicine will affect your driving
☐ **D.** Drive a short distance to see if the medicine is affecting your driving

308 You take the wrong route and find you are on a one-way street. You should

Mark one answer

☐ **A.** reverse out of the road
☐ **B.** turn round in a side road
☐ **C.** continue to the end of the road
☐ **D.** reverse into a driveway

309 Which THREE are likely to make you lose concentration while driving?

Mark three answers

- [ ] **A.** Looking at road maps
- [ ] **B.** Listening to loud music
- [ ] **C.** Using your windscreen washers
- [ ] **D.** Looking in your wing mirror
- [ ] **E.** Using a mobile phone

310 You are driving along this road. The driver on the left is reversing from a driveway. You should

Mark one answer

- [ ] **A.** move to the opposite side of the road
- [ ] **B.** drive through as you have priority
- [ ] **C.** sound your horn and be prepared to stop
- [ ] **D.** speed up and drive through quickly

311 You have been involved in an argument before starting your journey. This has made you feel angry. You should

Mark one answer

- [ ] **A.** start to drive, but open a window
- [ ] **B.** drive slower than normal and turn your radio on
- [ ] **C.** have an alcoholic drink to help you relax before driving
- [ ] **D.** calm down before you start to drive

312 You start to feel tired while driving. What should you do?

Mark one answer

- [ ] **A.** Increase your speed slightly
- [ ] **B.** Decrease your speed slightly
- [ ] **C.** Find a less busy route
- [ ] **D.** Pull over at a safe place to rest

313 You are driving on this dual carriageway. Why may you need to slow down?

Mark one answer

- [ ] **A.** There is a broken white line in the centre
- [ ] **B.** There are solid white lines either side
- [ ] **C.** There are road works ahead of you
- [ ] **D.** There are no footpaths

314 You have just been overtaken by this motorcyclist who is cutting in sharply. You should

Mark one answer

- [ ] **A.** sound the horn
- [ ] **B.** brake firmly
- [ ] **C.** keep a safe gap
- [ ] **D.** flash your lights

315 You are about to drive home. You cannot find the glasses you need to wear. You should

Mark one answer

- [ ] **A.** drive home slowly, keeping to quiet roads
- [ ] **B.** borrow a friend's glasses and use those
- [ ] **C.** drive home at night, so that the lights will help you
- [ ] **D.** find a way of getting home without driving

316 Which THREE result from drinking alcohol?

Mark three answers

- [ ] **A.** Less control
- [ ] **B.** A false sense of confidence
- [ ] **C.** Faster reactions
- [ ] **D.** Poor judgement of speed
- [ ] **E.** Greater awareness of danger

317 Which THREE of these are likely effects of drinking alcohol?

Mark three answers

- [ ] **A.** Reduced co-ordination
- [ ] **B.** Increased confidence
- [ ] **C.** Poor judgement
- [ ] **D.** Increased concentration
- [ ] **E.** Faster reactions
- [ ] **F.** Colour blindness

318 How does alcohol affect you?

Mark one answer

- [ ] **A.** It speeds up your reactions
- [ ] **B.** It increases your awareness
- [ ] **C.** It improves your co-ordination
- [ ] **D.** It reduces your concentration

319 Your doctor has given you a course of medicine. Why should you ask how it will affect you?

Mark one answer

- [ ] **A.** Drugs make you a better driver by quickening your reactions
- [ ] **B.** You will have to let your insurance company know about the medicine
- [ ] **C.** Some types of medicine can cause your reactions to slow down
- [ ] **D.** The medicine you take may affect your hearing

320 **You are not sure if your cough medicine will affect you. What TWO things should you do?**

Mark two answers

- [ ] **A.** Ask your doctor
- [ ] **B.** Check the medicine label
- [ ] **C.** Drive if you feel alright
- [ ] **D.** Ask a friend or relative for advice

321 **You are on a motorway. You feel tired. You should**

Mark one answer

- [ ] **A.** carry on but go slowly
- [ ] **B.** leave the motorway at the next exit
- [ ] **C.** complete your journey as quickly as possible
- [ ] **D.** stop on the hard shoulder

322 **You find that you need glasses to read vehicle number plates at the required distance. When MUST you wear them?**

Mark one answer

- [ ] **A.** Only in bad weather conditions
- [ ] **B.** At all times when driving
- [ ] **C.** Only when you think it necessary
- [ ] **D.** Only in bad light or at night time

323 **Which TWO things would help to keep you alert during a long journey?**

Mark two answers

- [ ] **A.** Finishing your journey as fast as you can
- [ ] **B.** Keeping off the motorways and using country roads
- [ ] **C.** Making sure that you get plenty of fresh air
- [ ] **D.** Making regular stops for refreshments

324 **Which of the following types of glasses should NOT be worn when driving at night?**

Mark one answer

- [ ] **A.** Half-moon
- [ ] **B.** Round
- [ ] **C.** Bi-focal
- [ ] **D.** Tinted

325 **Drinking any amount of alcohol is likely to**

Mark three answers

- [ ] **A.** slow down your reactions to hazards
- [ ] **B.** increase the speed of your reactions
- [ ] **C.** worsen your judgement of speed
- [ ] **D.** improve your awareness of danger
- [ ] **E.** give a false sense of confidence

326 **What else can seriously affect your concentration, other than alcoholic drinks?**

Mark three answers

- [ ] **A.** Drugs
- [ ] **B.** Tiredness
- [ ] **C.** Tinted windows
- [ ] **D.** Contact lenses
- [ ] **E.** Loud music

327 **As a driver you find that your eyesight has become very poor. Your optician says they cannot help you. The law says that you should tell**

Mark one answer

- [ ] **A.** the licensing authority
- [ ] **B.** your own doctor
- [ ] **C.** the local police station
- [ ] **D.** another optician

328 For which of these may you use hazard warning lights?

Mark one answer

- [ ] **A.** When driving on a motorway to warn traffic behind of a hazard ahead
- [ ] **B.** When you are double parked on a two-way road
- [ ] **C.** When your direction indicators are not working
- [ ] **D.** When warning oncoming traffic that you intend to stop

329 When should you use hazard warning lights?

Mark one answer

- [ ] **A.** When you are double parked on a two-way road
- [ ] **B.** When your direction indicators are not working
- [ ] **C.** When warning oncoming traffic that you intend to stop
- [ ] **D.** When your vehicle has broken down and is causing an obstruction

330 You want to turn left at this junction. The view of the main road is restricted. What should you do?

Mark one answer

- [ ] **A.** Stay well back and wait to see if something comes
- [ ] **B.** Build up your speed so that you can emerge quickly
- [ ] **C.** Stop and apply the handbrake even if the road is clear
- [ ] **D.** Approach slowly and edge out until you can see more clearly

331 You are driving on a motorway. The traffic ahead is braking sharply because of an accident. How could you warn traffic behind you?

Mark one answer

- [ ] **A.** Briefly use the hazard warning lights
- [ ] **B.** Switch on the hazard warning lights continuously
- [ ] **C.** Briefly use the rear fog lights
- [ ] **D.** Switch on the headlights continuously

332 When may you use hazard warning lights?

Mark one answer

- [ ] **A.** To park alongside another car
- [ ] **B.** To park on double yellow lines
- [ ] **C.** When you are being towed
- [ ] **D.** When you have broken down

333 Hazard warning lights should be used when vehicles are

Mark one answer

- [ ] **A.** broken down and causing an obstruction
- [ ] **B.** faulty and moving slowly
- [ ] **C.** being towed along a road
- [ ] **D.** reversing into a side road

334 Some two-way roads are divided into three lanes. Why are these particularly dangerous?

Mark one answer

- [ ] **A.** Traffic in both directions can use the middle lane to overtake
- [ ] **B.** Traffic can travel faster in poor weather conditions
- [ ] **C.** Traffic can overtake on the left
- [ ] **D.** Traffic uses the middle lane for emergencies only

335 To avoid an accident when entering a contraflow system, you should

Mark three answers

- [ ] **A.** reduce speed in good time
- [ ] **B.** switch lanes any time to make progress
- [ ] **C.** choose an appropriate lane early
- [ ] **D.** keep the correct separation distance
- [ ] **E.** increase speed to pass through quickly
- [ ] **F.** follow other motorists closely to avoid long queues

336 When driving a car fitted with automatic transmission what would you use 'kick down' for?

Mark one answer

- [ ] **A.** Cruise control
- [ ] **B.** Quick acceleration
- [ ] **C.** Slow braking
- [ ] **D.** Fuel economy

337 Which sign means that there may be people walking along the road?

Mark one answer

- [ ] **A.**

- [ ] **B.**

- [ ] **C.**

- [ ] **D.**

338 You are turning left at a junction. Pedestrians have started to cross the road. You should

Mark one answer

- [ ] **A.** go on, giving them plenty of room
- [ ] **B.** stop and wave at them to cross
- [ ] **C.** blow your horn and proceed
- [ ] **D.** give way to them

339 You are turning left from a main road into a side road. People are already crossing the road into which you are turning. You should

Mark one answer

- [ ] **A.** continue, as it is your right of way
- [ ] **B.** signal to them to continue crossing
- [ ] **C.** wait and allow them to cross
- [ ] **D.** sound your horn to warn them of your presence

340 You are at a road junction, turning into a minor road. There are pedestrians crossing the minor road. You should

Mark one answer

- [ ] **A.** stop and wave the pedestrians across
- [ ] **B.** sound your horn to let the pedestrians know that you are there
- [ ] **C.** give way to the pedestrians who are already crossing
- [ ] **D.** carry on; the pedestrians should give way to you

341 You are turning left into a side road. What hazards should you be especially aware of?

Mark one answer
- [ ] **A.** One-way street
- [ ] **B.** Pedestrians
- [ ] **C.** Traffic congestion
- [ ] **D.** Parked vehicles

342 You intend to turn right into a side road. Just before turning you should check for motorcyclists who might be

Mark one answer
- [ ] **A.** overtaking on your left
- [ ] **B.** following you closely
- [ ] **C.** emerging from the side road
- [ ] **D.** overtaking on your right

343 A toucan crossing is different from other crossings because

Mark one answer
- [ ] **A.** moped riders can use it
- [ ] **B.** it is controlled by a traffic warden
- [ ] **C.** it is controlled by two flashing lights
- [ ] **D.** cyclists can use it

344 At toucan crossings

Mark two answers
- [ ] **A.** there is no flashing amber light
- [ ] **B.** cyclists are not permitted
- [ ] **C.** there is a continuously flashing amber beacon
- [ ] **D.** pedestrians and cyclists may cross
- [ ] **E.** you only stop if someone is waiting to cross

345 What does this sign tell you?

Mark one answer
- [ ] **A.** No cycling
- [ ] **B.** Cycle route ahead
- [ ] **C.** Route for cycles only
- [ ] **D.** End of cycle route

346 How will a school crossing patrol signal you to stop?

Mark one answer
- [ ] **A.** By pointing to children on the opposite pavement
- [ ] **B.** By displaying a red light
- [ ] **C.** By displaying a stop sign
- [ ] **D.** By giving you an arm signal

347 Where would you see this sign?

Mark one answer
- [ ] **A.** In the window of a car taking children to school
- [ ] **B.** At the side of the road
- [ ] **C.** At playground areas
- [ ] **D.** On the rear of a school bus or coach

348 Which sign tells you that pedestrians may be walking in the road as there is no pavement?

Mark one answer

- [ ] **A.**

- [ ] **B.**

- [ ] **C.**

- [ ] **D.**

349 What does this sign mean?

Mark one answer

- [ ] **A.** No route for pedestrians and cyclists
- [ ] **B.** A route for pedestrians only
- [ ] **C.** A route for cyclists only
- [ ] **D.** A route for pedestrians and cyclists

350 You see a pedestrian with a white stick and red band. This means that the person is

Mark one answer

- [ ] **A.** physically disabled
- [ ] **B.** deaf only
- [ ] **C.** blind only
- [ ] **D.** deaf and blind

351 What action would you take when elderly people are crossing the road?

Mark one answer

- [ ] **A.** Wave them across so they know that you have seen them
- [ ] **B.** Be patient and allow them to cross in their own time
- [ ] **C.** Rev the engine to let them know that you are waiting
- [ ] **D.** Tap the horn in case they are hard of hearing

352 You see two elderly pedestrians about to cross the road ahead. You should

Mark one answer

- [ ] **A.** expect them to wait for you to pass
- [ ] **B.** speed up to get past them quickly
- [ ] **C.** stop and wave them across the road
- [ ] **D.** be careful, they may misjudge your speed

353 What does this sign mean?

Mark one answer

- [ ] **A.** Contraflow pedal cycle lane
- [ ] **B.** With-flow pedal cycle lane
- [ ] **C.** Pedal cycles and buses only
- [ ] **D.** No pedal cycles or buses

354 **You are coming up to a roundabout. A cyclist is signalling to turn right. What should you do?**

Mark one answer
- A. Overtake on the right
- B. Give a horn warning
- C. Signal the cyclist to move across
- D. Give the cyclist plenty of room

355 **You are approaching this roundabout and see the cyclist signal right. Why is the cyclist keeping to the left?**

Mark one answer
- A. It is a quicker route for the cyclist
- B. The cyclist is going to turn left instead
- C. The cyclist thinks *The Highway Code* does not apply to bicycles
- D. The cyclist is slower and more vulnerable

356 **When you are overtaking a cyclist you should leave as much room as you would give to a car. What is the main reason for this?**

Mark one answer
- A. The cyclist might change lanes
- B. The cyclist might get off the bike
- C. The cyclist might swerve
- D. The cyclist might have to make a right turn

357 **Which TWO should you allow extra room when overtaking?**

Mark two answers
- A. Motorcycles
- B. Tractors
- C. Bicycles
- D. Road-sweeping vehicles

358 **Why should you look particularly for motorcyclists and cyclists at junctions?**

Mark one answer
- A. They may want to turn into the side road
- B. They may slow down to let you turn
- C. They are harder to see
- D. They might not see you turn

359 **You are waiting to come out of a side road. Why should you watch carefully for motorcycles?**

Mark one answer
- A. Motorcycles are usually faster than cars
- B. Police patrols often use motorcycles
- C. Motorcycles are small and hard to see
- D. Motorcycles have right of way

360 **In daylight, an approaching motorcyclist is using a dipped headlight. Why?**

Mark one answer
- A. So that the rider can be seen more easily
- B. To stop the battery overcharging
- C. To improve the rider's vision
- D. The rider is inviting you to proceed

361 Motorcyclists should wear bright clothing mainly because

Mark one answer

- ☐ **A.** they must do so by law
- ☐ **B.** it helps keep them cool in summer
- ☐ **C.** the colours are popular
- ☐ **D.** drivers often do not see them

362 There is a slow-moving motorcyclist ahead of you. You are unsure what the rider is going to do. You should

Mark one answer

- ☐ **A.** pass on the left
- ☐ **B.** pass on the right
- ☐ **C.** stay behind
- ☐ **D.** move closer

363 Motorcyclists will often look round over their right shoulder just before turning right. This is because

Mark one answer

- ☐ **A.** they need to listen for following traffic
- ☐ **B.** motorcycles do not have mirrors
- ☐ **C.** looking around helps them balance as they turn
- ☐ **D.** they need to check for traffic in their blind area

364 At road junctions which of the following are most vulnerable?

Mark three answers

- ☐ **A.** Cyclists
- ☐ **B.** Motorcyclists
- ☐ **C.** Pedestrians
- ☐ **D.** Car drivers
- ☐ **E.** Lorry drivers

365 Motorcyclists are particularly vulnerable

Mark one answer

- ☐ **A.** when moving off
- ☐ **B.** on dual carriageways
- ☐ **C.** when approaching junctions
- ☐ **D.** on motorways

366 An injured motorcyclist is lying unconscious in the road. You should

Mark one answer

- ☐ **A.** remove the safety helmet
- ☐ **B.** seek medical assistance
- ☐ **C.** move the person off the road
- ☐ **D.** remove the leather jacket

367 You notice horse riders in front. What should you do FIRST?

Mark one answer

- ☐ **A.** Pull out to the middle of the road
- ☐ **B.** Slow down and be ready to stop
- ☐ **C.** Accelerate around them
- ☐ **D.** Signal right

368 **You are approaching a roundabout. There are horses just ahead of you. You should**

Mark two answers
- [ ] **A.** be prepared to stop
- [ ] **B.** treat them like any other vehicle
- [ ] **C.** give them plenty of room
- [ ] **D.** accelerate past as quickly as possible
- [ ] **E.** sound your horn as a warning

369 **Which THREE should you do when passing sheep on a road?**

Mark three answers
- [ ] **A.** Allow plenty of room
- [ ] **B.** Go very slowly
- [ ] **C.** Pass quickly but quietly
- [ ] **D.** Be ready to stop
- [ ] **E.** Briefly sound your horn

370 **At night you see a pedestrian wearing reflective clothing and carrying a bright red light. What does this mean?**

Mark one answer
- [ ] **A.** You are approaching road works
- [ ] **B.** You are approaching an organised walk
- [ ] **C.** You are approaching a slow-moving vehicle
- [ ] **D.** You are approaching an accident black spot

371 **As you approach a pelican crossing the lights change to green. Elderly people are half-way across. You should**

Mark one answer
- [ ] **A.** wave them to cross as quickly as they can
- [ ] **B.** rev your engine to make them hurry
- [ ] **C.** flash your lights in case they have not heard you
- [ ] **D.** wait because they will take longer to cross

372 **There are flashing amber lights under a school warning sign. What action should you take?**

Mark one answer
- [ ] **A.** Reduce speed until you are clear of the area
- [ ] **B.** Keep up your speed and sound the horn
- [ ] **C.** Increase your speed to clear the area quickly
- [ ] **D.** Wait at the lights until they change to green

373 You are approaching this crossing. You should

Mark one answer

- ☐ **A.** prepare to slow down and stop
- ☐ **B.** stop and wave the pedestrians across
- ☐ **C.** speed up and pass by quickly
- ☐ **D.** drive on unless the pedestrians step out

374 You see a pedestrian with a dog. The dog has a bright orange lead and collar. This especially warns you that the pedestrian is

Mark one answer

- ☐ **A.** elderly
- ☐ **B.** dog training
- ☐ **C.** colour blind
- ☐ **D.** deaf

375 These road markings must be kept clear to allow

Mark one answer

- ☐ **A.** schoolchildren to be dropped off
- ☐ **B.** for teachers to park
- ☐ **C.** schoolchildren to be picked up
- ☐ **D.** a clear view of the crossing area

376 You must not stop on these road markings because you may obstruct

Mark one answer

- ☐ **A.** children's view of the crossing area
- ☐ **B.** teachers' access to the school
- ☐ **C.** delivery vehicles' access to the school
- ☐ **D.** emergency vehicles' access to the school

377 The left-hand pavement is closed due to street repairs. What should you do?

Mark one answer

- ☐ **A.** Watch out for pedestrians walking in the road
- ☐ **B.** Use your right-hand mirror more often
- ☐ **C.** Speed up to get past the road works quicker
- ☐ **D.** Position close to the left-hand kerb

378 Where would you see this sign?

Mark one answer

- ☐ **A.** Near a school crossing
- ☐ **B.** At a playground entrance
- ☐ **C.** On a school bus
- ☐ **D.** At a 'pedestrians only' area

379 You are following a motorcyclist on an uneven road. You should

Mark one answer

- [ ] **A.** allow less room so you can be seen in their mirrors
- [ ] **B.** overtake immediately
- [ ] **C.** allow extra room in case they swerve to avoid potholes
- [ ] **D.** allow the same room as normal because road surfaces do not affect motorcyclists

380 You are following two cyclists. They approach a roundabout in the left-hand lane. In which direction should you expect the cyclists to go?

Mark one answer

- [ ] **A.** Left
- [ ] **B.** Right
- [ ] **C.** Any direction
- [ ] **D.** Straight ahead

381 You are travelling behind a moped. You want to turn left just ahead. You should

Mark one answer

- [ ] **A.** overtake the moped before the junction
- [ ] **B.** pull alongside the moped and stay level until just before the junction
- [ ] **C.** sound your horn as a warning and pull in front of the moped
- [ ] **D.** stay behind until the moped has passed the junction

382 Which THREE of the following are hazards motorcyclists present in queues of traffic?

Mark three answers

- [ ] **A.** Cutting in just in front of you
- [ ] **B.** Riding in single file
- [ ] **C.** Passing very close to you
- [ ] **D.** Riding with their headlight on dipped beam
- [ ] **E.** Filtering between the lanes

383 You see a horse rider as you approach a roundabout. They are signalling right but keeping well to the left. You should

Mark one answer

- [ ] **A.** proceed as normal
- [ ] **B.** keep close to them
- [ ] **C.** cut in front of them
- [ ] **D.** stay well back

384 How would you react to drivers who appear to be inexperienced?

Mark one answer

- [ ] **A.** Sound your horn to warn them of your presence
- [ ] **B.** Be patient and prepare for them to react more slowly
- [ ] **C.** Flash your headlights to indicate that it is safe for them to proceed
- [ ] **D.** Overtake them as soon as possible

385 You are following a learner driver who stalls at a junction. You should

Mark one answer

- [ ] **A.** be patient as you expect them to make mistakes
- [ ] **B.** stay very close behind and flash your headlights
- [ ] **C.** start to rev your engine if they take too long to restart
- [ ] **D.** immediately steer around them and drive on

386 You are on a country road. What should you expect to see coming towards you on YOUR side of the road?

Mark one answer

- [ ] **A.** Motorcycles
- [ ] **B.** Bicycles
- [ ] **C.** Pedestrians
- [ ] **D.** Horse riders

387 You are turning left into a side road. Pedestrians are crossing the road near the junction. You must

Mark one answer

- [ ] **A.** wave them on
- [ ] **B.** sound your horn
- [ ] **C.** switch on your hazard lights
- [ ] **D.** wait for them to cross

388 You are following a car driven by an elderly driver. You should

Mark one answer

- [ ] **A.** expect the driver to drive badly
- [ ] **B.** flash your lights and overtake
- [ ] **C.** be aware that the driver's reactions may not be as fast as yours
- [ ] **D.** stay very close behind but be careful

389 You are following a cyclist. You wish to turn left just ahead. You should

Mark one answer

- [ ] **A.** overtake the cyclist before the junction
- [ ] **B.** pull alongside the cyclist and stay level until after the junction
- [ ] **C.** hold back until the cyclist has passed the junction
- [ ] **D.** go around the cyclist on the junction

390 A horse rider is in the left-hand lane approaching a roundabout. You should expect the rider to

Mark one answer

- [ ] **A.** go in any direction
- [ ] **B.** turn right
- [ ] **C.** turn left
- [ ] **D.** go ahead

391 **You have just passed your test. How can you decrease your risk of accidents on the motorway?**

Mark one answer
- ☐ **A.** By keeping up with the car in front
- ☐ **B.** By never going over 40mph
- ☐ **C.** By staying only in the left-hand lane
- ☐ **D.** By taking further training

392 **Powered vehicles used by disabled people are small and hard to see. How do they give early warning when on a dual carriageway?**

Mark one answer
- ☐ **A.** They will have a flashing red light
- ☐ **B.** They will have a flashing green light
- ☐ **C.** They will have a flashing blue light
- ☐ **D.** They will have a flashing amber light

393 **You should never attempt to overtake a cyclist**

Mark one answer
- ☐ **A.** just before you turn left
- ☐ **B.** on a left-hand bend
- ☐ **C.** on a one-way street
- ☐ **D.** on a dual carriageway

394 **Ahead of you there is a moving vehicle with a flashing amber beacon. This means it is**

Mark one answer
- ☐ **A.** slow moving
- ☐ **B.** broken down
- ☐ **C.** a doctor's car
- ☐ **D.** a school crossing patrol

395 **You want to reverse into a side road. You are not sure that the area behind your car is clear. What should you do?**

Mark one answer
- ☐ **A.** Look through the rear window only
- ☐ **B.** Get out and check
- ☐ **C.** Check the mirrors only
- ☐ **D.** Carry on, assuming it is clear

396 **You are about to reverse into a side road. A pedestrian wishes to cross behind you. You should**

Mark one answer
- ☐ **A.** wave to the pedestrian to stop
- ☐ **B.** give way to the pedestrian
- ☐ **C.** wave to the pedestrian to cross
- ☐ **D.** reverse before the pedestrian starts to cross

397 **Who is especially in danger of not being seen as you reverse your car?**

Mark one answer
- ☐ **A.** Motorcyclists
- ☐ **B.** Car drivers
- ☐ **C.** Cyclists
- ☐ **D.** Children

398 **You are reversing around a corner when you notice a pedestrian walking behind you. What should you do?**

Mark one answer
- ☐ **A.** Slow down and wave the pedestrian across
- ☐ **B.** Continue reversing and steer round the pedestrian
- ☐ **C.** Stop and give way
- ☐ **D.** Continue reversing and sound your horn

399

You want to turn right from a junction but your view is restricted by parked vehicles. What should you do?

Mark one answer

- [ ] **A.** Move out quickly, but be prepared to stop
- [ ] **B.** Sound your horn and pull out if there is no reply
- [ ] **C.** Stop, then move slowly forward until you have a clear view
- [ ] **D.** Stop, get out and look along the main road to check

400

You are at the front of a queue of traffic waiting to turn right into a side road. Why is it important to check your right mirror just before turning?

Mark one answer

- [ ] **A.** To look for pedestrians about to cross
- [ ] **B.** To check for overtaking vehicles
- [ ] **C.** To make sure the side road is clear
- [ ] **D.** To check for emerging traffic

401

What must a driver do at a pelican crossing when the amber light is flashing?

Mark one answer

- [ ] **A.** Signal the pedestrian to cross
- [ ] **B.** Always wait for the green light before proceeding
- [ ] **C.** Give way to any pedestrians on the crossing
- [ ] **D.** Wait for the red-and-amber light before proceeding

402

You have stopped at a pelican crossing. A disabled person is crossing slowly in front of you. The lights have now changed to green. You should

Mark two answers

- [ ] **A.** allow the person to cross
- [ ] **B.** drive in front of the person
- [ ] **C.** drive behind the person
- [ ] **D.** sound your horn
- [ ] **E.** be patient
- [ ] **F.** edge forward slowly

403

You are driving past parked cars. You notice a bicycle wheel sticking out between them. What should you do?

Mark one answer

- [ ] **A.** Accelerate past quickly and sound your horn
- [ ] **B.** Slow down and wave the cyclist across
- [ ] **C.** Brake sharply and flash your headlights
- [ ] **D.** Slow down and be prepared to stop for a cyclist

404 You are driving past a line of parked cars. You notice a ball bouncing out into the road ahead. What should you do?

Mark one answer

- [ ] **A.** Continue driving at the same speed and sound your horn
- [ ] **B.** Continue driving at the same speed and flash your headlights
- [ ] **C.** Slow down and be prepared to stop for children
- [ ] **D.** Stop and wave the children across to fetch their ball

405 You want to turn right from a main road into a side road. Just before turning you should

Mark one answer

- [ ] **A.** cancel your right-turn signal
- [ ] **B.** select first gear
- [ ] **C.** check for traffic overtaking on your right
- [ ] **D.** stop and set the handbrake

406 You are driving in slow-moving queues of traffic. Just before changing lane you should

Mark one answer

- [ ] **A.** sound the horn
- [ ] **B.** look for motorcyclists filtering through the traffic
- [ ] **C.** give a 'slowing down' arm signal
- [ ] **D.** change down to first gear

407 You are driving in town. There is a bus at the bus stop on the other side of the road. Why should you be careful?

Mark one answer

- [ ] **A.** The bus may have broken down
- [ ] **B.** Pedestrians may come from behind the bus
- [ ] **C.** The bus may move off suddenly
- [ ] **D.** The bus may remain stationary

408 How should you overtake horse riders?

Mark one answer

- [ ] **A.** Drive up close and overtake as soon as possible
- [ ] **B.** Speed is not important but allow plenty of room
- [ ] **C.** Use your horn just once to warn them
- [ ] **D.** Drive slowly and leave plenty of room

409 A friend wants to help you learn to drive. They must be

Mark one answer

- [ ] **A.** over 21 and have held a full licence for at least two years
- [ ] **B.** over 18 and hold an advanced driver's certificate
- [ ] **C.** over 18 and have fully comprehensive insurance
- [ ] **D.** over 21 and have held a full licence for at least three years

410 You are dazzled at night by a vehicle behind you. You should

Mark one answer

- [ ] **A.** set your mirror to anti-dazzle
- [ ] **B.** set your mirror to dazzle the other driver
- [ ] **C.** brake sharply to a stop
- [ ] **D.** switch your rear lights on and off

411 You have a collision whilst your car is moving. What is the first thing you must do?

Mark one answer

- [ ] **A.** Stop only if there are injured people
- [ ] **B.** Call the emergency services
- [ ] **C.** Stop at the scene of the accident
- [ ] **D.** Call your insurance company

412 Yellow zigzag lines on the road outside schools mean

Mark one answer

- [ ] **A.** sound your horn to alert other road users
- [ ] **B.** stop to allow children to cross
- [ ] **C.** you must not wait or park on these lines
- [ ] **D.** you must not drive over these lines

413 What do these road markings outside a school mean?

Mark one answer

- [ ] **A.** You may park here if you are a teacher
- [ ] **B.** Sound your horn before parking
- [ ] **C.** When parking, use your hazard warning lights
- [ ] **D.** You must not, wait or park your vehicle here

414 You are driving on a main road. You intend to turn right into a side road. Just before turning you should

Mark one answer

- [ ] **A.** adjust your interior mirror
- [ ] **B.** flash your headlamps
- [ ] **C.** steer over to the left
- [ ] **D.** check for traffic overtaking on your right

415 Why should you allow extra room when overtaking a motorcyclist on a windy day?

Mark one answer

- [ ] **A.** The rider may turn off suddenly to get out of the wind
- [ ] **B.** The rider may be blown across in front of you
- [ ] **C.** The rider may stop suddenly
- [ ] **D.** The rider may be travelling faster than normal

416 Which age group of drivers is most likely to be involved in a road accident?

Mark one answer

- [ ] **A.** 17 to 25-year-olds
- [ ] **B.** 36 to 45-year-olds
- [ ] **C.** 46 to 55-year-olds
- [ ] **D.** over 55-year-olds

417

You are driving towards a zebra crossing. A person in a wheelchair is waiting to cross. What should you do?

Mark one answer

- [ ] **A.** Continue on your way
- [ ] **B.** Wave to the person to cross
- [ ] **C.** Wave to the person to wait
- [ ] **D.** Be prepared to stop

418

Where in particular should you look out for motorcyclists?

Mark one answer

- [ ] **A.** In a filling station
- [ ] **B.** At a road junction
- [ ] **C.** Near a service area
- [ ] **D.** When entering a car park

419

Where should you take particular care to look out for motorcyclists and cyclists?

Mark one answer

- [ ] **A.** On dual carriageways
- [ ] **B.** At junctions
- [ ] **C.** At zebra crossings
- [ ] **D.** On one-way streets

420

The road outside this school is marked with yellow zigzag lines. What do these lines mean?

Mark one answer

- [ ] **A.** You may park on the lines when dropping off schoolchildren
- [ ] **B.** You may park on the lines when picking schoolchildren up
- [ ] **C.** You must not wait or park your vehicle here at all
- [ ] **D.** You must stay with your vehicle if you park here

421 The road is wet. Why might a motorcyclist steer round drain covers on a bend?

Mark one answer

- [ ] **A.** To avoid puncturing the tyres on the edge of the drain covers
- [ ] **B.** To prevent the motorcycle sliding on the metal drain covers
- [ ] **C.** To help judge the bend using the drain covers as marker points
- [ ] **D.** To avoid splashing pedestrians on the pavement

422 You are about to overtake a slow-moving motorcyclist. Which one of these signs would make you take special care?

Mark one answer

- [ ] **A.** 
- [ ] **B.** 
- [ ] **C.** 
- [ ] **D.** 

423 You are waiting to emerge left from a minor road. A large vehicle is approaching from the right. You have time to turn, but you should wait. Why?

Mark one answer

- [ ] **A.** The large vehicle can easily hide an overtaking vehicle
- [ ] **B.** The large vehicle can turn suddenly
- [ ] **C.** The large vehicle is difficult to steer in a straight line
- [ ] **D.** The large vehicle can easily hide vehicles from the left

424 You are following a long vehicle. It approaches a crossroads and signals left, but moves out to the right. You should

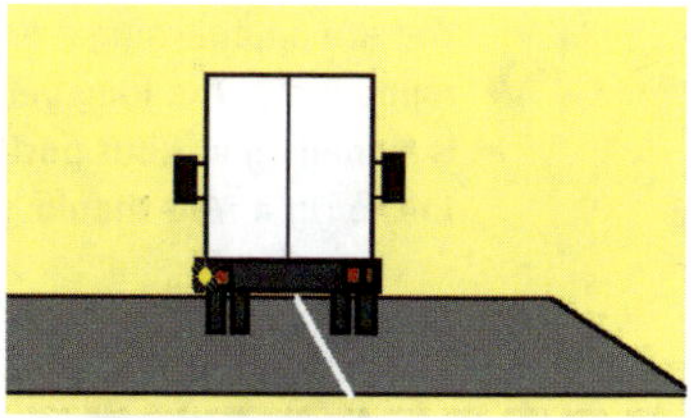

Mark one answer

- [ ] **A.** get closer in order to pass it quickly
- [ ] **B.** stay well back and give it room
- [ ] **C.** assume the signal is wrong and it is really turning right
- [ ] **D.** overtake as it starts to slow down

425 You are following a long vehicle approaching a crossroads. The driver signals right but moves close to the left-hand kerb. What should you do?

Mark one answer

- [ ] **A.** Warn the driver of the wrong signal
- [ ] **B.** Wait behind the long vehicle
- [ ] **C.** Report the driver to the police
- [ ] **D.** Overtake on the right-hand side

426 You are approaching a mini-roundabout. The long vehicle in front is signalling left but positioned over to the right. You should

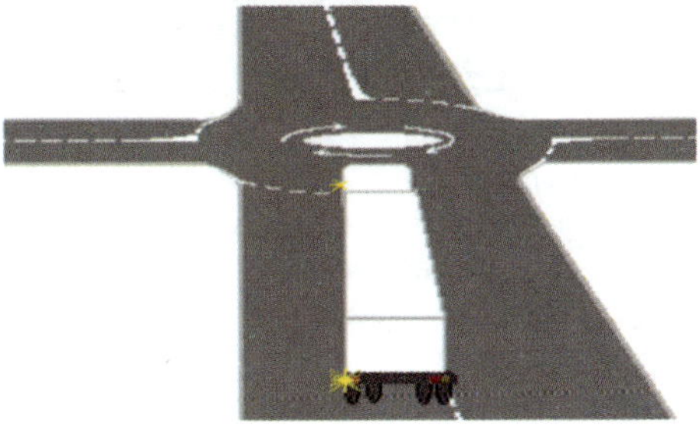

Mark one answer

- [ ] **A.** sound your horn
- [ ] **B.** overtake on the left
- [ ] **C.** follow the same course as the lorry
- [ ] **D.** keep well back

427 Before overtaking a large vehicle you should keep well back. Why is this?

Mark one answer

- [ ] **A.** To give acceleration space to overtake quickly on blind bends
- [ ] **B.** To get the best view of the road ahead
- [ ] **C.** To leave a gap in case the vehicle stops and rolls back
- [ ] **D.** To offer other drivers a safe gap if they want to overtake you

428 Why is passing a lorry more risky than passing a car?

Mark one answer

- [ ] **A.** Lorries are longer than cars
- [ ] **B.** Lorries may suddenly pull up
- [ ] **C.** The brakes of lorries are not as good
- [ ] **D.** Lorries climb hills more slowly

429 You are travelling behind a bus that pulls up at a bus stop. What should you do?

Mark two answers

- [ ] **A.** Accelerate past the bus sounding your horn
- [ ] **B.** Watch carefully for pedestrians
- [ ] **C.** Be ready to give way to the bus
- [ ] **D.** Pull in closely behind the bus

430 When you approach a bus signalling to move off from a bus stop you should

Mark one answer

- [ ] **A.** get past before it moves
- [ ] **B.** allow it to pull away, if it is safe to do so
- [ ] **C.** flash your headlights as you approach
- [ ] **D.** signal left and wave the bus on

431 Which of these is LEAST likely to be affected by crosswinds?

Mark one answer

- [ ] **A.** Cyclists
- [ ] **B.** Motorcyclists
- [ ] **C.** High-sided vehicles
- [ ] **D.** Cars

432 You are following a large lorry on a wet road. Spray makes it difficult to see. You should

Mark one answer

- [ ] **A.** drop back until you can see better
- [ ] **B.** put your headlights on full beam
- [ ] **C.** keep close to the lorry, away from the spray
- [ ] **D.** speed up and overtake quickly

433 What should you do as you approach this lorry?

Mark one answer

- [ ] **A.** Slow down and be prepared to wait
- [ ] **B.** Make the lorry wait for you
- [ ] **C.** Flash your lights at the lorry
- [ ] **D.** Move to the right-hand side of the road

434 You are following a large articulated vehicle. It is going to turn left into a narrow road. What action should you take?

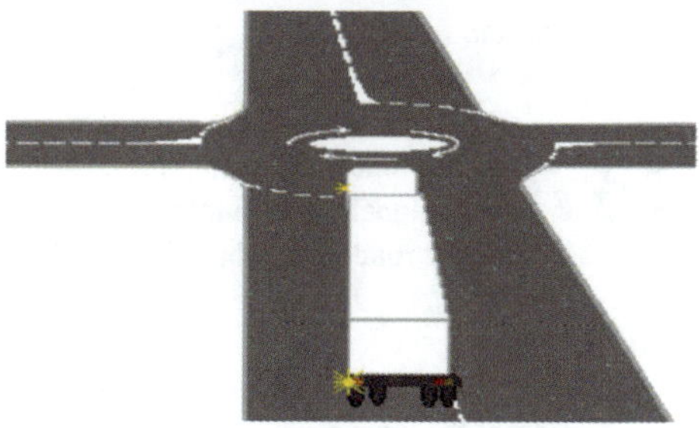

Mark one answer

- [ ] **A.** Move out and overtake on the right
- [ ] **B.** Pass on the left as the vehicle moves out
- [ ] **C.** Be prepared to stop behind
- [ ] **D.** Overtake quickly before the lorry moves out

435 You keep well back while waiting to overtake a large vehicle. A car fills the gap. You should

Mark one answer

- [ ] **A.** sound your horn
- [ ] **B.** drop back further
- [ ] **C.** flash your headlights
- [ ] **D.** start to overtake

436 You are following a large vehicle approaching crossroads. The driver signals to turn left. What should you do?

Mark one answer

- [ ] **A.** Overtake if you can leave plenty of room
- [ ] **B.** Overtake only if there are no oncoming vehicles
- [ ] **C.** Do not overtake until the vehicle begins to turn
- [ ] **D.** Do not overtake when at or approaching a junction

437 You are following a long lorry. The driver signals to turn left into a narrow road. What should you do?

Mark one answer

- [ ] **A.** Overtake on the left before the lorry reaches the junction
- [ ] **B.** Overtake on the right as soon as the lorry slows down
- [ ] **C.** Do not overtake unless you can see there is no oncoming traffic
- [ ] **D.** Do not overtake, stay well back and be prepared to stop

438 You wish to overtake a long, slow-moving vehicle on a busy road. You should

Mark one answer

- [ ] **A.** follow it closely and keep moving out to see the road ahead
- [ ] **B.** flash your headlights for the oncoming traffic to give way
- [ ] **C.** stay behind until the driver waves you past
- [ ] **D.** keep well back until you can see that it is clear

439 It is very windy. You are behind a motorcyclist who is overtaking a high-sided vehicle. What should you do?

Mark one answer

- [ ] **A.** Overtake the motorcyclist immediately
- [ ] **B.** Keep well back
- [ ] **C.** Stay level with the motorcyclist
- [ ] **D.** Keep close to the motorcyclist

440 It is very windy. You are about to overtake a motorcyclist. You should

Mark one answer

- [ ] **A.** overtake slowly
- [ ] **B.** allow extra room
- [ ] **C.** sound your horn
- [ ] **D.** keep close as you pass

441 You are towing a caravan. Which is the safest type of rear-view mirror to use?

Mark one answer

- [ ] **A.** Interior wide-angle mirror
- [ ] **B.** Extended-arm side mirrors
- [ ] **C.** Ordinary door mirrors
- [ ] **D.** Ordinary interior mirror

442
You are driving in town. Ahead of you a bus is at a bus stop. Which TWO of the following should you do?

Mark two answers

- [ ] **A.** Be prepared to give way if the bus suddenly moves off
- [ ] **B.** Continue at the same speed but sound your horn as a warning
- [ ] **C.** Watch carefully for the sudden appearance of pedestrians
- [ ] **D.** Pass the bus as quickly as you possibly can

443
You are driving in heavy traffic on a wet road. Spray makes it difficult to be seen. You should use your

Mark two answers

- [ ] **A.** full beam headlights
- [ ] **B.** rear fog lights if visibility is less than 100 metres (328 feet)
- [ ] **C.** rear fog lights if visibility is more than 100 metres (328 feet)
- [ ] **D.** dipped headlights
- [ ] **E.** sidelights only

444
You are driving along this road. What should you be prepared to do?

Mark one answer

- [ ] **A.** Sound your horn and continue
- [ ] **B.** Slow down and give way
- [ ] **C.** Report the driver to the police
- [ ] **D.** Squeeze through the gap

445
As a driver why should you be more careful where trams operate?

Mark one answer

- [ ] **A.** Because they do not have a horn
- [ ] **B.** Because they do not stop for cars
- [ ] **C.** Because they do not have lights
- [ ] **D.** Because they cannot steer to avoid you

446 In which THREE of these situations may you overtake another vehicle on the left?

Mark three answers

- [ ] A. When you are in a one-way street
- [ ] B. When approaching a motorway slip road where you will be turning off
- [ ] C. When the vehicle in front is signalling to turn right
- [ ] D. When a slower vehicle is travelling in the right-hand lane of a dual carriageway
- [ ] E. In slow-moving traffic queues when traffic in the right-hand lane is moving more slowly

447 You are travelling in very heavy rain. Your overall stopping distance is likely to be

Mark one answer

- [ ] A. doubled
- [ ] B. halved
- [ ] C. up to ten times greater
- [ ] D. no different

448 Which TWO of the following are correct? When overtaking at night you should

Mark two answers

- [ ] A. wait until a bend so that you can see the oncoming headlights
- [ ] B. sound your horn twice before moving out
- [ ] C. be careful because you can see less
- [ ] D. beware of bends in the road ahead
- [ ] E. put headlights on full beam

449 When may you wait in a box junction?

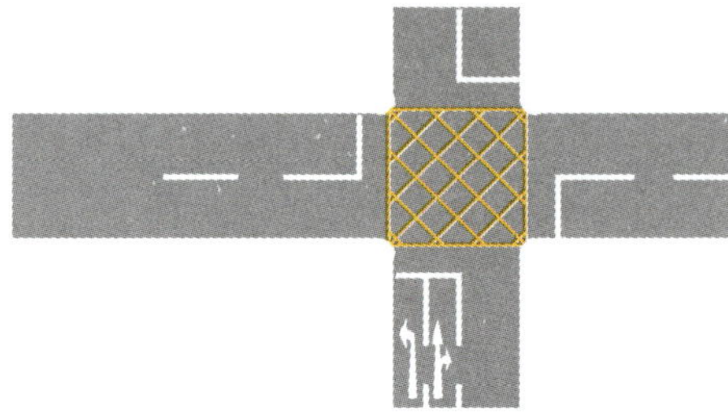

Mark one answer

- [ ] A. When you are stationary in a queue of traffic
- [ ] B. When approaching a pelican crossing
- [ ] C. When approaching a zebra crossing
- [ ] D. When oncoming traffic prevents you turning right

450 Which of these plates normally appear with this road sign?

Mark one answer

- [ ] A.

- [ ] B.

- [ ] C.

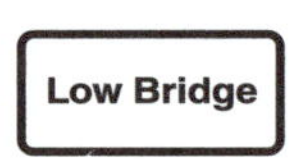

- [ ] D.

451 Areas reserved for trams may have

Mark three answers

- [ ] **A.** metal studs around them
- [ ] **B.** white line markings
- [ ] **C.** zigzag markings
- [ ] **D.** a different coloured surface
- [ ] **E.** yellow hatch markings
- [ ] **F.** a different surface texture

452 Traffic calming measures are used to

Mark one answer

- [ ] **A.** stop road rage
- [ ] **B.** help overtaking
- [ ] **C.** slow traffic down
- [ ] **D.** help parking

453 Why should you always reduce your speed when travelling in fog?

Mark one answer

- [ ] **A.** Because the brakes do not work as well
- [ ] **B.** Because you could be dazzled by other people's fog lights
- [ ] **C.** Because the engine is colder
- [ ] **D.** Because it is more difficult to see events ahead

454 You are on a motorway in fog. The left-hand edge of the motorway can be identified by reflective studs. What colour are they?

Mark one answer

- [ ] **A.** Green
- [ ] **B.** Amber
- [ ] **C.** Red
- [ ] **D.** White

455 A rumble device is designed to

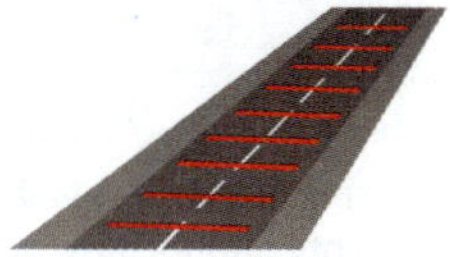

Mark two answers

- [ ] **A.** give directions
- [ ] **B.** prevent cattle escaping
- [ ] **C.** alert you to low tyre pressure
- [ ] **D.** alert you to a hazard
- [ ] **E.** encourage you to reduce speed

456 You are on a narrow road at night. A slower-moving vehicle ahead has been signalling right for some time. What should you do?

Mark one answer

- [ ] **A.** Overtake on the left
- [ ] **B.** Flash your headlights before overtaking
- [ ] **C.** Signal right and sound your horn
- [ ] **D.** Wait for the signal to be cancelled before overtaking

457 Why should you test your brakes after this hazard?

Mark one answer

- [ ] **A.** Because you will be on a slippery road
- [ ] **B.** Because your brakes will be soaking wet
- [ ] **C.** Because you will have gone down a long hill
- [ ] **D.** Because you will have just crossed a long bridge

458 You have to make a journey in foggy conditions. You should

Mark one answer
- [ ] **A.** follow other vehicles' tail-lights closely
- [ ] **B.** avoid using dipped headlights
- [ ] **C.** leave plenty of time for your journey
- [ ] **D.** keep two seconds behind other vehicles

459 You see a vehicle coming towards you on a single-track road. You should

Mark one answer
- [ ] **A.** go back to the main road
- [ ] **B.** do an emergency stop
- [ ] **C.** stop at a passing place
- [ ] **D.** put on your hazard warning lights

460 You are overtaking a car at night. You must be sure that

Mark one answer
- [ ] **A.** you flash your headlights before overtaking
- [ ] **B.** you select a higher gear
- [ ] **C.** you have switched your lights to full beam before overtaking
- [ ] **D.** you do not dazzle other road users

461 You are on a road which has speed humps. A driver in front is travelling slower than you. You should

Mark one answer
- [ ] **A.** sound your horn
- [ ] **B.** overtake as soon as you can
- [ ] **C.** flash your headlights
- [ ] **D.** slow down and stay behind

462 You are following other vehicles in fog with your lights on. How else can you reduce the chances of being involved in an accident?

Mark one answer
- [ ] **A.** Keep close to the vehicle in front
- [ ] **B.** Use your main beam instead of dipped headlights
- [ ] **C.** Keep together with the faster vehicles
- [ ] **D.** Reduce your speed and increase the gap

463 You see these markings on the road. Why are they there?

Mark one answer
- [ ] **A.** To show a safe distance between vehicles
- [ ] **B.** To keep the area clear of traffic
- [ ] **C.** To make you aware of your speed
- [ ] **D.** To warn you to change direction

464 When MUST you use dipped headlights during the day?

Mark one answer
- [ ] **A.** All the time
- [ ] **B.** Along narrow streets
- [ ] **C.** In poor visibility
- [ ] **D.** When parking

465 What are TWO main reasons why coasting downhill is wrong?

Mark two answers

- [ ] **A.** Fuel consumption will be higher
- [ ] **B.** The vehicle will pick up speed
- [ ] **C.** It puts more wear and tear on the tyres
- [ ] **D.** You have less braking and steering control
- [ ] **E.** It damages the engine

466 Hills can affect the performance of your vehicle. Which TWO apply when driving up steep hills?

Mark two answers

- [ ] **A.** Higher gears will pull better
- [ ] **B.** You will slow down sooner
- [ ] **C.** Overtaking will be easier
- [ ] **D.** The engine will work harder
- [ ] **E.** The steering will feel heavier

467 Why is coasting wrong?

Mark one answer

- [ ] **A.** It will cause the car to skid
- [ ] **B.** It will make the engine stall
- [ ] **C.** The engine will run faster
- [ ] **D.** There is no engine braking

468 You are driving on the motorway in windy conditions. When passing high-sided vehicles you should

Mark one answer

- [ ] **A.** increase your speed
- [ ] **B.** be wary of a sudden gust
- [ ] **C.** drive alongside very closely
- [ ] **D.** expect normal conditions

469 To correct a rear-wheel skid you should

Mark one answer

- [ ] **A.** not steer at all
- [ ] **B.** steer away from it
- [ ] **C.** steer into it
- [ ] **D.** apply your handbrake

470 You have to make a journey in fog. What are the TWO most important things you should do before you set out?

Mark two answers

- [ ] **A.** Top up the radiator with antifreeze
- [ ] **B.** Make sure that you have a warning triangle in the vehicle
- [ ] **C.** Check that your lights are working
- [ ] **D.** Check the battery
- [ ] **E.** Make sure that the windows are clean

471 You are driving in fog. Why should you keep well back from the vehicle in front?

Mark one answer

- [ ] **A.** In case it changes direction suddenly
- [ ] **B.** In case its fog lights dazzle you
- [ ] **C.** In case it stops suddenly
- [ ] **D.** In case its brake lights dazzle you

472 You should switch your rear fog lights on when visibility drops below

Mark one answer

- [ ] **A.** your overall stopping distance
- [ ] **B.** ten car lengths
- [ ] **C.** 200 metres (656 feet)
- [ ] **D.** 100 metres (328 feet)

473 **Whilst driving, the fog clears and you can see more clearly. You must remember to**

Mark one answer
- A. switch off the fog lights
- B. reduce your speed
- C. switch off the demister
- D. close any open windows

474 **You have to park on the road in fog. You should**

Mark one answer
- A. leave sidelights on
- B. leave dipped headlights and fog lights on
- C. leave dipped headlights on
- D. leave main beam headlights on

475 **On a foggy day you unavoidably have to park your car on the road. You should**

Mark one answer
- A. leave your headlights on
- B. leave your fog lights on
- C. leave your sidelights on
- D. leave your hazard lights on

476 **You are travelling at night. You are dazzled by headlights coming towards you. You should**

Mark one answer
- A. pull down your sun visor
- B. slow down or stop
- C. switch on your main beam headlights
- D. put your hand over your eyes

477 **Which of the following may apply when dealing with this hazard?**

Mark four answers
- A. It could be more difficult in winter
- B. Use a low gear and drive slowly
- C. Use a high gear to prevent wheelspin
- D. Test your brakes afterwards
- E. Always switch on fog lamps
- F. There may be a depth gauge

478 **Front fog lights may be used ONLY if**

Mark one answer
- A. visibility is seriously reduced
- B. they are fitted above the bumper
- C. they are not as bright as the headlights
- D. an audible warning device is used

479 **Front fog lights may be used ONLY if**

Mark one answer
- A. your headlights are not working
- B. they are operated with rear fog lights
- C. they were fitted by the vehicle manufacturer
- D. visibility is seriously reduced

480 You are driving with your front fog lights switched on. Earlier fog has now cleared. What should you do?

Mark one answer

- A. Leave them on if other drivers have their lights on
- B. Switch them off as long as visibility remains good
- C. Flash them to warn oncoming traffic that it is foggy
- D. Drive with them on instead of your headlights

481 Front fog lights should be used ONLY when

Mark one answer

- A. travelling in very light rain
- B. visibility is seriously reduced
- C. daylight is fading
- D. driving after midnight

482 Why is it dangerous to leave rear fog lights on when they are not needed?

Mark two answers

- A. Brake lights are less clear
- B. Following drivers can be dazzled
- C. Electrical systems could be overloaded
- D. Direction indicators may not work properly
- E. The battery could fail

483 You are driving on a clear dry night with your rear fog lights switched on. This may

Mark two answers

- A. reduce glare from the road surface
- B. make other drivers think you are braking
- C. give a better view of the road ahead
- D. dazzle following drivers
- E. help your indicators to be seen more clearly

484 You have just driven out of fog. Visibility is now good. You MUST

Mark one answer

- A. switch off all your fog lights
- B. keep your rear fog lights on
- C. keep your front fog lights on
- D. leave fog lights on in case fog returns

485 You forget to switch off your rear fog lights when the fog has cleared. This may

Mark three answers

- A. dazzle other road users
- B. reduce battery life
- C. cause brake lights to be less clear
- D. be breaking the law
- E. seriously affect engine power

486 You have been driving in thick fog which has now cleared. You must switch OFF your rear fog lights because

Mark one answer

- A. they use a lot of power from the battery
- B. they make your brake lights less clear
- C. they will cause dazzle in your rear-view mirror
- D. they may not be properly adjusted

487 Front fog lights should be used

Mark one answer

- [ ] **A.** when visibility is reduced to 100 metres (328 feet)
- [ ] **B.** as a warning to oncoming traffic
- [ ] **C.** when driving during the hours of darkness
- [ ] **D.** in any conditions and at any time

488 Using rear fog lights in clear daylight will

Mark one answer

- [ ] **A.** be useful when towing a trailer
- [ ] **B.** give extra protection
- [ ] **C.** dazzle other drivers
- [ ] **D.** make following drivers keep back

489 Using front fog lights in clear daylight will

Mark one answer

- [ ] **A.** flatten the battery
- [ ] **B.** dazzle other drivers
- [ ] **C.** improve your visibility
- [ ] **D.** increase your awareness

490 You may use front fog lights with headlights ONLY when visibility is reduced to less than

Mark one answer

- [ ] **A.** 100 metres (328 feet)
- [ ] **B.** 200 metres (656 feet)
- [ ] **C.** 300 metres (984 feet)
- [ ] **D.** 400 metres (1,312 feet)

491 You may drive with front fog lights switched on

Mark one answer

- [ ] **A.** when visibility is less than 100 metres (328 feet)
- [ ] **B.** at any time to be noticed
- [ ] **C.** instead of headlights on high-speed roads
- [ ] **D.** when dazzled by the lights of oncoming vehicles

492 Chains can be fitted to your wheels to help prevent

Mark one answer

- [ ] **A.** damage to the road surface
- [ ] **B.** wear to the tyres
- [ ] **C.** skidding in deep snow
- [ ] **D.** the brakes locking

493 Holding the clutch pedal down or rolling in neutral for too long while driving will

Mark one answer

- [ ] **A.** use more fuel
- [ ] **B.** cause the engine to overheat
- [ ] **C.** reduce your control
- [ ] **D.** improve tyre wear

494
How can you use the engine of your vehicle to control your speed?

Mark one answer
- ☐ **A.** By changing to a lower gear
- ☐ **B.** By selecting reverse gear
- ☐ **C.** By changing to a higher gear
- ☐ **D.** By selecting neutral

495
You are driving down a steep hill. Why could keeping the clutch down or rolling in neutral for too long be dangerous?

Mark one answer
- ☐ **A.** Fuel consumption will be higher
- ☐ **B.** Your vehicle will pick up speed
- ☐ **C.** It will damage the engine
- ☐ **D.** It will wear tyres out more quickly

496
Why could keeping the clutch down or selecting neutral for long periods of time be dangerous?

Mark one answer
- ☐ **A.** Fuel spillage will occur
- ☐ **B.** Engine damage may be caused
- ☐ **C.** You will have less steering and braking control
- ☐ **D.** It will wear tyres out more quickly

497
You are driving on an icy road. What distance should you drive from the car in front?

Mark one answer
- ☐ **A.** four times the normal distance
- ☐ **B.** six times the normal distance
- ☐ **C.** eight times the normal distance
- ☐ **D.** ten times the normal distance

498
You are on a well-lit motorway at night. You must

Mark one answer
- ☐ **A.** use only your sidelights
- ☐ **B.** always use your headlights
- ☐ **C.** always use rear fog lights
- ☐ **D.** use headlights only in bad weather

499
You are on a motorway at night with other vehicles just ahead of you. Which lights should you have on?

Mark one answer
- ☐ **A.** Front fog lights
- ☐ **B.** Main beam headlights
- ☐ **C.** Sidelights only
- ☐ **D.** Dipped headlights

500
Which THREE of the following will affect your stopping distance?

Mark three answers
- ☐ **A.** How fast you are going
- ☐ **B.** The tyres on your vehicle
- ☐ **C.** The time of day
- ☐ **D.** The weather
- ☐ **E.** The street lighting

501
You are on a motorway at night. You MUST have your headlights switched on unless

Mark one answer
- ☐ **A.** there are vehicles close in front of you
- ☐ **B.** you are travelling below 50mph
- ☐ **C.** the motorway is lit
- ☐ **D.** your vehicle is broken down on the hard shoulder

502 You will feel the effects of engine braking when you

Mark one answer

- [ ] **A.** only use the handbrake
- [ ] **B.** only use neutral
- [ ] **C.** change to a lower gear
- [ ] **D.** change to a higher gear

503 Daytime visibility is poor but not seriously reduced. You should switch on

Mark one answer

- [ ] **A.** headlights and fog lights
- [ ] **B.** front fog lights
- [ ] **C.** dipped headlights
- [ ] **D.** rear fog lights

504 Why are vehicles fitted with rear fog lights?

Mark one answer

- [ ] **A.** To be seen when driving at high speed
- [ ] **B.** To use if broken down in a dangerous position
- [ ] **C.** To make them more visible in thick fog
- [ ] **D.** To warn drivers following closely to drop back

505 While you are driving in fog, it becomes necessary to use front fog lights. You should

Mark one answer

- [ ] **A.** only turn them on in heavy traffic conditions
- [ ] **B.** remember not to use them on motorways
- [ ] **C.** only use them on dual carriageways
- [ ] **D.** remember to switch them off as visibility improves

506 When snow is falling heavily you should

Mark one answer

- [ ] **A.** only drive with your hazard lights on
- [ ] **B.** not drive unless you have a mobile phone
- [ ] **C.** only drive when your journey is short
- [ ] **D.** not drive unless it is essential

507 You are driving down a long steep hill. You suddenly notice your brakes are not working as well as normal. What is the usual cause of this?

Mark one answer

- [ ] **A.** The brakes overheating
- [ ] **B.** Air in the brake fluid
- [ ] **C.** Oil on the brakes
- [ ] **D.** Badly adjusted brakes

508 **Which FOUR of these must NOT use motorways?**

Mark four answers

- [ ] **A.** Learner car drivers
- [ ] **B.** Motorcycles over 50cc
- [ ] **C.** Double-deck buses
- [ ] **D.** Farm tractors
- [ ] **E.** Horse riders
- [ ] **F.** Cyclists

509 **Which FOUR of these must NOT use motorways?**

Mark four answers

- [ ] **A.** Learner car drivers
- [ ] **B.** Motorcycles over 50cc
- [ ] **C.** Double-deck buses
- [ ] **D.** Farm tractors
- [ ] **E.** Learner motorcyclists
- [ ] **F.** Cyclists

510 **Immediately after joining a motorway you should normally**

Mark one answer

- [ ] **A.** try to overtake
- [ ] **B.** re-adjust your mirrors
- [ ] **C.** position your vehicle in the centre lane
- [ ] **D.** keep in the left-hand lane

511 **When joining a motorway you must always**

Mark one answer

- [ ] **A.** use the hard shoulder
- [ ] **B.** stop at the end of the acceleration lane
- [ ] **C.** come to a stop before joining the motorway
- [ ] **D.** give way to traffic already on the motorway

512 **What is the national speed limit for cars and motorcycles in the centre lane of a three-lane motorway?**

Mark one answer

- [ ] **A.** 40mph
- [ ] **B.** 50mph
- [ ] **C.** 60mph
- [ ] **D.** 70mph

513 **What is the national speed limit on motorways for cars and motorcycles?**

Mark one answer

- [ ] **A.** 30mph
- [ ] **B.** 50mph
- [ ] **C.** 60mph
- [ ] **D.** 70mph

514 **The left-hand lane on a three-lane motorway is for use by**

Mark one answer

- [ ] **A.** any vehicle
- [ ] **B.** large vehicles only
- [ ] **C.** emergency vehicles only
- [ ] **D.** slow vehicles only

515 **What is the right-hand lane used for on a three-lane motorway?**

Mark one answer

- [ ] **A.** Emergency vehicles only
- [ ] **B.** Overtaking
- [ ] **C.** Vehicles towing trailers
- [ ] **D.** Coaches only

516 Which of these IS NOT allowed to travel in the right-hand lane of a three-lane motorway?

Mark one answer

- [ ] **A.** A small delivery van
- [ ] **B.** A motorcycle
- [ ] **C.** A vehicle towing a trailer
- [ ] **D.** A motorcycle and sidecar

517 You are travelling on a motorway. You decide you need a rest. You should

Mark two answers

- [ ] **A.** stop on the hard shoulder
- [ ] **B.** go to a service area
- [ ] **C.** park on the slip road
- [ ] **D.** park on the central reservation
- [ ] **E.** leave at the next exit

518 You break down on a motorway. You need to call for help. Why may it be better to use an emergency roadside telephone rather than a mobile phone?

Mark one answer

- [ ] **A.** It connects you to a local garage
- [ ] **B.** Using a mobile phone will distract other drivers
- [ ] **C.** It allows easy location by the emergency services
- [ ] **D.** Mobile phones do not work on motorways

519 What should you use the hard shoulder of a motorway for?

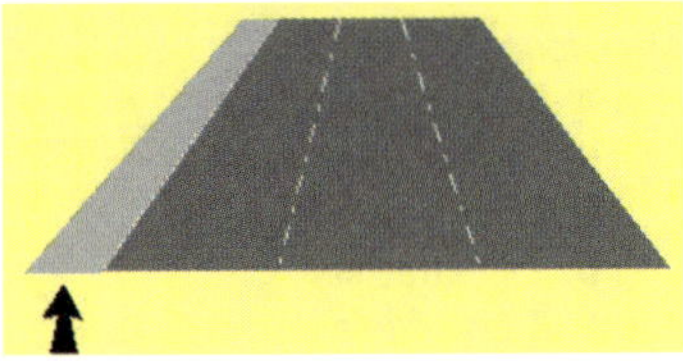

Mark one answer

- [ ] **A.** Stopping in an emergency
- [ ] **B.** Leaving the motorway
- [ ] **C.** Stopping when you are tired
- [ ] **D.** Joining the motorway

520 After a breakdown you need to rejoin the main carriageway of a motorway from the hard shoulder. You should

Mark one answer

- [ ] **A.** move out onto the carriageway then build up your speed
- [ ] **B.** move out onto the carriageway using your hazard lights
- [ ] **C.** gain speed on the hard shoulder before moving out onto the carriageway
- [ ] **D.** wait on the hard shoulder until someone flashes their headlights at you

521 A crawler lane on a motorway is found

Mark one answer

- [ ] **A.** on a steep gradient
- [ ] **B.** before a service area
- [ ] **C.** before a junction
- [ ] **D.** along the hard shoulder

522
You are driving on a motorway. There are red flashing lights above every lane. You must

Mark one answer
- [ ] **A.** pull on to the hard shoulder
- [ ] **B.** slow down and watch for further signals
- [ ] **C.** leave at the next exit
- [ ] **D.** stop and wait

523
You are in the right-hand lane on a motorway. You see these overhead signs. This means

Mark one answer
- [ ] **A.** move to the left and reduce your speed to 50mph
- [ ] **B.** there are road works 50 metres (55 yards) ahead
- [ ] **C.** use the hard shoulder until you have passed the hazard
- [ ] **D.** leave the motorway at the next exit

524
What do these motorway signs show?

Mark one answer
- [ ] **A.** They are countdown markers to a bridge
- [ ] **B.** They are distance markers to the next telephone
- [ ] **C.** They are countdown markers to the next exit
- [ ] **D.** They warn of a police control ahead

525
On a motorway the amber reflective studs can be found between

Mark one answer
- [ ] **A.** the hard shoulder and the carriageway
- [ ] **B.** the acceleration lane and the carriageway
- [ ] **C.** the central reservation and the carriageway
- [ ] **D.** each pair of the lanes

526
What colour are the reflective studs between the lanes on a motorway?

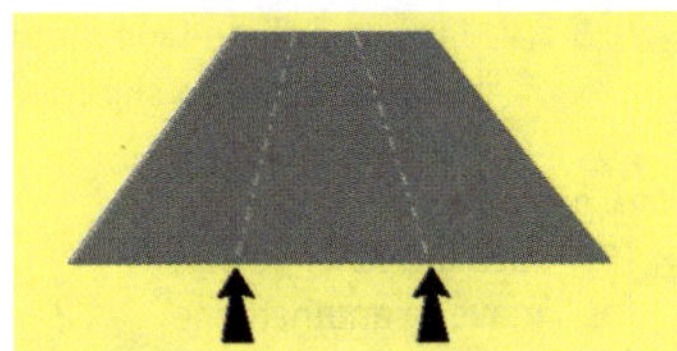

Mark one answer
- [ ] **A.** Green
- [ ] **B.** Amber
- [ ] **C.** White
- [ ] **D.** Red

527
What colour are the reflective studs between a motorway and its slip road?

Mark one answer
- [ ] **A.** Amber
- [ ] **B.** White
- [ ] **C.** Green
- [ ] **D.** Red

528
You are allowed to stop on a motorway when you

Mark one answer
- [ ] **A.** need to walk and get fresh air
- [ ] **B.** wish to pick up hitchhikers
- [ ] **C.** are told to do so by fashing red lights
- [ ] **D.** need to use a mobile telephone

529 **You have broken down on a motorway. To find the nearest emergency telephone you should always walk**

Mark one answer

- [ ] **A.** with the traffic flow
- [ ] **B.** facing oncoming traffic
- [ ] **C.** in the direction shown on the marker posts
- [ ] **D.** in the direction of the nearest exit

530 **You are travelling along the left-hand lane of a three-lane motorway. Traffic is joining from a slip road. You should**

Mark one answer

- [ ] **A.** race the other vehicles
- [ ] **B.** move to another lane
- [ ] **C.** maintain a steady speed
- [ ] **D.** switch on your hazard flashers

531 **You are joining a motorway. Why is it important to make full use of the slip road?**

Mark one answer

- [ ] **A.** Because there is space available to turn round if you need to
- [ ] **B.** To allow you direct access to the overtaking lanes
- [ ] **C.** To build up a speed similar to traffic on the motorway
- [ ] **D.** Because you can continue on the hard shoulder

532 **How should you use the emergency telephone on a motorway?**

Mark one answer

- [ ] **A.** Stay close to the carriageway
- [ ] **B.** Face the oncoming traffic
- [ ] **C.** Keep your back to the traffic
- [ ] **D.** Stand on the hard shoulder

533 **You are on a motorway. What colour are the reflective studs on the left of the carriageway?**

Mark one answer

- [ ] **A.** Green
- [ ] **B.** Red
- [ ] **C.** White
- [ ] **D.** Amber

534 **On a three-lane motorway which lane should you normally use?**

Mark one answer

- [ ] **A.** Left
- [ ] **B.** Right
- [ ] **C.** Centre
- [ ] **D.** Either the right or centre

535 **A basic rule when on motorways is**

Mark one answer

- [ ] **A.** use the lane that has least traffic
- [ ] **B.** keep to the left-hand lane unless overtaking
- [ ] **C.** overtake on the side that is clearest
- [ ] **D.** try to keep above 50mph to prevent congestion

536 When going through a contraflow system on a motorway you should

Mark one answer

- A. ensure that you do not exceed 30mph
- B. keep a good distance from the vehicle ahead
- C. switch lanes to keep the traffic flowing
- D. stay close to the vehicle ahead to reduce queues

537 You are on a three-lane motorway. There are red reflective studs on your left and white ones to your right. Where are you?

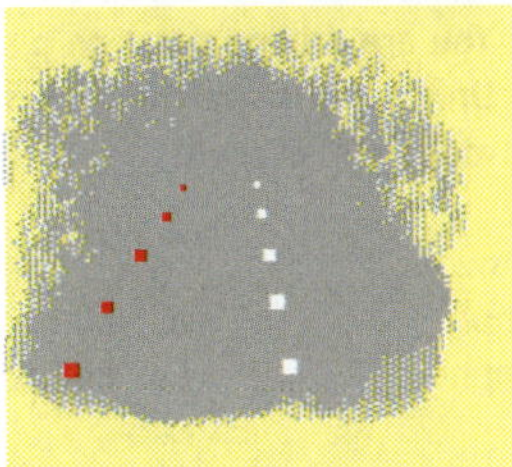

Mark one answer

- A. In the right-hand lane
- B. In the middle lane
- C. On the hard shoulder
- D. In the left-hand lane

538 When may you stop on a motorway?

Mark three answers

- A. If you have to read a map
- B. When you are tired and need a rest
- C. If red lights show above every lane
- D. When told to by the police
- E. If your mobile phone rings
- F. In an emergency or a breakdown

539 You are approaching road works on a motorway. What should you do?

Mark one answer

- A. Speed up to clear the area quickly
- B. Always use the hard shoulder
- C. Obey all speed limits
- D. Stay very close to the vehicle in front

540 On motorways you should never overtake on the left unless

Mark one answer

- A. you can see well ahead that the hard shoulder is clear
- B. the traffic in the right-hand lane is signalling right
- C. you warn drivers behind by signalling left
- D. there is a queue of slow-moving traffic to your right that is moving more slowly than you are

541 You are towing a trailer on a motorway. What is your maximum speed limit?

Mark one answer
- [ ] A. 40mph
- [ ] B. 50mph
- [ ] C. 60mph
- [ ] D. 70mph

542 The left-hand lane of a motorway should be used for

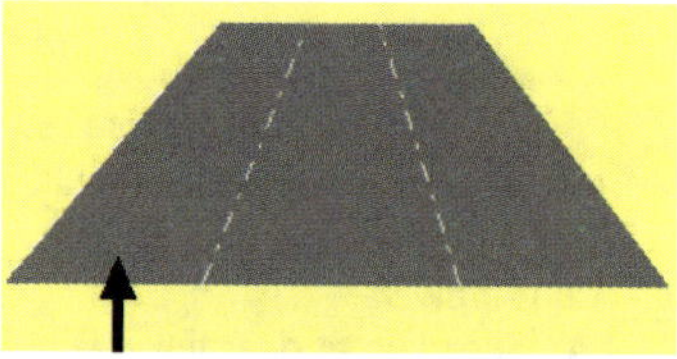

Mark one answer
- [ ] A. breakdowns and emergencies only
- [ ] B. overtaking slower traffic in the other lanes
- [ ] C. slow vehicles only
- [ ] D. normal driving

543 You are driving on a motorway. You have to slow down quickly due to a hazard. You should

Mark one answer
- [ ] A. switch on your hazard lights
- [ ] B. switch on your headlights
- [ ] C. sound your horn
- [ ] D. flash your headlights

544 You get a puncture on the motorway. You manage to get your vehicle on to the hard shoulder. You should

Mark one answer
- [ ] A. change the wheel yourself immediately
- [ ] B. use the emergency telephone and call for assistance
- [ ] C. try to wave down another vehicle for help
- [ ] D. only change the wheel if you have a passenger to help you

545 You are driving on a motorway. By mistake, you go past the exit that you wanted to take. You should

Mark one answer
- [ ] A. carefully reverse on the hard shoulder
- [ ] B. carry on to the next exit
- [ ] C. carefully reverse in the left-hand lane
- [ ] D. make a U-turn at the next gap in the central reservation

546 Your vehicle breaks down on the hard shoulder of a motorway. You decide to use your mobile phone to call for help. You should

Mark one answer
- [ ] A. stand at the rear of the vehicle while making the call
- [ ] B. try to repair the vehicle yourself
- [ ] C. get out of the vehicle by the right-hand door
- [ ] D. check your location from the marker posts on the left

547 You are driving a car on a motorway. Unless signs show otherwise you must NOT exceed

Mark one answer **NI**
- [ ] A. 50mph
- [ ] B. 60mph
- [ ] C. 70mph
- [ ] D. 80mph

548 You are on a three-lane motorway towing a trailer. You may use the right-hand lane when

Mark one answer **NI**
- [ ] A. there are lane closures
- [ ] B. there is slow-moving traffic
- [ ] C. you can maintain a high speed
- [ ] D. large vehicles are in the left and centre lanes

549 **You are on a motorway. There is a contraflow system ahead. What would you expect to find?**

Mark one answer
- [ ] **A.** Temporary traffic lights
- [ ] **B.** Lower speed limits
- [ ] **C.** Wider lanes than normal
- [ ] **D.** Speed humps

550 **You are driving at 70mph on a three-lane motorway. There is no traffic ahead. Which lane should you use?**

Mark one answer
- [ ] **A.** Any lane
- [ ] **B.** Middle lane
- [ ] **C.** Right lane
- [ ] **D.** Left lane

551 **Your vehicle has broken down on a motorway. You are not able to stop on the hard shoulder. What should you do?**

Mark one answer
- [ ] **A.** Switch on your hazard warning lights
- [ ] **B.** Stop following traffic and ask for help
- [ ] **C.** Attempt to repair your vehicle quickly
- [ ] **D.** Stand behind your vehicle to warn others

552 **Why is it particularly important to carry out a check on your vehicle before making a long motorway journey?**

Mark one answer
- [ ] **A.** You will have to do more harsh braking on motorways
- [ ] **B.** Motorway service stations do not deal with breakdowns
- [ ] **C.** The road surface will wear down the tyres faster
- [ ] **D.** Continuous high speeds may increase the risk of your vehicle breaking down

553 **For what reason may you use the right-hand lane of a motorway?**

Mark one answer
- [ ] **A.** For keeping out of the way of lorries
- [ ] **B.** For driving at more than 70mph
- [ ] **C.** For turning right
- [ ] **D.** For overtaking other vehicles

554 **On a motorway you may ONLY stop on the hard shoulder**

Mark one answer
- [ ] **A.** in an emergency
- [ ] **B.** if you feel tired and need to rest
- [ ] **C.** if you accidentally go past the exit that you wanted to take
- [ ] **D.** to pick up a hitchhiker

555 You are driving on a motorway. The car ahead shows its hazard lights for a short time. This tells you that

Mark one answer
- A. the driver wants you to overtake
- B. the other car is going to change lanes
- C. traffic ahead is slowing or stopping suddenly
- D. there is a police speed check ahead

556 The emergency telephones on a motorway are connected to the

Mark one answer
- A. ambulance service
- B. police control
- C. fire brigade
- D. breakdown service

557 You are intending to leave the motorway at the next exit. Before you reach the exit you should normally position your vehicle

Mark one answer
- A. in the middle lane
- B. in the left-hand lane
- C. on the hard shoulder
- D. in any lane

558 As a provisional licence holder you should not drive a car

Mark one answer
- A. over 30mph
- B. at night
- C. on the motorway
- D. with passengers in rear seats

559 Motorway emergency telephones are usually linked to the police. In some areas they are now linked to

Mark one answer NI
- A. the Highways Agency Control Centre
- B. the Driver Vehicle Licensing Agency
- C. the Driving Standards Agency
- D. the local Vehicle Registration Office

560 An Emergency Refuge Area is an area

Mark one answer
- A. on a motorway for use in cases of emergency or breakdown
- B. for use if you think you will be involved in a road rage incident
- C. on a motorway for a police patrol to park and watch traffic
- D. for construction and road workers to store emergency equipment

561 What is an Emergency Refuge Area on a motorway for?

Mark one answer
- A. An area to park in when you want to use a mobile phone
- B. To use in cases of emergency or breakdown
- C. For an emergency recovery vehicle to park in a contra-flow system
- D. To drive in when there is queuing traffic ahead

562 Highways Agency Traffic Officers

Mark one answer NI

- [ ] **A.** will not be able to assist at a breakdown or emergency
- [ ] **B.** are not able to stop and direct anyone on a motorway
- [ ] **C.** will tow a broken down vehicle and it's passengers home
- [ ] **D.** are able to stop and direct anyone on a motorway

563 You are on a motorway. A red cross is displayed above the hard shoulder. What does this mean?

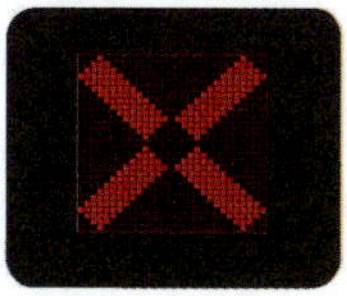

Mark one answer

- [ ] **A.** Pull up in this lane to answer your mobile phone
- [ ] **B.** Use this lane as a running lane
- [ ] **C.** This lane can be used if you need a rest
- [ ] **D.** You should not travel in this lane

564 You are on a motorway in an Active Traffic Management (ATM) area. A mandatory speed limit is displayed above the hard shoulder. What does this mean?

Mark one answer NI

- [ ] **A.** You should not travel in this lane
- [ ] **B.** The hard shoulder can be used as a running lane
- [ ] **C.** You can park on the hard shoulder if you feel tired
- [ ] **D.** You can pull up in this lane to answer a mobile phone

565 The aim of an Active Traffic Management scheme on a motorway is to

Mark one answer NI

- [ ] **A.** prevent overtaking
- [ ] **B.** reduce rest stops
- [ ] **C.** prevent tailgating
- [ ] **D.** reduce congestion

566 You are in an Active Traffic Management area on a motorway. When the Actively Managed mode is operating

Mark one answer NI

- [ ] **A.** speed limits are only advisory
- [ ] **B.** the national speed limit will apply
- [ ] **C.** the speed limit is always 30 mph
- [ ] **D.** all speed limit signals are set

567

You are travelling on a motorway. A red cross is shown above the hard shoulder and mandatory speed limits above all other lanes. This means

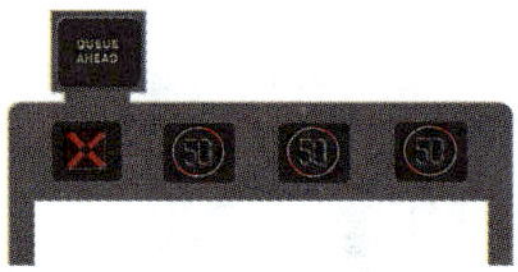

Mark one answer NI

- A. the hard shoulder can be used as a rest area if you feel tired
- B. the hard shoulder is for emergency or breakdown use only
- C. the hard shoulder can be used as a normal running lane
- D. the hard shoulder has a speed limit of 50 mph

568

You are travelling on a motorway. A red cross is shown above the hard shoulder. What does this mean?

Mark one answer NI

- A. Use this lane as a rest area
- B. Use this as a normal running lane
- C. Do not use this lane to travel in
- D. National speed limit applies in this lane

569

You see this sign on a motorway. It means you can use

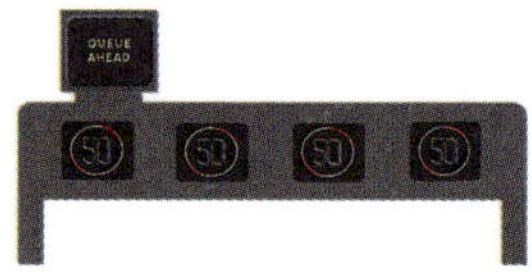

Mark one answer NI

- A. any lane except the hard shoulder
- B. the hard shoulder only
- C. the three right hand lanes only
- D. all the lanes including the hard shoulder

570

Why can it be an advantage for traffic speed to stay constant over a longer distance?

Mark one answer

- A. You will do more stop-start driving
- B. You will use far more fuel
- C. You will be able to use more direct routes
- D. Your overall journey time will normally improve

571

You should not normally travel on the hard shoulder of a motorway. When can you use it?

Mark one answer NI

- A. When taking the next exit
- B. When traffic is stopped
- C. When signs direct you to
- D. When traffic is slow moving

572 **What is the meaning of this sign?**

Mark one answer

- [ ] **A.** Local speed limit applies
- [ ] **B.** No waiting on the carriageway
- [ ] **C.** National speed limit applies
- [ ] **D.** No entry to vehicular traffic

573 **What is the national speed limit on a single carriageway road for cars and motorcycles?**

Mark one answer

- [ ] **A.** 70mph
- [ ] **B.** 60mph
- [ ] **C.** 50mph
- [ ] **D.** 30mph

574 **What is the national speed limit for cars and motorcycles on a dual carriageway?**

Mark one answer

- [ ] **A.** 30mph
- [ ] **B.** 50mph
- [ ] **C.** 60mph
- [ ] **D.** 70mph

575 **There are no speed limit signs on the road. How is a 30mph limit indicated?**

Mark one answer

- [ ] **A.** By hazard warning lines
- [ ] **B.** By street lighting
- [ ] **C.** By pedestrian islands
- [ ] **D.** By double or single yellow lines

576 **Where you see street lights but no speed limit signs the limit is usually**

Mark one answer

- [ ] **A.** 30mph
- [ ] **B.** 40mph
- [ ] **C.** 50mph
- [ ] **D.** 60mph

577 **What does this sign mean?**

Mark one answer

- [ ] **A.** Minimum speed 30mph
- [ ] **B.** End of maximum speed
- [ ] **C.** End of minimum speed
- [ ] **D.** Maximum speed 30mph

578 **There is a tractor ahead of you. You wish to overtake but you are NOT sure if it is safe to do so. You should**

Mark one answer

- [ ] **A.** follow another overtaking vehicle through
- [ ] **B.** sound your horn to the slow vehicle to pull over
- [ ] **C.** speed through but flash your lights to oncoming traffic
- [ ] **D.** not overtake if you are in doubt

579 Which three of the following are most likely to take an unusual course at roundabouts?

Mark three answers

- [ ] **A.** Horse riders
- [ ] **B.** Milk floats
- [ ] **C.** Delivery vans
- [ ] **D.** Long vehicles
- [ ] **E.** Estate cars
- [ ] **F.** Cyclists

580 In which TWO places should you NOT park?

Mark two answers

- [ ] **A.** Near a school entrance
- [ ] **B.** Near a police station
- [ ] **C.** In a side road
- [ ] **D.** At a bus stop
- [ ] **E.** In a one-way street

581 On a clearway you must not stop

Mark one answer

- [ ] **A.** at any time
- [ ] **B.** when it is busy
- [ ] **C.** in the rush hour
- [ ] **D.** during daylight hours

582 What is the meaning of this sign?

Mark one answer

- [ ] **A.** No entry
- [ ] **B.** Waiting restrictions
- [ ] **C.** National speed limit
- [ ] **D.** School crossing patrol

583 You can park on the right-hand side of a road at night

Mark one answer

- [ ] **A.** in a one-way street
- [ ] **B.** with your sidelights on
- [ ] **C.** more than 10 metres (32 feet) from a junction
- [ ] **D.** under a lamppost

584 On a three-lane dual carriageway the right-hand lane can be used for

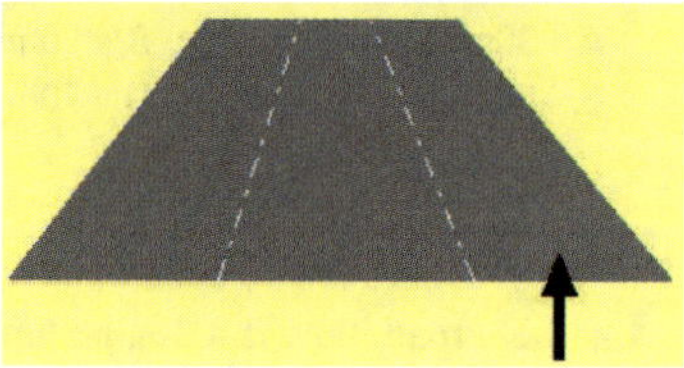

Mark one answer

- [ ] **A.** overtaking only, never turning right
- [ ] **B.** overtaking or turning right
- [ ] **C.** fast-moving traffic only
- [ ] **D.** turning right only, never overtaking

585 You are approaching a busy junction. There are several lanes with road markings. At the last moment you realise that you are in the wrong lane. You should

Mark one answer

- [ ] **A.** continue in that lane
- [ ] **B.** force your way across
- [ ] **C.** stop until the area has cleared
- [ ] **D.** use clear arm signals to cut across

586 Where may you overtake on a one-way street?

Mark one answer

- [ ] **A.** Only on the left-hand side
- [ ] **B.** Overtaking is not allowed
- [ ] **C.** Only on the right-hand side
- [ ] **D.** Either on the right or the left

587 When going straight ahead at a roundabout you should

Mark one answer

- [ ] **A.** indicate left before leaving the roundabout
- [ ] **B.** not indicate at any time
- [ ] **C.** indicate right when approaching the roundabout
- [ ] **D.** indicate left when approaching the roundabout

588 Which vehicle might have to use a different course to normal at roundabouts?

Mark one answer

- [ ] **A.** Sports car
- [ ] **B.** Van
- [ ] **C.** Estate car
- [ ] **D.** Long vehicle

589 You are going straight ahead at a roundabout. How should you signal?

Mark one answer

- [ ] **A.** Signal right on the approach and then left to leave the roundabout
- [ ] **B.** Signal left as you leave the roundabout
- [ ] **C.** Signal left on the approach to the roundabout and keep the signal on until you leave
- [ ] **D.** Signal left just after you pass the exit before the one you will take

590 You may only enter a box junction when

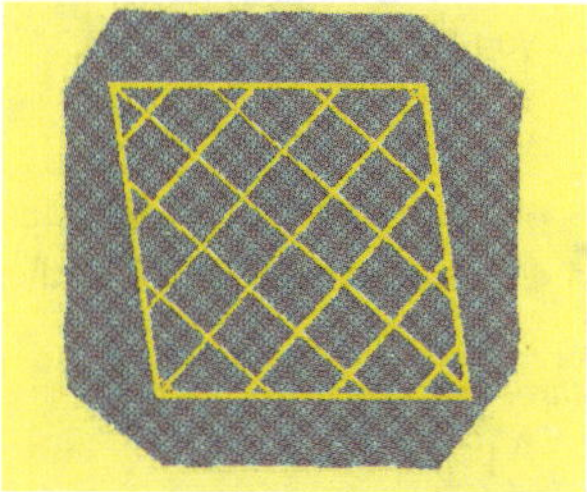

Mark one answer

- [ ] **A.** there are less than two vehicles in front of you
- [ ] **B.** the traffic lights show green
- [ ] **C.** your exit road is clear
- [ ] **D.** you need to turn left

591 **You may wait in a yellow box junction when**

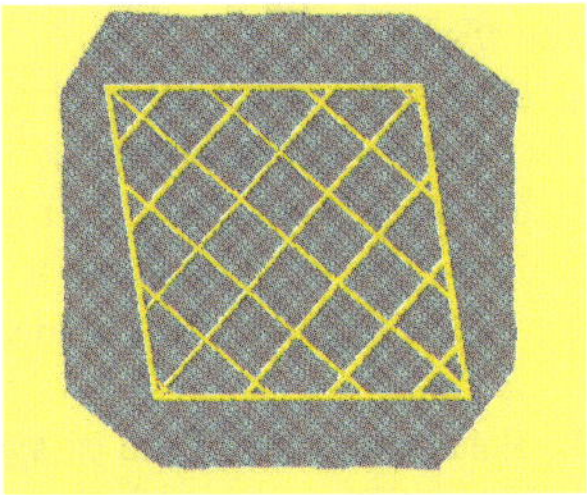

Mark one answer
- [ ] **A.** oncoming traffic is preventing you from turning right
- [ ] **B.** you are in a queue of traffic turning left
- [ ] **C.** you are in a queue of traffic to go ahead
- [ ] **D.** you are on a roundabout

592 **You MUST stop when signalled to do so by which THREE of these?**

Mark three answers
- [ ] **A.** A police officer
- [ ] **B.** A pedestrian
- [ ] **C.** A school crossing patrol
- [ ] **D.** A bus driver
- [ ] **E.** A red traffic light

593 **You will see these markers when approaching**

Mark one answer
- [ ] **A.** the end of a motorway
- [ ] **B.** a concealed level crossing
- [ ] **C.** a concealed speed limit sign
- [ ] **D.** the end of a dual carriageway

594 **Someone is waiting to cross at a zebra crossing. They are standing on the pavement. You should normally**

Mark one answer
- [ ] **A.** go on quickly before they step on to the crossing
- [ ] **B.** stop before you reach the zigzag lines and let them cross
- [ ] **C.** stop, let them cross, wait patiently
- [ ] **D.** ignore them as they are still on the pavement

595 **At toucan crossings, apart from pedestrians you should be aware of**

Mark one answer
- [ ] **A.** emergency vehicles emerging
- [ ] **B.** buses pulling out
- [ ] **C.** trams crossing in front
- [ ] **D.** cyclists riding across

596 Who can use a toucan crossing?

Mark two answers

- [ ] **A.** Trains
- [ ] **B.** Cyclists
- [ ] **C.** Buses
- [ ] **D.** Pedestrians
- [ ] **E.** Trams

597 At a pelican crossing, what does a flashing amber light mean?

Mark one answer

- [ ] **A.** You must not move off until the lights stop flashing
- [ ] **B.** You must give way to pedestrians still on the crossing
- [ ] **C.** You can move off, even if pedestrians are still on the crossing
- [ ] **D.** You must stop because the lights are about to change to red

598 You are waiting at a pelican crossing. The red light changes to flashing amber. This means you must

Mark one answer

- [ ] **A.** wait for pedestrians on the crossing to clear
- [ ] **B.** move off immediately without any hesitation
- [ ] **C.** wait for the green light before moving off
- [ ] **D.** get ready and go when the continuous amber light shows

599 You are travelling on a well-lit road at night in a built-up area. By using dipped headlights you will be able to

Mark one answer

- [ ] **A.** see further along the road
- [ ] **B.** go at a much faster speed
- [ ] **C.** switch to main beam quickly
- [ ] **D.** be easily seen by others

600 When can you park on the left opposite these road markings?

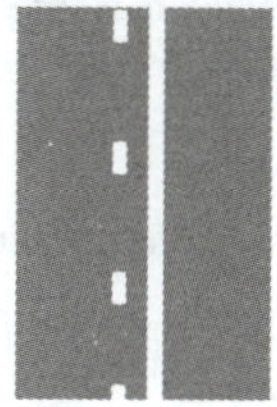

Mark one answer

- [ ] **A.** If the line nearest to you is broken
- [ ] **B.** When there are no yellow lines
- [ ] **C.** To pick up or set down passengers
- [ ] **D.** During daylight hours only

601 You are intending to turn right at a crossroads. An oncoming driver is also turning right. It will normally be safer to

Mark one answer

- [ ] **A.** keep the other vehicle to your RIGHT and turn behind it (offside to offside)
- [ ] **B.** keep the other vehicle to your LEFT and turn in front of it (nearside to nearside)
- [ ] **C.** carry on and turn at the next junction instead
- [ ] **D.** hold back and wait for the other driver to turn first

602 You are on a road that has no traffic signs. There are street lights. What is the speed limit?

Mark one answer

- [ ] **A.** 20mph
- [ ] **B.** 30mph
- [ ] **C.** 40mph
- [ ] **D.** 60mph

603 You are going along a street with parked vehicles on the left-hand side. For which THREE reasons should you keep your speed down?

Mark three answers

- ☐ **A.** So that oncoming traffic can see you more clearly
- ☐ **B.** You may set off car alarms
- ☐ **C.** Vehicles may be pulling out
- ☐ **D.** Drivers' doors may open
- ☐ **E.** Children may run out from between the vehicles

604 You meet an obstruction on your side of the road. You should

Mark one answer

- ☐ **A.** carry on, you have priority
- ☐ **B.** give way to oncoming traffic
- ☐ **C.** wave oncoming vehicles through
- ☐ **D.** accelerate to get past first

605 You are on a two-lane dual carriageway. For which TWO of the following would you use the right-hand lane?

Mark two answers

- ☐ **A.** Turning right
- ☐ **B.** Normal progress
- ☐ **C.** Staying at the minimum allowed speed
- ☐ **D.** Constant high speed
- ☐ **E.** Overtaking slower traffic
- ☐ **F.** Mending punctures

606 Who has priority at an unmarked crossroads?

Mark one answer

- ☐ **A.** The larger vehicle
- ☐ **B.** No one has priority
- ☐ **C.** The faster vehicle
- ☐ **D.** The smaller vehicle

607 What is the nearest you may park to a junction?

Mark one answer **NI**

- ☐ **A.** 10 metres (32 feet)
- ☐ **B.** 12 metres (39 feet)
- ☐ **C.** 15 metres (49 feet)
- ☐ **D.** 20 metres (66 feet)

608 In which THREE places must you NOT park?

Mark three answers **NI**

- ☐ **A.** Near the brow of a hill
- ☐ **B.** At or near a bus stop
- ☐ **C.** Where there is no pavement
- ☐ **D.** Within 10 metres (32 feet) of a junction
- ☐ **E.** On a 40mph road

609 You are waiting at a level crossing. A train has passed but the lights keep flashing. You must

Mark one answer

- ☐ **A.** carry on waiting
- ☐ **B.** phone the signal operator
- ☐ **C.** edge over the stop line and look for trains
- ☐ **D.** park and investigate

610 You park overnight on a road with a 40mph speed limit. You should park

Mark one answer

- [ ] **A.** facing the traffic
- [ ] **B.** with parking lights on
- [ ] **C.** with dipped headlights on
- [ ] **D.** near a street light

611 The dual carriageway you are turning right on to has a very narrow central reservation. What should you do?

Mark one answer

- [ ] **A.** Proceed to the central reservation and wait
- [ ] **B.** Wait until the road is clear in both directions
- [ ] **C.** Stop in the first lane so that other vehicles give way
- [ ] **D.** Emerge slightly to show your intentions

612 At a crossroads there are no signs or road markings. Two vehicles approach. Which has priority?

Mark one answer

- [ ] **A.** Neither of the vehicles
- [ ] **B.** The vehicle travelling the fastest
- [ ] **C.** Oncoming vehicles turning right
- [ ] **D.** Vehicles approaching from the right

613 What does this sign tell you?

Mark one answer

- [ ] **A.** That it is a no-through road
- [ ] **B.** End of traffic calming zone
- [ ] **C.** Free parking zone ends
- [ ] **D.** No waiting zone ends

614 You are entering an area of road works. There is a temporary speed limit displayed. You should

Mark one answer

- [ ] **A.** not exceed the speed limit
- [ ] **B.** obey the limit only during rush hour
- [ ] **C.** ignore the displayed limit
- [ ] **D.** obey the limit except at night

615 You may drive over a footpath

Mark one answer

- [ ] **A.** to overtake slow-moving traffic
- [ ] **B.** when the pavement is very wide
- [ ] **C.** if no pedestrians are near
- [ ] **D.** to get into a property

616 A single-carriageway road has this sign. What is the maximum permitted speed for a car towing a trailer?

Mark one answer

- [ ] A. 30mph
- [ ] B. 40mph
- [ ] C. 50mph
- [ ] D. 60mph

617 You are towing a small caravan on a dual carriageway. You must not exceed

Mark one answer

- [ ] A. 50mph
- [ ] B. 40mph
- [ ] C. 70mph
- [ ] D. 60mph

618 You want to park and you see this sign. On the days and times shown you should

Mark one answer

- [ ] A. park in a bay and not pay
- [ ] B. park on yellow lines and pay
- [ ] C. park on yellow lines and not pay
- [ ] D. park in a bay and pay

619 As a car driver which THREE lanes are you NOT normally allowed to use?

Mark three answers

- [ ] A. Crawler lane
- [ ] B. Bus lane
- [ ] C. Overtaking lane
- [ ] D. Acceleration lane
- [ ] E. Cycle lane
- [ ] F. Tram lane

620 You are driving along a road that has a cycle lane. The lane is marked by a solid white line. This means that during its period of operation

Mark one answer

- [ ] A. the lane may be used for parking your car
- [ ] B. you may drive in that lane at any time
- [ ] C. the lane may be used when necessary
- [ ] D. you must not drive in that lane

621 A cycle lane is marked by a solid white line. You must not drive or park in it

Mark one answer

- [ ] A. at any time
- [ ] B. during the rush hour
- [ ] C. if a cyclist is using it
- [ ] D. during its period of operation

622 While driving, you intend to turn left into a minor road. On the approach you should

Mark one answer

- [ ] A. keep just left of the middle of the road
- [ ] B. keep in the middle of the road
- [ ] C. swing out wide just before turning
- [ ] D. keep well to the left of the road

623 **You are waiting at a level crossing. The red warning lights continue to flash after a train has passed by. What should you do?**

Mark one answer
- [ ] **A.** Get out and investigate
- [ ] **B.** Telephone the signal operator
- [ ] **C.** Continue to wait
- [ ] **D.** Drive across carefully

624 **You are driving over a level crossing. The warning lights come on and a bell rings. What should you do?**

Mark one answer
- [ ] **A.** Get everyone out of the vehicle immediately
- [ ] **B.** Stop and reverse back to clear the crossing
- [ ] **C.** Keep going and clear the crossing
- [ ] **D.** Stop immediately and use your hazard warning lights

625 **You are on a busy main road and find that you are travelling in the wrong direction. What should you do?**

Mark one answer
- [ ] **A.** Turn into a side road on the right and reverse into the main road
- [ ] **B.** Make a U-turn in the main road
- [ ] **C.** Make a 'three-point' turn in the main road
- [ ] **D.** Turn round in a side road

626 **You may remove your seat belt when carrying out a manoeuvre that involves**

Mark one answer
- [ ] **A.** reversing
- [ ] **B.** a hill start
- [ ] **C.** an emergency stop
- [ ] **D.** driving slowly

627 **You must not reverse**

Mark one answer
- [ ] **A.** for longer than necessary
- [ ] **B.** for more than a car's length
- [ ] **C.** into a side road
- [ ] **D.** in a built-up area

628 **You are parked in a busy high street. What is the safest way to turn your vehicle around so you can go the opposite way?**

Mark one answer
- [ ] **A.** Find a quiet side road to turn round in
- [ ] **B.** Drive into a side road and reverse into the main road
- [ ] **C.** Get someone to stop the traffic
- [ ] **D.** Do a U-turn

629 When you are NOT sure that it is safe to reverse your vehicle you should

Mark one answer
- [ ] A. use your horn
- [ ] B. rev your engine
- [ ] C. get out and check
- [ ] D. reverse slowly

630 When may you reverse from a side road into a main road?

Mark one answer
- [ ] A. Only if both roads are clear of traffic
- [ ] B. Not at any time
- [ ] C. At any time
- [ ] D. Only if the main road is clear of traffic

631 You want to turn right at a box junction. There is oncoming traffic. You should

Mark one answer
- [ ] A. wait in the box junction if your exit is clear
- [ ] B. wait before the junction until it is clear of all traffic
- [ ] C. drive on, you cannot turn right at a box junction
- [ ] D. drive slowly into the box junction when signalled by oncoming traffic

632 You are reversing your vehicle into a side road. When would the greatest hazard to passing traffic occur?

Mark one answer
- [ ] A. After you've completed the manoeuvre
- [ ] B. Just before you actually begin to manoeuvre
- [ ] C. After you've entered the side road
- [ ] D. When the front of your vehicle swings out

633 You are driving on a road that has a cycle lane. The lane is marked by a broken white line. This means that

Mark two answers
- [ ] A. you should not drive in the lane unless it is unavoidable
- [ ] B. you should not park in the lane unless it is unavoidable
- [ ] C. you can drive in the lane at any time
- [ ] D. the lane must be used by motorcyclists in heavy traffic

634 Where is the safest place to park your vehicle at night?

Mark one answer
- [ ] A. In a garage
- [ ] B. On a busy road
- [ ] C. In a quiet car park
- [ ] D. Near a red route

635 To help keep your vehicle secure at night where should you park?

Mark one answer
- [ ] A. Near a police station
- [ ] B. In a quiet road
- [ ] C. On a red route
- [ ] D. In a well-lit area

636 **You are in the right-hand lane of a dual carriageway. You see signs showing that the right-hand lane is closed 800 yards ahead. You should**

Mark one answer

- [ ] **A.** keep in that lane until you reach the queue
- [ ] **B.** move to the left immediately
- [ ] **C.** wait and see which lane is moving faster
- [ ] **D.** move to the left in good time

637 **You are driving on an urban clearway. You may stop only to**

Mark one answer

- [ ] **A.** set down and pick up passengers
- [ ] **B.** use a mobile telephone
- [ ] **C.** ask for directions
- [ ] **D.** load or unload goods

638 **You are looking for somewhere to park your vehicle. The area is full EXCEPT for spaces marked 'disabled use'. You can**

Mark one answer

- [ ] **A.** use these spaces when elsewhere is full
- [ ] **B.** park if you stay with your vehicle
- [ ] **C.** use these spaces, disabled or not
- [ ] **D.** not park there unless permitted

639 **Your vehicle is parked on the road at night. When must you use sidelights?**

Mark one answer

- [ ] **A.** Where there are continuous white lines in the middle of the road
- [ ] **B.** Where the speed limit exceeds 30mph
- [ ] **C.** Where you are facing oncoming traffic
- [ ] **D.** Where you are near a bus stop

640 **On which THREE occasions MUST you stop your vehicle?**

Mark three answers

- [ ] **A.** When in an accident where damage or injury is caused
- [ ] **B.** At a red traffic light
- [ ] **C.** When signalled to do so by a police officer
- [ ] **D.** At a junction with double broken white lines
- [ ] **E.** At a pelican crossing when the amber light is flashing and no pedestrians are crossing

641 **You are on a road that is only wide enough for one vehicle. There is a car coming towards you. What should you do?**

Mark one answer

- [ ] **A.** Pull into a passing place on your right
- [ ] **B.** Force the other driver to reverse
- [ ] **C.** Pull into a passing place if your vehicle is wider
- [ ] **D.** Pull into a passing place on your left

642 What MUST you have to park in a disabled space?

Mark one answer

- [ ] **A.** An orange or blue badge
- [ ] **B.** A wheelchair
- [ ] **C.** An advanced driver certificate
- [ ] **D.** A modified vehicle

643 You are driving at night with full beam headlights on. A vehicle is overtaking you. You should dip your lights

Mark one answer

- [ ] **A.** some time after the vehicle has passed you
- [ ] **B.** before the vehicle starts to pass you
- [ ] **C.** only if the other driver dips their headlights
- [ ] **D.** as soon as the vehicle passes you

644 When may you drive a motor car in this bus lane?

Mark one answer

- [ ] **A.** Outside its hours of operation
- [ ] **B.** To get to the front of a traffic queue
- [ ] **C.** You may not use it at any time
- [ ] **D.** To overtake slow-moving traffic

645 Signals are normally given by direction indicators and

Mark one answer

- [ ] **A.** brake lights
- [ ] **B.** sidelights
- [ ] **C.** fog lights
- [ ] **D.** interior lights

646 You MUST obey signs giving orders. These signs are mostly in

Mark one answer

- [ ] **A.** green rectangles
- [ ] **B.** red triangles
- [ ] **C.** blue rectangles
- [ ] **D.** red circles

647 Traffic signs giving orders are generally which shape?

Mark one answer

- [ ] **A.**

- [ ] **B.**

- [ ] **C.**

- [ ] **D.**

648 Which type of sign tells you NOT to do something?

Mark one answer

- [ ] **A.**

- [ ] **B.**

- [ ] **C.**

- [ ] **D.**

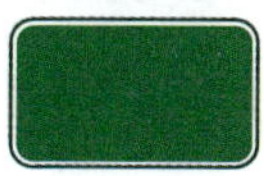

649 What does this sign mean?

Mark one answer

- [ ] **A.** Maximum speed limit with traffic calming
- [ ] **B.** Minimum speed limit with traffic calming
- [ ] **C.** '20 cars only' parking zone
- [ ] **D.** Only 20 cars allowed at any one time

650 Which sign means no motor vehicles are allowed?

Mark one answer

- [ ] **A.**

- [ ] **B.**

- [ ] **C.**

- [ ] **D.**

651 Which of these signs means no motor vehicles?

Mark one answer

- [ ] **A.**

- [ ] **B.**

- [ ] **C.**

- [ ] **D.**

652 What does this sign mean?

Mark one answer

- [ ] **A.** New speed limit 20mph
- [ ] **B.** No vehicles over 30 tonnes
- [ ] **C.** Minimum speed limit 30mph
- [ ] **D.** End of 20mph zone

653 What does this sign mean?

Mark one answer

- [ ] **A.** No overtaking
- [ ] **B.** No motor vehicles
- [ ] **C.** Clearway (no stopping)
- [ ] **D.** Cars and motorcycles only

654 What does this sign mean?

Mark one answer

- [ ] **A.** No parking
- [ ] **B.** No road markings
- [ ] **C.** No through road
- [ ] **D.** No entry

655 What does this sign mean?

Mark one answer

- [ ] **A.** Bend to the right
- [ ] **B.** Road on the right closed
- [ ] **C.** No traffic from the right
- [ ] **D.** No right turn

656 Which sign means 'no entry'?

Mark one answer

- [ ] **A.**

- [ ] **B.**

- [ ] **C.**

- [ ] **D.**

657 What does this sign mean?

Mark one answer

- [ ] **A.** Route for trams only
- [ ] **B.** Route for buses only
- [ ] **C.** Parking for buses only
- [ ] **D.** Parking for trams only

658 Which type of vehicle does this sign apply to?

Mark one answer
- [ ] **A.** Wide vehicles
- [ ] **B.** Long vehicles
- [ ] **C.** High vehicles
- [ ] **D.** Heavy vehicles

659 Which sign means NO motor vehicles allowed?

Mark one answer

- [ ] **A.**

- [ ] **B.**

- [ ] **C.**

- [ ] **D.**

660 What does this sign mean?

Mark one answer
- [ ] **A.** You have priority
- [ ] **B.** No motor vehicles
- [ ] **C.** Two-way traffic
- [ ] **D.** No overtaking

661 What does this sign mean?

Mark one answer
- [ ] **A.** Keep in one lane
- [ ] **B.** Give way to oncoming traffic
- [ ] **C.** Do not overtake
- [ ] **D.** Form two lanes

662 Which sign means no overtaking?

Mark one answer

- [ ] **A.**

- [ ] **B.**

- [ ] **C.**

- [ ] **D.**

663 What does this sign mean?

Mark one answer
- [ ] **A.** Waiting restrictions apply
- [ ] **B.** Waiting permitted
- [ ] **C.** National speed limit applies
- [ ] **D.** Clearway (no stopping)

664 What does this sign mean?

Mark one answer

- [ ] **A.** End of restricted speed area
- [ ] **B.** End of restricted parking area
- [ ] **C.** End of clearway
- [ ] **D.** End of cycle route

665 Which sign means 'no stopping'?

Mark one answer

- [ ] **A.**

- [ ] **B.**

- [ ] **C.**

- [ ] **D.**

666 What does this sign mean?

Mark one answer

- [ ] **A.** Roundabout
- [ ] **B.** Crossroads
- [ ] **C.** No stopping
- [ ] **D.** No entry

667 You see this sign ahead. It means

Mark one answer

- [ ] **A.** national speed limit applies
- [ ] **B.** waiting restrictions apply
- [ ] **C.** no stopping
- [ ] **D.** no entry

668 What does this sign mean?

Mark one answer

- [ ] **A.** Distance to parking place ahead
- [ ] **B.** Distance to public telephone ahead
- [ ] **C.** Distance to public house ahead
- [ ] **D.** Distance to passing place ahead

669 What does this sign mean?

Mark one answer

- [ ] **A.** Vehicles may not park on the verge or footway
- [ ] **B.** Vehicles may park on the left-hand side of the road only
- [ ] **C.** Vehicles may park fully on the verge or footway
- [ ] **D.** Vehicles may park on the right-hand side of the road only

670 What does this traffic sign mean?

Mark one answer

- [ ] **A.** No overtaking allowed
- [ ] **B.** Give priority to oncoming traffic
- [ ] **C.** Two-way traffic
- [ ] **D.** One-way traffic only

671 What is the meaning of this traffic sign?

Mark one answer

- [ ] **A.** End of two-way road
- [ ] **B.** Give priority to vehicles coming towards you
- [ ] **C.** You have priority over vehicles coming towards you
- [ ] **D.** Bus lane ahead

672 What MUST you do when you see this sign?

Mark one answer

- [ ] **A.** Stop, only if traffic is approaching
- [ ] **B.** Stop, even if the road is clear
- [ ] **C.** Stop, only if children are waiting to cross
- [ ] **D.** Stop, only if a red light is showing

673 What does this sign mean?

Mark one answer

- [ ] **A.** No overtaking
- [ ] **B.** You are entering a one-way street
- [ ] **C.** Two-way traffic ahead
- [ ] **D.** You have priority over vehicles from the opposite direction

674 What shape is a STOP sign at a junction?

Mark one answer

- [ ] **A.**

- [ ] **B.**

- [ ] **C.**

- [ ] **D.**

675 At a junction you see this sign partly covered by snow. What does it mean?

Mark one answer

- [ ] **A.** Crossroads
- [ ] **B.** Give way
- [ ] **C.** Stop
- [ ] **D.** Turn right

676 Which shape is used for a 'give way' sign?

Mark one answer

- [ ] A.

- [ ] B.

- [ ] C.

- [ ] D.

677 What does this sign mean?

Mark one answer

- [ ] A. Service area 30 miles ahead
- [ ] B. Maximum speed 30mph
- [ ] C. Minimum speed 30mph
- [ ] D. Lay-by 30 miles ahead

678 Which of these signs means turn left ahead?

Mark one answer

- [ ] A.

- [ ] B.

- [ ] C.

- [ ] D.

679 What does this sign mean?

Mark one answer

- [ ] A. Buses turning
- [ ] B. Ring road
- [ ] C. Mini-roundabout
- [ ] D. Keep right

680 What does this sign mean?

Mark one answer

- [ ] A. Give way to oncoming vehicles
- [ ] B. Approaching traffic passes you on both sides
- [ ] C. Turn off at the next available junction
- [ ] D. Pass either side to get to the same destination

681 What does this sign mean?

Mark one answer

- [ ] A. Route for trams
- [ ] B. Give way to trams
- [ ] C. Route for buses
- [ ] D. Give way to buses

682 What does a circular traffic sign with a blue background do?

Mark one answer

- [ ] **A.** Give warning of a motorway ahead
- [ ] **B.** Give directions to a car park
- [ ] **C.** Give motorway information
- [ ] **D.** Give an instruction

683 Which of these signs means that you are entering a one-way street?

Mark one answer

- [ ] **A.**

- [ ] **B.**

- [ ] **C.**

- [ ] **D.**

684 Where would you see a contraflow bus and cycle lane?

Mark one answer

- [ ] **A.** On a dual carriageway
- [ ] **B.** On a roundabout
- [ ] **C.** On an urban motorway
- [ ] **D.** On a one-way street

685 What does this sign mean?

Mark one answer

- [ ] **A.** Bus station on the right
- [ ] **B.** Contraflow bus lane
- [ ] **C.** With-flow bus lane
- [ ] **D.** Give way to buses

686 What does this sign mean?

Mark one answer

- [ ] **A.** With-flow bus and cycle lane
- [ ] **B.** Contraflow bus and cycle lane
- [ ] **C.** No buses and cycles allowed
- [ ] **D.** No waiting for buses and cycles

687 What does a sign with a brown background show?

Mark one answer

- [ ] **A.** Tourist directions
- [ ] **B.** Primary roads
- [ ] **C.** Motorway routes
- [ ] **D.** Minor routes

688 This sign means

Mark one answer

- [ ] A. tourist attraction
- [ ] B. beware of trains
- [ ] C. level crossing
- [ ] D. beware of trams

689 What are triangular signs for?

Mark one answer

- [ ] A. To give warnings
- [ ] B. To give information
- [ ] C. To give orders
- [ ] D. To give directions

690 What does this sign mean?

Mark one answer

- [ ] A. Turn left ahead
- [ ] B. T-junction
- [ ] C. No through road
- [ ] D. Give way

691 What does this sign mean?

Mark one answer

- [ ] A. Multi-exit roundabout
- [ ] B. Risk of ice
- [ ] C. Six roads converge
- [ ] D. Place of historical interest

692 What does this sign mean?

Mark one answer

- [ ] A. Crossroads
- [ ] B. Level crossing with gate
- [ ] C. Level crossing without gate
- [ ] D. Ahead only

693 What does this sign mean?

Mark one answer

- [ ] A. Ring road
- [ ] B. Mini-roundabout
- [ ] C. No vehicles
- [ ] D. Roundabout

694 Which FOUR of these would be indicated by a triangular road sign?

Mark four answers

- [ ] **A.** Road narrows
- [ ] **B.** Ahead only
- [ ] **C.** Low bridge
- [ ] **D.** Minimum speed
- [ ] **E.** Children crossing
- [ ] **F.** T-junction

695 What does this sign mean?

Mark one answer

- [ ] **A.** Cyclists must dismount
- [ ] **B.** Cycles are not allowed
- [ ] **C.** Cycle route ahead
- [ ] **D.** Cycle in single file

696 Which sign means that pedestrians may be walking along the road?

Mark one answer

- [ ] **A.**

- [ ] **B.**

- [ ] **C.**

- [ ] **D.**

697 Which of these signs warn you of a pedestrian crossing?

Mark one answer

- [ ] **A.**

- [ ] **B.**

- [ ] **C.**

- [ ] **D.**

698 What does this sign mean?

Mark one answer

- [ ] **A.** No footpath ahead
- [ ] **B.** Pedestrians only ahead
- [ ] **C.** Pedestrian crossing ahead
- [ ] **D.** School crossing ahead

699 What does this sign mean?

Mark one answer

- [ ] **A.** School crossing patrol
- [ ] **B.** No pedestrians allowed
- [ ] **C.** Pedestrian zone – no vehicles
- [ ] **D.** Pedestrian crossing ahead

700 Which of these signs means there is a double bend ahead?

Mark one answer

☐ A.

☐ B.

☐ C.

☐ D.

701 What does this sign mean?

Mark one answer

☐ **A.** Wait at the barriers
☐ **B.** Wait at the crossroads
☐ **C.** Give way to trams
☐ **D.** Give way to farm vehicles

702 What does this sign mean?

Mark one answer

☐ **A.** Humpback bridge
☐ **B.** Humps in the road
☐ **C.** Entrance to tunnel
☐ **D.** Soft verges

703 What does this sign mean?

Mark one answer

☐ **A.** Low bridge ahead
☐ **B.** Tunnel ahead
☐ **C.** Ancient monument ahead
☐ **D.** Accident black spot ahead

704 What does this sign mean?

Mark one answer

☐ **A.** Two-way traffic straight ahead
☐ **B.** Two-way traffic crosses a one-way road
☐ **C.** Two-way traffic over a bridge
☐ **D.** Two-way traffic crosses a two-way road

705 Which sign means 'two-way traffic crosses a one-way road'?

Mark one answer

☐ A.

☐ B.

☐ C.

☐ D.

706 Which of these signs means the end of a dual carriageway?

Mark one answer

- [ ] **A.**

- [ ] **B.**

- [ ] **C.**

- [ ] **D.**

707 What does this sign mean?

Mark one answer

- [ ] **A.** End of dual carriageway
- [ ] **B.** Tall bridge
- [ ] **C.** Road narrows
- [ ] **D.** End of narrow bridge

708 What does this sign mean?

Mark one answer

- [ ] **A.** Two-way traffic ahead across a one-way road
- [ ] **B.** Traffic approaching you has priority
- [ ] **C.** Two-way traffic straight ahead
- [ ] **D.** Motorway contraflow system ahead

709 What does this sign mean?

Mark one answer

- [ ] **A.** Crosswinds
- [ ] **B.** Road noise
- [ ] **C.** Airport
- [ ] **D.** Adverse camber

710 What does this traffic sign mean?

Mark one answer

- [ ] **A.** Slippery road ahead
- [ ] **B.** Tyres liable to punctures ahead
- [ ] **C.** Danger ahead
- [ ] **D.** Service area ahead

711 You are about to overtake when you see this sign. You should

Mark one answer

- [ ] **A.** overtake the other driver as quickly as possible
- [ ] **B.** move to the right to get a better view
- [ ] **C.** switch your headlights on before overtaking
- [ ] **D.** hold back until you can see clearly ahead

712 What does this sign mean?

Mark one answer
- [ ] **A.** Level crossing with gate or barrier
- [ ] **B.** Gated road ahead
- [ ] **C.** Level crossing without gate or barrier
- [ ] **D.** Cattle grid ahead

713 What does this sign mean?

Mark one answer
- [ ] **A.** No trams ahead
- [ ] **B.** Oncoming trams
- [ ] **C.** Trams crossing ahead
- [ ] **D.** Trams only

714 What does this sign mean?

Mark one answer
- [ ] **A.** Adverse camber
- [ ] **B.** Steep hill downwards
- [ ] **C.** Uneven road
- [ ] **D.** Steep hill upwards

715 What does this sign mean?

Mark one answer
- [ ] **A.** Uneven road surface
- [ ] **B.** Bridge over the road
- [ ] **C.** Road ahead ends
- [ ] **D.** Water across the road

716 What does this sign mean?

Mark one answer
- [ ] **A.** Humpback bridge
- [ ] **B.** Traffic calming hump
- [ ] **C.** Low bridge
- [ ] **D.** Uneven road

717 What does this sign mean?

Mark one answer
- [ ] **A.** Turn left for parking area
- [ ] **B.** No through road on the left
- [ ] **C.** No entry for traffic turning left
- [ ] **D.** Turn left for ferry terminal

718 What does this sign mean?

Mark one answer
- ☐ **A.** T-junction
- ☐ **B.** No through road
- ☐ **C.** Telephone box ahead
- ☐ **D.** Toilet ahead

719 Which sign means 'no through road'?

Mark one answer

☐ **A.**

☐ **B.**

☐ **C.**

☐ **D.**

720 Which of the following signs informs you that you are coming to a 'no through road'?

Mark one answer

☐ **A.**

☐ **B.**

☐ **C.**

☐ **D.**

721 What does this sign mean?

Mark one answer
- ☐ **A.** Direction to park-and-ride car park
- ☐ **B.** No parking for buses or coaches
- ☐ **C.** Directions to bus and coach park
- ☐ **D.** Parking area for cars and coaches

722 You are driving through a tunnel and you see this sign. What does it mean?

Mark one answer
- ☐ **A.** Direction to emergency pedestrian exit
- ☐ **B.** Beware of pedestrians, no footpath ahead
- ☐ **C.** No access for pedestrians
- ☐ **D.** Beware of pedestrians crossing ahead

723 Which is the sign for a ring road?

Mark one answer

☐ **A.**

☐ **B.**

☐ **C.**

☐ **D.**

724 **At a railway level crossing the red light signal continues to flash after a train has gone by. What should you do?**

Mark one answer
- [ ] **A.** Phone the signal operator
- [ ] **B.** Alert drivers behind you
- [ ] **C.** Wait
- [ ] **D.** Proceed with caution

725 **At a junction you see this signal. It means**

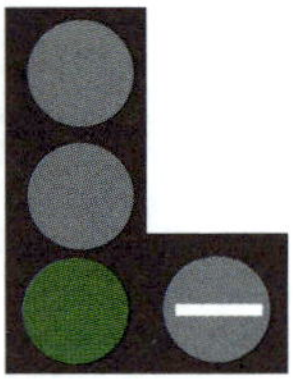

Mark one answer
- [ ] **A.** cars must stop
- [ ] **B.** trams must stop
- [ ] **C.** both trams and cars must stop
- [ ] **D.** both trams and cars can continue

726 **What does this sign mean?**

Mark one answer
- [ ] **A.** The right-hand lane ahead is narrow
- [ ] **B.** Right-hand lane for buses only
- [ ] **C.** Right-hand lane for turning right
- [ ] **D.** The right-hand lane is closed

727 **What does this sign mean?**

Mark one answer
- [ ] **A.** Change to the left lane
- [ ] **B.** Leave at the next exit
- [ ] **C.** Contraflow system
- [ ] **D.** One-way street

728 **What does this sign mean?**

Mark one answer
- [ ] **A.** Leave motorway at next exit
- [ ] **B.** Lane for heavy and slow vehicles
- [ ] **C.** All lorries use the hard shoulder
- [ ] **D.** Rest area for lorries

729 You are approaching a red traffic light. The signal will change from red to

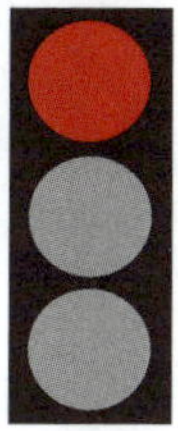

Mark one answer

- ☐ **A.** red and amber, then green
- ☐ **B.** green, then amber
- ☐ **C.** amber, then green
- ☐ **D.** green and amber, then green

730 A red traffic light means

Mark one answer

- ☐ **A.** you should stop unless turning left
- ☐ **B.** stop, if you are able to brake safely
- ☐ **C.** you must stop and wait behind the stop line
- ☐ **D.** proceed with caution

731 At traffic lights, amber on its own means

Mark one answer

- ☐ **A.** prepare to go
- ☐ **B.** go if the way is clear
- ☐ **C.** go if no pedestrians are crossing
- ☐ **D.** stop at the stop line

732 You are approaching traffic lights. Red and amber are showing. This means

Mark one answer

- ☐ **A.** pass the lights if the road is clear
- ☐ **B.** there is a fault with the lights – take care
- ☐ **C.** wait for the green light before you cross the stop line
- ☐ **D.** the lights are about to change to red

733 You are at a junction controlled by traffic lights. When should you NOT proceed at green?

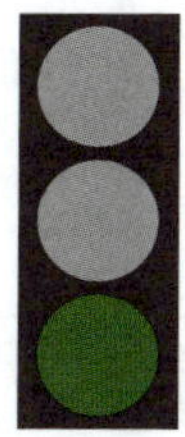

Mark one answer

- ☐ **A.** When pedestrians are waiting to cross
- ☐ **B.** When your exit from the junction is blocked
- ☐ **C.** When you think the lights may be about to change
- ☐ **D.** When you intend to turn right

734 You are in the left-hand lane at traffic lights. You are waiting to turn left. At which of these traffic lights must you NOT move on?

Mark one answer

☐ **A.**

☐ **B.**

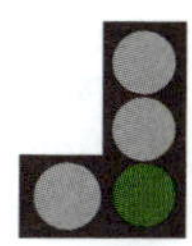

☐ **C.**

☐ **D.**

735 What does this sign mean?

Mark one answer

- [ ] **A.** Traffic lights out of order
- [ ] **B.** Amber signal out of order
- [ ] **C.** Temporary traffic lights ahead
- [ ] **D.** New traffic lights ahead

736 When traffic lights are out of order, who has priority?

Mark one answer

- [ ] **A.** Traffic going straight on
- [ ] **B.** Traffic turning right
- [ ] **C.** Nobody
- [ ] **D.** Traffic turning left

737 These flashing red lights mean STOP. In which THREE of the following places could you find them?

Mark three answers

- [ ] **A.** Pelican crossings
- [ ] **B.** Lifting bridges
- [ ] **C.** Zebra crossings
- [ ] **D.** Level crossings
- [ ] **E.** Motorway exits
- [ ] **F.** Fire stations

738 What do these zigzag lines at pedestrian crossings mean?

Mark one answer

- [ ] **A.** No parking at any time
- [ ] **B.** Parking allowed only for a short time
- [ ] **C.** Slow down to 20mph
- [ ] **D.** Sounding horns is not allowed

739 When may you cross a double solid white line in the middle of the road?

Mark one answer

- [ ] **A.** To pass traffic that is queuing back at a junction
- [ ] **B.** To pass a car signalling to turn left ahead
- [ ] **C.** To pass a road maintenance vehicle travelling at 10mph or less
- [ ] **D.** To pass a vehicle that is towing a trailer

740 What does this road marking mean?

Mark one answer
- [ ] **A.** Do not cross the line
- [ ] **B.** No stopping allowed
- [ ] **C.** You are approaching a hazard
- [ ] **D.** No overtaking allowed

741 This marking appears on the road just before a

Mark one answer
- [ ] **A.** 'no entry' sign
- [ ] **B.** 'give way' sign
- [ ] **C.** 'stop' sign
- [ ] **D.** 'no through road' sign

742 Where would you see this road marking?

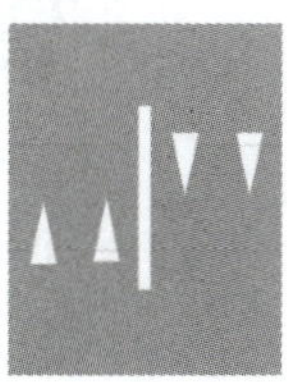

Mark one answer
- [ ] **A.** At traffic lights
- [ ] **B.** On road humps
- [ ] **C.** Near a level crossing
- [ ] **D.** At a box junction

743 Which is a hazard warning line?

Mark one answer
- [ ] **A.**

- [ ] **B.**

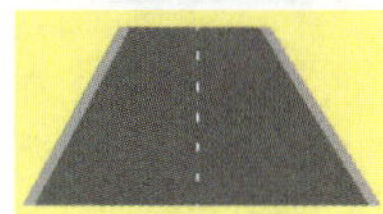

- [ ] **C.**

- [ ] **D.**

744 At this junction there is a stop sign with a solid white line on the road surface. Why is there a stop sign here?

Mark one answer
- [ ] **A.** Speed on the major road is de-restricted
- [ ] **B.** It is a busy junction
- [ ] **C.** Visibility along the major road is restricted
- [ ] **D.** There are hazard warning lines in the centre of the road

745 **You see this line across the road at the entrance to a roundabout. What does it mean?**

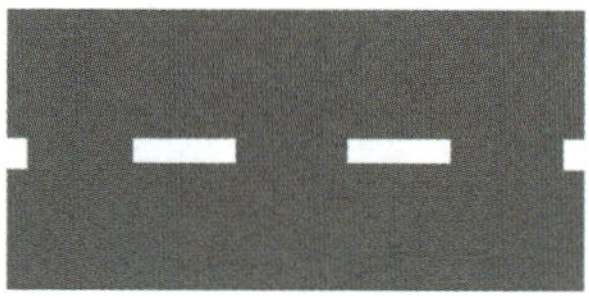

Mark one answer

- [ ] **A.** Give way to traffic from the right
- [ ] **B.** Traffic from the left has right of way
- [ ] **C.** You have right of way
- [ ] **D.** Stop at the line

746 **Where would you find these road markings?**

Mark one answer

- [ ] **A.** At a railway crossing
- [ ] **B.** At a junction
- [ ] **C.** On a motorway
- [ ] **D.** On a pedestrian crossing

747 **How will a police officer in a patrol vehicle normally get you to stop?**

Mark one answer

- [ ] **A.** Flash the headlights, indicate left and point to the left
- [ ] **B.** Wait until you stop, then approach you
- [ ] **C.** Use the siren, overtake, cut in front and stop
- [ ] **D.** Pull alongside you, use the siren and wave you to stop

748 **There is a police car following you. The police officer flashes the headlights and points to the left. What should you do?**

Mark one answer

- [ ] **A.** Turn left at the next junction
- [ ] **B.** Pull up on the left
- [ ] **C.** Stop immediately
- [ ] **D.** Move over to the left

749 **You approach a junction. The traffic lights are not working. A police officer gives this signal. You should**

Mark one answer

- [ ] **A.** turn left only
- [ ] **B.** turn right only
- [ ] **C.** stop level with the officer's arm
- [ ] **D.** stop at the stop line

750 **The driver of the car in front is giving this arm signal. What does it mean?**

Mark one answer

- [ ] **A.** The driver is slowing down
- [ ] **B.** The driver intends to turn right
- [ ] **C.** The driver wishes to overtake
- [ ] **D.** The driver intends to turn left

751 Where would you see these road markings?

Mark one answer

- [ ] **A.** At a level crossing
- [ ] **B.** On a motorway slip road
- [ ] **C.** At a pedestrian crossing
- [ ] **D.** On a single-track road

752 When may you NOT overtake on the left?

Mark one answer

- [ ] **A.** On a free-flowing motorway or dual carriageway
- [ ] **B.** When the traffic is moving slowly in queues
- [ ] **C.** On a one-way street
- [ ] **D.** When the car in front is signalling to turn right

753 What does this motorway sign mean?

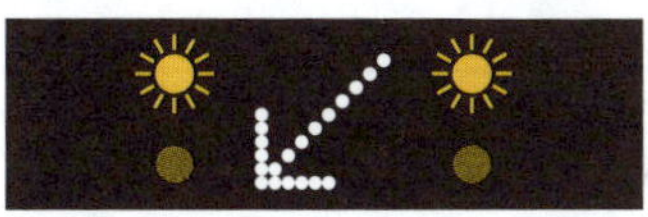

Mark one answer

- [ ] **A.** Change to the lane on your left
- [ ] **B.** Leave the motorway at the next exit
- [ ] **C.** Change to the opposite carriageway
- [ ] **D.** Pull up on the hard shoulder

754 What does this motorway sign mean?

Mark one answer

- [ ] **A.** Temporary minimum speed 50mph
- [ ] **B.** No services for 50 miles
- [ ] **C.** Obstruction 50 metres (164 feet) ahead
- [ ] **D.** Temporary maximum speed 50mph

755 What does this sign mean?

Mark one answer

- [ ] **A.** Through traffic to use left lane
- [ ] **B.** Right-hand lane T-junction only
- [ ] **C.** Right-hand lane closed ahead
- [ ] **D.** 11 tonne weight limit

756 On a motorway this sign means

Mark one answer

- [ ] **A.** move over on to the hard shoulder
- [ ] **B.** overtaking on the left only
- [ ] **C.** leave the motorway at the next exit
- [ ] **D.** move to the lane on your left

757 What does '25' mean on this motorway sign?

Mark one answer

- [ ] **A.** The distance to the nearest town
- [ ] **B.** The route number of the road
- [ ] **C.** The number of the next junction
- [ ] **D.** The speed limit on the slip road

758 The right-hand lane of a three-lane motorway is

Mark one answer

- [ ] **A.** for lorries only
- [ ] **B.** an overtaking lane
- [ ] **C.** the right-turn lane
- [ ] **D.** an acceleration lane

759 Where can you find reflective amber studs on a motorway?

Mark one answer

- [ ] **A.** Separating the slip road from the motorway
- [ ] **B.** On the left-hand edge of the road
- [ ] **C.** On the right-hand edge of the road
- [ ] **D.** Separating the lanes

760 Where on a motorway would you find green reflective studs?

Mark one answer

- [ ] **A.** Separating driving lanes
- [ ] **B.** Between the hard shoulder and the carriageway
- [ ] **C.** At slip road entrances and exits
- [ ] **D.** Between the carriageway and the central reservation

761 You are travelling along a motorway. You see this sign. You should

Mark one answer

- [ ] **A.** leave the motorway at the next exit
- [ ] **B.** turn left immediately
- [ ] **C.** change lane
- [ ] **D.** move on to the hard shoulder

762 What does this sign mean?

Mark one answer

- [ ] **A.** No motor vehicles
- [ ] **B.** End of motorway
- [ ] **C.** No through road
- [ ] **D.** End of bus lane

763 Which of these signs means that the national speed limit applies?

Mark one answer

☐ **A.**

☐ **B.**

☐ **C.**

☐ **D.**

764 What is the maximum speed on a single carriageway road?

Mark one answer

☐ **A.** 50mph
☐ **B.** 60mph
☐ **C.** 40mph
☐ **D.** 70mph

765 What does this sign mean?

Mark one answer

☐ **A.** End of motorway
☐ **B.** End of restriction
☐ **C.** Lane ends ahead
☐ **D.** Free recovery ends

766 This sign is advising you to

Mark one answer

☐ **A.** follow the route diversion
☐ **B.** follow the signs to the picnic area
☐ **C.** give way to pedestrians
☐ **D.** give way to cyclists

767 Why would this temporary speed limit sign be shown?

Mark one answer

☐ **A.** To warn of the end of the motorway
☐ **B.** To warn you of a low bridge
☐ **C.** To warn you of a junction ahead
☐ **D.** To warn of road works ahead

768 This traffic sign means there is

Mark one answer

☐ **A.** a compulsory maximum speed limit
☐ **B.** an advisory maximum speed limit
☐ **C.** a compulsory minimum speed limit
☐ **D.** an advised separation distance

769 **You see this sign at a crossroads. You should**

Mark one answer

- [ ] **A.** maintain the same speed
- [ ] **B.** carry on with great care
- [ ] **C.** find another route
- [ ] **D.** telephone the police

770 **You are signalling to turn right in busy traffic. How would you confirm your intention safely?**

Mark one answer

- [ ] **A.** Sound the horn
- [ ] **B.** Give an arm signal
- [ ] **C.** Flash your headlights
- [ ] **D.** Position over the centre line

771 **What does this sign mean?**

Mark one answer

- [ ] **A.** Motorcycles only
- [ ] **B.** No cars
- [ ] **C.** Cars only
- [ ] **D.** No motorcycles

772 **You are on a motorway. You see this sign on a lorry that has stopped in the right-hand lane. You should**

Mark one answer

- [ ] **A.** move into the right-hand lane
- [ ] **B.** stop behind the flashing lights
- [ ] **C.** pass the lorry on the left
- [ ] **D.** leave the motorway at the next exit

773 **You are on a motorway. Red flashing lights appear above your lane only. What should you do?**

Mark one answer

- [ ] **A.** Continue in that lane and look for further information
- [ ] **B.** Move into another lane in good time
- [ ] **C.** Pull on to the hard shoulder
- [ ] **D.** Stop and wait for an instruction to proceed

774 **A red traffic light means**

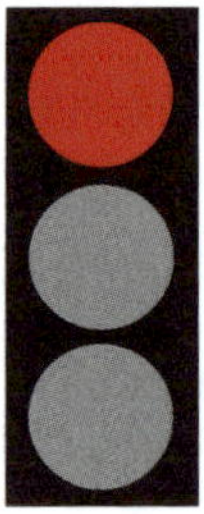

Mark one answer

- [ ] **A.** you must stop behind the white stop line
- [ ] **B.** you may go straight on if there is no other traffic
- [ ] **C.** you may turn left if it is safe to do so
- [ ] **D.** you must slow down and prepare to stop if traffic has started to cross

775 The driver of this car is giving an arm signal. What are they about to do?

Mark one answer

- [ ] **A.** Turn to the right
- [ ] **B.** Turn to the left
- [ ] **C.** Go straight ahead
- [ ] **D.** Let pedestrians cross

776 Which arm signal tells you that the car you are following is going to turn left?

Mark one answer

- [ ] **A.**

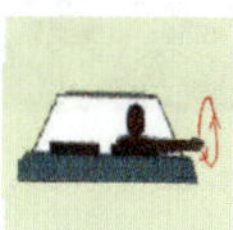

- [ ] **B.**

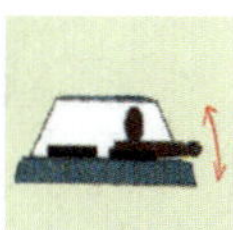

- [ ] **C.**

- [ ] **D.**

777 When may you sound the horn?

Mark one answer

- [ ] **A.** To give you right of way
- [ ] **B.** To attract a friend's attention
- [ ] **C.** To warn others of your presence
- [ ] **D.** To make slower drivers move over

778 You must not use your horn when you are stationary

Mark one answer

- [ ] **A.** unless a moving vehicle may cause you danger
- [ ] **B.** at any time whatsoever
- [ ] **C.** unless it is used only briefly
- [ ] **D.** except for signalling that you have just arrived

779 What does this sign mean?

Mark one answer

- [ ] **A.** You can park on the days and times shown
- [ ] **B.** No parking on the days and times shown
- [ ] **C.** No parking at all from Monday to Friday
- [ ] **D.** End of the urban clearway restrictions

780 What does this sign mean?

Mark one answer

- [ ] **A.** Quayside or river bank
- [ ] **B.** Steep hill downwards
- [ ] **C.** Uneven road surface
- [ ] **D.** Road liable to flooding

781 You see this amber traffic light ahead. Which light or lights will come on next?

Mark one answer
- [ ] A. Red alone
- [ ] B. Red and amber together
- [ ] C. Green and amber together
- [ ] D. Green alone

782 This broken white line painted in the centre of the road means

Mark one answer
- [ ] A. oncoming vehicles have priority over you
- [ ] B. you should give priority to oncoming vehicles
- [ ] C. there is a hazard ahead of you
- [ ] D. the area is a national speed limit zone

783 Which sign means you have priority over oncoming vehicles?

Mark one answer
- [ ] A.

- [ ] B.

- [ ] C.

- [ ] D.

784 You see this signal overhead on the motorway. What does it mean?

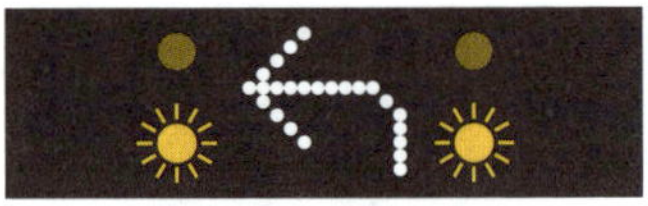

Mark one answer
- [ ] A. Leave the motorway at the next exit
- [ ] B. All vehicles use the hard shoulder
- [ ] C. Sharp bend to the left ahead
- [ ] D. Stop, all lanes ahead closed

785 A white line like this along the centre of the road is a

Mark one answer
- [ ] A. bus lane marking
- [ ] B. hazard warning
- [ ] C. give way marking
- [ ] D. lane marking

786 What is the purpose of these yellow criss-cross lines on the road?

Mark one answer

- [ ] **A.** To make you more aware of the traffic lights
- [ ] **B.** To guide you into position as you turn
- [ ] **C.** To prevent the junction becoming blocked
- [ ] **D.** To show you where to stop when the lights change

787 What is the reason for the yellow criss-cross lines painted on the road here?

Mark one answer

- [ ] **A.** To mark out an area for trams only
- [ ] **B.** To prevent queuing traffic from blocking the junction on the left
- [ ] **C.** To mark the entrance lane to a car park
- [ ] **D.** To warn you of the tram lines crossing the road

788 What is the reason for the area marked in red and white along the centre of this road?

Mark one answer

- [ ] **A.** It is to separate traffic flowing in opposite directions
- [ ] **B.** It marks an area to be used by overtaking motorcyclists
- [ ] **C.** It is a temporary marking to warn of the road works
- [ ] **D.** It is separating the two sides of the dual carriageway

789 Other drivers may sometimes flash their headlights at you. In which situation are they allowed to do this?

Mark one answer

- [ ] **A.** To warn of a radar speed trap ahead
- [ ] **B.** To show that they are giving way to you
- [ ] **C.** To warn you of their presence
- [ ] **D.** To let you know there is a fault with your vehicle

790 At road works which of the following can control traffic flow?

Mark three answers

- [ ] **A.** A STOP–GO board
- [ ] **B.** Flashing amber lights
- [ ] **C.** A police officer
- [ ] **D.** Flashing red lights
- [ ] **E.** Temporary traffic lights

791 You are approaching a zebra crossing where pedestrians are waiting. Which arm signal might you give?

Mark one answer

- [ ] A. 
- [ ] B. 
- [ ] C. 
- [ ] D. 

792 The white line along the side of the road

Mark one answer

- [ ] A. shows the edge of the carriageway
- [ ] B. shows the approach to a hazard
- [ ] C. means no parking
- [ ] D. means no overtaking

793 You see this white arrow on the road ahead. It means

Mark one answer

- [ ] A. entrance on the left
- [ ] B. all vehicles turn left
- [ ] C. keep left of the hatched markings
- [ ] D. road bending to the left

794 How should you give an arm signal to turn left?

Mark one answer

- [ ] A. 
- [ ] B. 
- [ ] C. 
- [ ] D. 

795 You are waiting at a T-junction. A vehicle is coming from the right with the left signal flashing. What should you do?

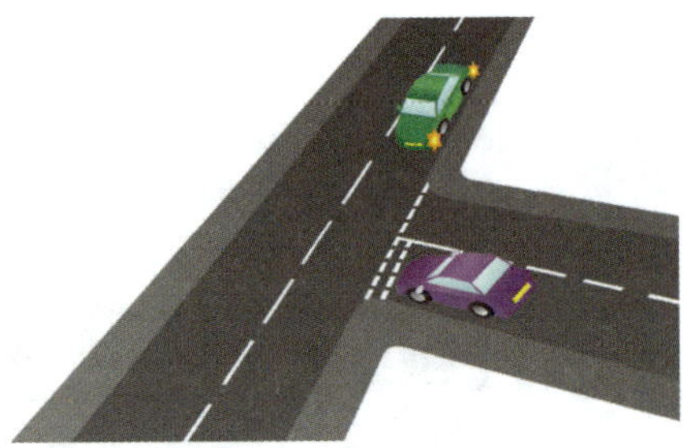

Mark one answer

- [ ] A. Move out and accelerate hard
- [ ] B. Wait until the vehicle starts to turn in
- [ ] C. Pull out before the vehicle reaches the junction
- [ ] D. Move out slowly

796 **When may you use hazard warning lights when driving?**

Mark one answer

- ☐ **A.** Instead of sounding the horn in a built-up area between 11.30pm and 7am
- ☐ **B.** On a motorway or unrestricted dual carriageway, to warn of a hazard ahead
- ☐ **C.** On rural routes, after a warning sign of animals
- ☐ **D.** On the approach to toucan crossings where cyclists are waiting to cross

797 **You are driving on a motorway. There is a slow-moving vehicle ahead. On the back you see this sign. You should**

Mark one answer

- ☐ **A.** pass on the right
- ☐ **B.** pass on the left
- ☐ **C.** leave at the next exit
- ☐ **D.** drive no further

798 **In some narrow residential streets you may find a speed limit of**

Mark one answer

- ☐ **A.** 20mph
- ☐ **B.** 25mph
- ☐ **C.** 35mph
- ☐ **D.** 40mph

799 **You should NOT normally stop on these markings near schools**

Mark one answer

- ☐ **A.** except when picking up children
- ☐ **B.** under any circumstances
- ☐ **C.** unless there is nowhere else available
- ☐ **D.** except to set down children

800 **Why should you make sure that your indicators are cancelled after turning?**

Mark one answer

- ☐ **A.** To avoid flattening the battery
- ☐ **B.** To avoid misleading other road users
- ☐ **C.** To avoid dazzling other road users
- ☐ **D.** To avoid damage to the indicator relay

801 **You are driving in busy traffic. You want to pull up on the left just after a junction on the left. When should you signal?**

Mark one answer

- ☐ **A.** As you are passing or just after the junction
- ☐ **B.** Just before you reach the junction
- ☐ **C.** Well before you reach the junction
- ☐ **D.** It would be better not to signal at all

802 An MOT certificate is normally valid for

Mark one answer

- [ ] **A.** three years after the date it was issued
- [ ] **B.** 10,000 miles
- [ ] **C.** one year after the date it was issued
- [ ] **D.** 30,000 miles

803 A cover note is a document issued before you receive your

Mark one answer

- [ ] **A.** driving licence
- [ ] **B.** insurance certificate
- [ ] **C.** registration document
- [ ] **D.** MOT certificate

804 A police officer asks to see your documents. You do not have them with you. You may produce them at a police station within

Mark one answer

- [ ] **A.** 5 days
- [ ] **B.** 7 days
- [ ] **C.** 14 days
- [ ] **D.** 21 days

805 You have just passed your practical test. You do not hold a full licence in another category. Within two years you get six penalty points on your licence. What will you have to do?

Mark two answers

- [ ] **A.** Retake only your theory test
- [ ] **B.** Retake your theory and practical tests
- [ ] **C.** Retake only your practical test
- [ ] **D.** Reapply for your full licence immediately
- [ ] **E.** Reapply for your provisional licence

806 To drive on the road learners MUST

Mark one answer

- [ ] **A.** have NO penalty points on their licence
- [ ] **B.** have taken professional instruction
- [ ] **C.** have a signed, valid provisional licence
- [ ] **D.** apply for a driving test within 12 months

807 Before driving anyone else's motor vehicle you should make sure that

Mark one answer

- [ ] **A.** the vehicle owner has third party insurance cover
- [ ] **B.** your own vehicle has insurance cover
- [ ] **C.** the vehicle is insured for your use
- [ ] **D.** the owner has left the insurance documents in the vehicle

808 Your car needs an MOT certificate. If you drive without one this could invalidate your

Mark one answer

- [ ] **A.** vehicle service record
- [ ] **B.** insurance
- [ ] **C.** road tax disc
- [ ] **D.** vehicle registration document

809 When is it legal to drive a car over three years old without an MOT certificate?

Mark one answer **NI**

- [ ] **A.** Up to seven days after the old certificate has run out
- [ ] **B.** When driving to an MOT centre to arrange an appointment
- [ ] **C.** Just after buying a second-hand car with no MOT
- [ ] **D.** When driving to an appointment at an MOT centre

810 To supervise a learner driver you must

Mark two answers

- [ ] **A.** have held a full licence for at least 3 years
- [ ] **B.** be at least 21 years old
- [ ] **C.** be an approved driving instructor
- [ ] **D.** hold an advanced driving certificate

811 How old must you be to supervise a learner driver?

Mark one answer

- [ ] **A.** 18 years old
- [ ] **B.** 19 years old
- [ ] **C.** 20 years old
- [ ] **D.** 21 years old

812 A newly qualified driver must

Mark one answer

- [ ] **A.** display green 'L' plates
- [ ] **B.** not exceed 40mph for 12 months
- [ ] **C.** be accompanied on a motorway
- [ ] **D.** have valid motor insurance

813 You have third party insurance. What does this cover?

Mark three answers

- [ ] **A.** Damage to your own vehicle
- [ ] **B.** Damage to your vehicle by fire
- [ ] **C.** Injury to another person
- [ ] **D.** Damage to someone's property
- [ ] **E.** Damage to other vehicles
- [ ] **F.** Injury to yourself

814 For which TWO of these must you show your motor insurance certificate?

Mark two answers

- [ ] **A.** When you are taking your driving test
- [ ] **B.** When buying or selling a vehicle
- [ ] **C.** When a police officer asks you for it
- [ ] **D.** When you are taxing your vehicle
- [ ] **E.** When having an MOT inspection

815 Vehicle excise duty is often called 'Road Tax' or 'The Tax Disc'. You must

Mark one answer

- [ ] **A.** keep it with your registration document
- [ ] **B.** display it clearly on your vehicle
- [ ] **C.** keep it concealed safely in your vehicle
- [ ] **D.** carry it on you at all times

816 Motor cars must first have an MOT test certificate when they are

Mark one answer **NI**

- [ ] **A.** one year old
- [ ] **B.** three years old
- [ ] **C.** five years old
- [ ] **D.** seven years old

817 Your vehicle needs a current MOT certificate. You do not have one. Until you do have one you will not be able to renew your

Mark one answer

- [ ] **A.** driving licence
- [ ] **B.** vehicle insurance
- [ ] **C.** road tax disc
- [ ] **D.** vehicle registration document

818 Which THREE pieces of information are found on a vehicle registration document?

Mark three answers

- [ ] **A.** Registered keeper
- [ ] **B.** Make of the vehicle
- [ ] **C.** Service history details
- [ ] **D.** Date of the MOT
- [ ] **E.** Type of insurance cover
- [ ] **F.** Engine size

819 You have a duty to contact the licensing authority when

Mark three answers

- A. you go abroad on holiday
- B. you change your vehicle
- C. you change your name
- D. your job status is changed
- E. your permanent address changes
- F. your job involves travelling abroad

820 You must notify the licensing authority when

Mark three answers

- A. your health affects your driving
- B. your eyesight does not meet a set standard
- C. you intend lending your vehicle
- D. your vehicle requires an MOT certificate
- E. you change your vehicle

821 Your vehicle is insured third party only. This covers

Mark two answers

- A. damage to your vehicle
- B. damage to other vehicles
- C. injury to yourself
- D. injury to others
- E. all damage and injury

822 Your motor insurance policy has an excess of £100. What does this mean?

Mark one answer

- A. The insurance company will pay the first £100 of any claim
- B. You will be paid £100 if you do not have an accident
- C. Your vehicle is insured for a value of £100 if it is stolen
- D. You will have to pay the first £100 of any claim

823 When you apply to renew your vehicle excise licence (tax disc) you must produce

Mark one answer

- A. a valid insurance certificate
- B. the old tax disc
- C. the vehicle handbook
- D. a valid driving licence

824 What is the legal minimum insurance cover you must have to drive on public roads?

Mark one answer

- A. Third party, fire and theft
- B. Comprehensive
- C. Third party only
- D. Personal injury cover

825 Which THREE of the following do you need before you can drive legally?

Mark three answers

- A. A valid driving licence with signature
- B. A valid tax disc displayed on your vehicle
- C. A vehicle service record
- D. Proper insurance cover
- E. Breakdown cover
- F. A vehicle handbook

826 The cost of your insurance may reduce if you

Mark one answer NI

- A. are under 25 years old
- B. do not wear glasses
- C. pass the driving test first time
- D. take the Pass Plus scheme

827 Which of the following may reduce the cost of your insurance?

Mark one answer NI

- A. Having a valid MOT certificate
- B. Taking a Pass Plus course
- C. Driving a powerful car
- D. Having penalty points on your licence

828 The Pass Plus scheme has been created for new drivers. What is its main purpose?

NI

Mark one answer
- [ ] **A.** To allow you to drive faster
- [ ] **B.** To allow you to carry passengers
- [ ] **C.** To improve your basic skills
- [ ] **D.** To let you drive on motorways

829 How long will a Statutory Off Road Notification (SORN) last for?

Mark one answer
- [ ] **A.** 12 months
- [ ] **B.** 24 months
- [ ] **C.** 3 years
- [ ] **D.** 10 years

830 What is a Statutory Off Road Notification (SORN) declaration?

NI

Mark one answer
- [ ] **A.** A notification to tell VOSA that a vehicle does not have a current MOT
- [ ] **B.** Information kept by the police about the owner of the vehicle
- [ ] **C.** A notification to tell DVLA that a vehicle is not being used on the road
- [ ] **D.** Information held by insurance companies to check the vehicle is insured

831 A Statutory Off Road Notification (SORN) declaration is

NI

Mark one answer
- [ ] **A.** to tell DVLA that your vehicle is being used on the road but the MOT has expired
- [ ] **B.** to tell DVLA that you no longer own the vehicle
- [ ] **C.** to tell DVLA that your vehicle is not being used on the road
- [ ] **D.** to tell DVLA that you are buying a personal number plate

832 You claim on your insurance to have your car repaired. Your policy has an excess of £100. What does this mean?

Mark one answer
- [ ] **A.** The insurance company will pay the first £100 of any claim
- [ ] **B.** You will be paid £100 if you do not claim within one year
- [ ] **C.** Your vehicle is insured for a value of £100 if it is stolen
- [ ] **D.** You will have to pay the first £100 of the cost of repair to your car

833 A Statutory Off Road Notification (SORN) is valid

Mark one answer
- [ ] **A.** for as long as the vehicle has an MOT
- [ ] **B.** for 12 months only
- [ ] **C.** only if the vehicle is more than 3 years old
- [ ] **D.** provided the vehicle is insured

834 A Statutory Off Road Notification (SORN) will last

Mark one answer
- [ ] **A.** for the life of the vehicle
- [ ] **B.** for as long as you own the vehicle
- [ ] **C.** for 12 months only
- [ ] **D..** until the vehicle warranty expires

835 What is the maximum specified fine for driving without insurance?

NI

Mark one answer
- [ ] **A.** £50
- [ ] **B.** £500
- [ ] **C.** £1000
- [ ] **D.** £5000

836 At the scene of an accident you should

Mark one answer

- ☐ **A.** not put yourself at risk
- ☐ **B.** go to those casualties who are screaming
- ☐ **C.** pull everybody out of their vehicles
- ☐ **D.** leave vehicle engines switched on

837 You are the first to arrive at the scene of an accident. Which FOUR of these should you do?

Mark four answers

- ☐ **A.** Leave as soon as another motorist arrives
- ☐ **B.** Switch off the vehicle engine(s)
- ☐ **C.** Move uninjured people away from the vehicle(s)
- ☐ **D.** Call the emergency services
- ☐ **E.** Warn other traffic

838 An accident has just happened. An injured person is lying in a busy road. What is the FIRST thing you should do to help?

Mark one answer

- ☐ **A.** Treat the person for shock
- ☐ **B.** Warn other traffic
- ☐ **C.** Place them in the recovery position
- ☐ **D.** Make sure the injured person is kept warm

839 You are the first person to arrive at an accident where people are badly injured. Which THREE should you do?

Mark three answers

- ☐ **A.** Switch on your own hazard warning lights
- ☐ **B.** Make sure that someone telephones for an ambulance
- ☐ **C.** Try and get people who are injured to drink something
- ☐ **D.** Move the people who are injured clear of their vehicles
- ☐ **E.** Get people who are not injured clear of the scene

840 You arrive at the scene of a motorcycle accident. The rider is injured. When should the helmet be removed?

Mark one answer

- ☐ **A.** Only when it is essential
- ☐ **B.** Always straight away
- ☐ **C.** Only when the motorcyclist asks
- ☐ **D.** Always, unless they are in shock

841 You arrive at a serious motorcycle accident. The motorcyclist is unconscious and bleeding. Your main priorities should be to

Mark three answers

- ☐ **A.** try to stop the bleeding
- ☐ **B.** make a list of witnesses
- ☐ **C.** check the casualty's breathing
- ☐ **D.** take the numbers of the vehicles involved
- ☐ **E.** sweep up any loose debris
- ☐ **F.** check the casualty's airways

842 **You arrive at an accident. A motorcyclist is unconscious. Your FIRST priority is the casualty's**

Mark one answer

- A. breathing
- B. bleeding
- C. broken bones
- D. bruising

843 **At an accident a casualty is unconscious. Which THREE of the following should you check urgently?**

Mark three answers

- A. Circulation
- B. Airway
- C. Shock
- D. Breathing
- E. Broken bones

844 **You arrive at the scene of an accident. It has just happened and someone is unconscious. Which of the following should be given urgent priority to help them?**

Mark three answers

- A. Clear the airway and keep it open
- B. Try to get them to drink water
- C. Check that they are breathing
- D. Look for any witnesses
- E. Stop any heavy bleeding
- F. Take the numbers of vehicles involved

845 **At an accident someone is unconscious. Your main priorities should be to**

Mark three answers

- A. sweep up the broken glass
- B. take the names of witnesses
- C. count the number of vehicles involved
- D. check the airway is clear
- E. make sure they are breathing
- F. stop any heavy bleeding

846 **You have stopped at the scene of an accident to give help. Which THREE things should you do?**

Mark three answers

- A. Keep injured people warm and comfortable
- B. Keep injured people calm by talking to them reassuringly
- C. Keep injured people on the move by walking them around
- D. Give injured people a warm drink
- E. Make sure that injured people are not left alone

847 **You arrive at the scene of an accident. It has just happened and someone is injured. Which THREE of the following should be given urgent priority?**

Mark three answers

- A. Stop any severe bleeding
- B. Get them a warm drink
- C. Check that their breathing is OK
- D. Take numbers of vehicles involved
- E. Look for witnesses
- F. Clear their airway and keep it open

848 **At an accident a casualty has stopped breathing. You should**

Mark two answers

- ☐ **A.** remove anything that is blocking the mouth
- ☐ **B.** keep the head tilted forwards as far as possible
- ☐ **C.** raise the legs to help with circulation
- ☐ **D.** try to give the casualty something to drink
- ☐ **E.** tilt the head back gently to clear the airway

849 **You are at the scene of an accident. Someone is suffering from shock. You should**

Mark four answers

- ☐ **A.** reassure them constantly
- ☐ **B.** offer them a cigarette
- ☐ **C.** keep them warm
- ☐ **D.** avoid moving them if possible
- ☐ **E.** avoid leaving them alone
- ☐ **F.** give them a warm drink

850 **Which of the following should you NOT do at the scene of an accident?**

Mark one answer

- ☐ **A.** Warn other traffic by switching on your hazard warning lights
- ☐ **B.** Call the emergency services immediately
- ☐ **C.** Offer someone a cigarette to calm them down
- ☐ **D.** Ask drivers to switch off their engines

851 **There has been an accident. The driver is suffering from shock. You should**

Mark two answers

- ☐ **A.** give them a drink
- ☐ **B.** reassure them
- ☐ **C.** not leave them alone
- ☐ **D.** offer them a cigarette
- ☐ **E.** ask who caused the accident

852 **You have to treat someone for shock at the scene of an accident. You should**

Mark one answer

- ☐ **A.** reassure them constantly
- ☐ **B.** walk them around to calm them down
- ☐ **C.** give them something cold to drink
- ☐ **D.** cool them down as soon as possible

853 **You arrive at the scene of a motorcycle accident. No other vehicle is involved. The rider is unconscious, lying in the middle of the road. The first thing you should do is**

Mark one answer

- ☐ **A.** move the rider out of the road
- ☐ **B.** warn other traffic
- ☐ **C.** clear the road of debris
- ☐ **D.** give the rider reassurance

854

At an accident a small child is not breathing. When giving mouth to mouth you should breathe

Mark one answer

- A. sharply
- B. gently
- C. heavily
- D. rapidly

855

To start mouth to mouth on a casualty you should

Mark three answers

- A. tilt their head forward
- B. clear the airway
- C. turn them on their side
- D. tilt their head back gently
- E. pinch the nostrils together
- F. put their arms across their chest

856

When you are giving mouth to mouth you should only stop when

Mark one answer

- A. you think the casualty is dead
- B. the casualty can breathe without help
- C. the casualty has turned blue
- D. you think the ambulance is coming

857

You arrive at the scene of an accident. There has been an engine fire and someone's hands and arms have been burnt. You should NOT

Mark one answer

- A. douse the burn thoroughly with cool liquid
- B. lay the casualty down
- C. remove anything sticking to the burn
- D. reassure them constantly

858

You arrive at an accident where someone is suffering from severe burns. You should

Mark one answer

- A. apply lotions to the injury
- B. burst any blisters
- C. remove anything stuck to the burns
- D. douse the burns with cool liquid

859

You arrive at the scene of an accident. A pedestrian has a severe bleeding wound on their leg, although it is not broken. What should you do?

Mark two answers

- A. Dab the wound to stop bleeding
- B. Keep both legs flat on the ground
- C. Apply firm pressure to the wound
- D. Raise the leg to lessen bleeding
- E. Fetch them a warm drink

860 **You arrive at the scene of an accident. A passenger is bleeding badly from an arm wound. What should you do?**

Mark one answer
- ☐ **A.** Apply pressure over the wound and keep the arm down
- ☐ **B.** Dab the wound
- ☐ **C.** Get them a drink
- ☐ **D.** Apply pressure over the wound and raise the arm

861 **You arrive at the scene of an accident. A pedestrian is bleeding heavily from a leg wound but the leg is not broken. What should you do?**

Mark one answer
- ☐ **A.** Dab the wound to stop the bleeding
- ☐ **B.** Keep both legs flat on the ground
- ☐ **C.** Apply firm pressure to the wound
- ☐ **D.** Fetch them a warm drink

862 **At an accident a casualty is unconscious but still breathing. You should only move them if**

Mark one answer
- ☐ **A.** an ambulance is on its way
- ☐ **B.** bystanders advise you to
- ☐ **C.** there is further danger
- ☐ **D.** bystanders will help you to

863 **At an accident you suspect a casualty has back injuries. The area is safe. You should**

Mark one answer
- ☐ **A.** offer them a drink
- ☐ **B.** not move them
- ☐ **C.** raise their legs
- ☐ **D.** offer them a cigarette

864 **At an accident it is important to look after the casualty. When the area is safe, you should**

Mark one answer
- ☐ **A.** get them out of the vehicle
- ☐ **B.** give them a drink
- ☐ **C.** give them something to eat
- ☐ **D.** keep them in the vehicle

865 **A tanker is involved in an accident. Which sign would show that the tanker is carrying dangerous goods?**

Mark one answer

☐ **A.**

☐ **B.**

☐ **C.**

☐ **D.**

866 **The police may ask you to produce which three of these documents following an accident?**

Mark three answers

- [ ] **A.** Vehicle registration document
- [ ] **B.** Driving licence
- [ ] **C.** Theory test certificate
- [ ] **D.** Insurance certificate
- [ ] **E.** MOT test certificate
- [ ] **F.** Road tax disc

867 **You see a car on the hard shoulder of a motorway with a HELP pennant displayed. This means the driver is most likely to be**

Mark one answer

- [ ] **A.** a disabled person
- [ ] **B.** first aid trained
- [ ] **C.** a foreign visitor
- [ ] **D.** a rescue patrol person

868 **On the motorway the hard shoulder should be used**

Mark one answer

- [ ] **A.** to answer a mobile phone
- [ ] **B.** when an emergency arises
- [ ] **C.** for a short rest when tired
- [ ] **D.** to check a road atlas

869 **For which TWO should you use hazard warning lights?**

Mark two answers

- [ ] **A.** When you slow down quickly on a motorway because of a hazard ahead
- [ ] **B.** When you have broken down
- [ ] **C.** When you wish to stop on double yellow lines
- [ ] **D.** When you need to park on the pavement

870 **When are you allowed to use hazard warning lights?**

Mark one answer

- [ ] **A.** When stopped and temporarily obstructing traffic
- [ ] **B.** When travelling during darkness without headlights
- [ ] **C.** When parked for shopping on double yellow lines
- [ ] **D.** When travelling slowly because you are lost

871 **You are on a motorway. A large box falls on to the road from a lorry. The lorry does not stop. You should**

Mark one answer

- [ ] **A.** go to the next emergency telephone and inform the police
- [ ] **B.** catch up with the lorry and try to get the driver's attention
- [ ] **C.** stop close to the box until the police arrive
- [ ] **D.** pull over to the hard shoulder, then remove the box

872 **There has been an accident. A motorcyclist is lying injured and unconscious. Why should you usually not attempt to remove their helmet?**

Mark one answer

- [ ] **A.** Because they may not want you to
- [ ] **B.** This could result in more serious injury
- [ ] **C.** They will get too cold if you do this
- [ ] **D.** Because you could scratch the helmet

873 **After an accident, someone is unconscious in their vehicle. When should you call the emergency services?**

Mark one answer

- [ ] **A.** Only as a last resort
- [ ] **B.** As soon as possible
- [ ] **C.** After you have woken them up
- [ ] **D.** After checking for broken bones

874 **An accident casualty has an injured arm. They can move it freely, but it is bleeding. Why should you get them to keep it in a raised position?**

Mark one answer

- [ ] **A.** Because it will ease the pain
- [ ] **B.** It will help them to be seen more easily
- [ ] **C.** To stop them touching other people
- [ ] **D.** It will help to reduce the bleeding

875 **You are going through a congested tunnel and have to stop. What should you do?**

Mark one answer

- [ ] **A.** Pull up very close to the vehicle in front to save space
- [ ] **B.** Ignore any message signs as they are never up to date
- [ ] **C.** Keep a safe distance from the vehicle in front
- [ ] **D.** Make a U-turn and find another route

876 **You are going through a tunnel. What should you look out for that warns of accidents or congestion?**

Mark one answer

- [ ] **A.** Hazard warning lines
- [ ] **B.** Other drivers flashing their lights
- [ ] **C.** Variable message signs
- [ ] **D.** Areas marked with hatch markings

877 **You are going through a tunnel. What systems are provided to warn of any accidents or congestion?**

Mark one answer

- [ ] **A.** Double white centre lines
- [ ] **B.** Variable message signs
- [ ] **C.** Chevron 'distance markers'
- [ ] **D.** Rumble strips

878 While driving, a warning light on your vehicle's instrument panel comes on. You should

Mark one answer

- ☐ **A.** continue if the engine sounds alright
- ☐ **B.** hope that it is just a temporary electrical fault
- ☐ **C.** deal with the problem when there is more time
- ☐ **D.** check out the problem quickly and safely

879 You have broken down on a two-way road. You have a warning triangle. You should place the warning triangle at least how far from your vehicle?

Mark one answer

- ☐ **A.** 5 metres (16 feet)
- ☐ **B.** 25 metres (82 feet)
- ☐ **C.** 45 metres (147 feet)
- ☐ **D.** 100 metres (328 feet)

880 You break down on a level crossing. The lights have not yet begun to flash. Which THREE things should you do?

Mark three answers

- ☐ **A.** Telephone the signal operator
- ☐ **B.** Leave your vehicle and get everyone clear
- ☐ **C.** Walk down the track and signal the next train
- ☐ **D.** Move the vehicle if a signal operator tells you to
- ☐ **E.** Tell drivers behind what has happened

881 Your vehicle has broken down on an automatic railway level crossing. What should you do FIRST?

Mark one answer

- ☐ **A.** Get everyone out of the vehicle and clear of the crossing
- ☐ **B.** Phone the signal operator so that trains can be stopped
- ☐ **C.** Walk along the track to give warning to any approaching trains
- ☐ **D.** Try to push the vehicle clear of the crossing as soon as possible

882 Your tyre bursts while you are driving. Which TWO things should you do?

Mark two answers

- ☐ **A.** Pull on the handbrake
- ☐ **B.** Brake as quickly as possible
- ☐ **C.** Pull up slowly at the side of the road
- ☐ **D.** Hold the steering wheel firmly to keep control
- ☐ **E.** Continue on at a normal speed

883 Which TWO things should you do when a front tyre bursts?

Mark two answers

- ☐ **A.** Apply the handbrake to stop the vehicle
- ☐ **B.** Brake firmly and quickly
- ☐ **C.** Let the vehicle roll to a stop
- ☐ **D.** Hold the steering wheel lightly
- ☐ **E.** Grip the steering wheel firmly

884 Your vehicle has a puncture on a motorway. What should you do?

Mark one answer

- [ ] **A.** Drive slowly to the next service area to get assistance
- [ ] **B.** Pull up on the hard shoulder. Change the wheel as quickly as possible
- [ ] **C.** Pull up on the hard shoulder. Use the emergency phone to get assistance
- [ ] **D.** Switch on your hazard lights. Stop in your lane

885 Which of these items should you carry in your vehicle for use in the event of an accident?

Mark three answers

- [ ] **A.** Road map
- [ ] **B.** Can of petrol
- [ ] **C.** Jump leads
- [ ] **D.** Fire extinguisher
- [ ] **E.** First aid kit
- [ ] **F.** Warning triangle

886 You are in an accident on a two-way road. You have a warning triangle with you. At what distance before the obstruction should you place the warning triangle?

Mark one answer

- [ ] **A.** 25 metres (82 feet)
- [ ] **B.** 45 metres (147 feet)
- [ ] **C.** 100 metres (328 feet)
- [ ] **D.** 150 metres (492 feet)

887 You have broken down on a two-way road. You have a warning triangle. It should be displayed

Mark one answer

- [ ] **A.** on the roof of your vehicle
- [ ] **B.** at least 150 metres (492 feet) behind your vehicle
- [ ] **C.** at least 45 metres (147 feet) behind your vehicle
- [ ] **D.** just behind your vehicle

888 You have stalled in the middle of a level crossing and cannot restart the engine. The warning bell starts to ring. You should

Mark one answer

- [ ] **A.** get out and clear of the crossing
- [ ] **B.** run down the track to warn the signal operator
- [ ] **C.** carry on trying to restart the engine
- [ ] **D.** push the vehicle clear of the crossing

889 You are on the motorway. Luggage falls from your vehicle. What should you do?

Mark one answer

- [ ] **A.** Stop at the next emergency telephone and contact the police
- [ ] **B.** Stop on the motorway and put on hazard lights while you pick it up
- [ ] **C.** Walk back up the motorway to pick it up
- [ ] **D.** Pull up on the hard shoulder and wave traffic down

890 You are on a motorway. When can you use hazard warning lights?

Mark two answers

- [ ] **A.** When a vehicle is following too closely
- [ ] **B.** When you slow down quickly because of danger ahead
- [ ] **C.** When you are towing another vehicle
- [ ] **D.** When driving on the hard shoulder
- [ ] **E.** When you have broken down on the hard shoulder

891 You are involved in an accident with another vehicle. Someone is injured. Your vehicle is damaged. Which FOUR of the following should you find out?

Mark four answers

- [ ] **A.** Whether the driver owns the other vehicle involved
- [ ] **B.** The other driver's name, address and telephone number
- [ ] **C.** The make and registration number of the other vehicle
- [ ] **D.** The occupation of the other driver
- [ ] **E.** The details of the other driver's vehicle insurance
- [ ] **F.** Whether the other driver is licensed to drive

892 You have broken down on a motorway. When you use the emergency telephone you will be asked

Mark three answers

- [ ] **A.** for the number on the telephone that you are using
- [ ] **B.** for your driving licence details
- [ ] **C.** for the name of your vehicle insurance company
- [ ] **D.** for details of yourself and your vehicle
- [ ] **E.** whether you belong to a motoring organisation

893 You lose control of your car and damage a garden wall. No one is around. What must you do?

Mark one answer **NI**

- [ ] **A.** Report the accident to the police within 24 hours
- [ ] **B.** Go back to tell the house owner the next day
- [ ] **C.** Report the accident to your insurance company when you get home
- [ ] **D.** Find someone in the area to tell them about it immediately

894 Your engine catches fire. What should you do first?

Mark one answer

- [ ] **A.** Lift the bonnet and disconnect the battery
- [ ] **B.** Lift the bonnet and warn other traffic
- [ ] **C.** Call the breakdown service
- [ ] **D.** Call the fire brigade

895 Before driving through a tunnel what should you do?

Mark one answer

- [ ] **A.** Switch your radio off
- [ ] **B.** Remove any sunglasses
- [ ] **C.** Close your sunroof
- [ ] **D.** Switch on windscreen wipers

896 You are driving through a tunnel and the traffic is flowing normally. What should you do?

Mark one answer

- [ ] **A.** Use parking lights
- [ ] **B.** Use front spot lights
- [ ] **C.** Use dipped headlights
- [ ] **D.** Use rear fog lights

897 **Before entering a tunnel it is good advice to**

Mark one answer

- [ ] **A.** put on your sunglasses
- [ ] **B.** check tyre pressures
- [ ] **C.** change to a lower gear
- [ ] **D.** tune your radio to a local channel

898 **You are driving through a tunnel. Your vehicle breaks down. What should you do?**

Mark one answer

- [ ] **A.** Switch on hazard warning lights
- [ ] **B.** Remain in your vehicle
- [ ] **C.** Wait for the police to find you
- [ ] **D.** Rely on CCTV cameras seeing you

899 **Your vehicle breaks down in a tunnel. What should you do?**

Mark one answer

- [ ] **A.** Stay in your vehicle and wait for the police
- [ ] **B.** Stand in the lane behind your vehicle to warn others
- [ ] **C.** Stand in front of your vehicle to warn oncoming drivers
- [ ] **D.** Switch on hazard lights then go and call for help immediately

900 **You have an accident while driving through a tunnel. You are not injured but your vehicle CANNOT be driven. What should you do first?**

Mark one answer

- [ ] **A.** Rely on other drivers phoning for the police
- [ ] **B.** Switch off the engine and switch on hazard lights
- [ ] **C.** Take the names of witnesses and other drivers
- [ ] **D.** Sweep up any debris that is in the road

901 **When driving through a tunnel you should**

Mark one answer

- [ ] **A.** Look out for variable message signs
- [ ] **B.** Use your air conditioning system
- [ ] **C.** Switch on your rear fog lights
- [ ] **D.** Always use your windscreen wipers

902 **What TWO safeguards could you take against fire risk to your vehicle?**

Mark two answers

- [ ] **A.** Keep water levels above maximum
- [ ] **B.** Carry a fire extinguisher
- [ ] **C.** Avoid driving with a full tank of petrol
- [ ] **D.** Use unleaded petrol
- [ ] **E.** Check out any strong smell of petrol
- [ ] **F.** Use low octane fuel

903 You are towing a small trailer on a busy three-lane motorway. All the lanes are open. You must

Mark two answers

- ☐ **A.** not exceed 60mph
- ☐ **B.** not overtake
- ☐ **C.** have a stabiliser fitted
- ☐ **D.** use only the left and centre lanes

904 Any load that is carried on a roof rack MUST be

Mark one answer

- ☐ **A.** securely fastened when driving
- ☐ **B.** carried only when strictly necessary
- ☐ **C.** as light as possible
- ☐ **D.** covered with plastic sheeting

905 You are planning to tow a caravan. Which of these will mostly help to aid the vehicle handling?

Mark one answer

- ☐ **A.** A jockey wheel fitted to the tow bar
- ☐ **B.** Power steering fitted to the towing vehicle
- ☐ **C.** Anti-lock brakes fitted to the towing vehicle
- ☐ **D.** A stabiliser fitted to the tow bar

906 If a trailer swerves or snakes when you are towing it you should

Mark one answer

- ☐ **A.** ease off the accelerator and reduce your speed
- ☐ **B.** let go of the steering wheel and let it correct itself
- ☐ **C.** brake hard and hold the pedal down
- ☐ **D.** increase your speed as quickly as possible

907 How can you stop a caravan snaking from side to side?

Mark one answer

- ☐ **A.** Turn the steering wheel slowly to each side
- ☐ **B.** Accelerate to increase your speed
- ☐ **C.** Stop as quickly as you can
- ☐ **D.** Slow down very gradually

908 On which TWO occasions might you inflate your tyres to more than the recommended normal pressure?

Mark two answers

- ☐ **A.** When the roads are slippery
- ☐ **B.** When driving fast for a long distance
- ☐ **C.** When the tyre tread is worn below 2mm
- ☐ **D.** When carrying a heavy load
- ☐ **E.** When the weather is cold
- ☐ **F.** When the vehicle is fitted with anti-lock brakes

909 A heavy load on your roof rack will

Mark one answer

- ☐ **A.** improve the road holding
- ☐ **B.** reduce the stopping distance
- ☐ **C.** make the steering lighter
- ☐ **D.** reduce stability

910 Are passengers allowed to ride in a caravan that is being towed?

Mark one answer

- ☐ **A.** Yes, if they are over 14
- ☐ **B.** No, not at any time
- ☐ **C.** Only if all the seats in the towing vehicle are full
- ☐ **D.** Only if a stabiliser is fitted

911 You are towing a caravan along a motorway. The caravan begins to swerve from side to side. What should you do?

Mark one answer

- [ ] **A.** Ease off the accelerator slowly
- [ ] **B.** Steer sharply from side to side
- [ ] **C.** Do an emergency stop
- [ ] **D.** Speed up very quickly

912 A trailer must stay securely hitched up to the towing vehicle. What additional safety device can be fitted to the trailer braking system?

Mark one answer

- [ ] **A.** Stabiliser
- [ ] **B.** Jockey wheel
- [ ] **C.** Corner steadies
- [ ] **D.** Breakaway cable

913 Overloading your vehicle can seriously affect the

Mark two answers

- [ ] **A.** gearbox
- [ ] **B.** steering
- [ ] **C.** handling
- [ ] **D.** battery life
- [ ] **E.** journey time

914 Who is responsible for making sure that a vehicle is not overloaded?

Mark one answer

- [ ] **A.** The driver of the vehicle
- [ ] **B.** The owner of the items being carried
- [ ] **C.** The person who loaded the vehicle
- [ ] **D.** The licensing authority

915 Which of these is a suitable restraint for a child under three years?

Mark one answer

- [ ] **A.** A child seat
- [ ] **B.** An adult holding a child
- [ ] **C.** An adult seat belt
- [ ] **D.** A lap belt

916 A child under three years is being carried in your vehicle. They should be secured in a restraint. Which of these is suitable?

Mark one answer

- [ ] **A.** An adult holding a child
- [ ] **B.** A lap belt
- [ ] **C.** A baby carrier
- [ ] **D.** An adult seat belt

Part 5
Glossary

Accelerate
To make the vehicle move faster by pressing the right-hand pedal.

Advanced stop lines
A marked area on the road at traffic lights, which permits cyclists or buses to wait in front of other traffic.

Adverse weather
Bad weather that makes driving difficult or dangerous.

Alert
Quick to notice possible hazards.

Anticipation
Looking out for hazards and taking action before a problem starts.

Anti-lock brakes
Brakes that stop the wheels locking so that you are less likely to skid on a slippery road.

Aquaplane
To slide out of control on a wet road surface.

Articulated vehicle
A long vehicle that is divided into two or more sections joined by cables.

Attitude
The way you think or feel, which affects the way you drive. Especially, whether you are patient and polite, or impatient and aggressive.

Automatic
A vehicle with gears that change by themselves as you speed up or slow down.

Awareness
Taking notice of the road and traffic conditions around you at all times.

Black ice
An invisible film of ice that forms over the road surface, creating very dangerous driving conditions.

Blind spot
The section of road behind you which you cannot see in your mirrors. You 'cover' your blind spot by looking over your shoulder before moving off or overtaking.

Brake fade
Loss of power to the brakes when you have been using them for a long time without taking your foot off the brake pedal. For example, when driving down a steep hill. The brakes will overheat and not work properly.

Braking distance
The distance you must allow to slow the vehicle in order to come to a stop.

Brow
The highest point of a hill.

Built-up area
A town, or place with lots of buildings.

Carriageway
One side of a road or motorway. A 'dual carriageway' has two lanes on each side of a central reservation.

Catalytic converter
A piece of equipment fitted in the exhaust system that changes harmful gases into less harmful ones.

Chicane
A sharp double bend that has been put into a road to make traffic slow down.

Child restraint
A child seat or special seat belt for children. It keeps them safe and stops them moving around in the car.

Clearway
A road where no stopping is allowed at any time. The sign for a clearway is a red cross in a red circle on a blue background.

Coasting
Driving a vehicle without using any of the gears. That is, with your foot on the clutch pedal and the car in neutral.

Commentary driving
Talking to yourself about what you see on the road ahead and what action you are going to take – an aid to concentration.

Comprehensive insurance
A motor insurance policy that pays for repairs even if you cause an accident.

Concentration
Keeping all your attention on your driving.

Conditions
How good or bad the road surface is, volume of traffic on the road, and what the weather is like.

Congestion
Heavy traffic that makes it difficult to get to where you want to go.

Consideration
Thinking about other road users and not just yourself. For example, letting another driver go first at a junction, or stopping at a zebra crossing to let pedestrians cross over.

Contraflow
When traffic on a motorway follows signs to move to the opposite carriageway for a short distance because of roadworks. (During a contraflow, there is traffic driving in both directions on the same side of the motorway.)

Coolant
Liquid in the radiator that removes heat from the engine.

Defensive driving
Driving safely without taking risks, looking out for hazards and thinking for others.

Disqualified
Stopped from doing something (eg driving) by law, because you have broken the law.

Distraction
Anything that stops you concentrating on your driving, such as chatting to passengers or on your mobile phone.

Document
An official paper or card, eg your driving licence.

Dual carriageway
One side of a road or motorway, with two lanes on each side of a central reservation.

Engine braking – see also gears
Using the low gears to keep your speed down. For example, when you are driving down a steep hill and you want to stop the vehicle running away. Using the gears instead of braking will help to prevent brake fade.

Environment
The world around us and the air we breathe.

Exceed
Go higher than an upper limit.

Exhaust emissions
Gases that come out of the exhaust pipe to form part of the outside air.

Field of vision
How far you can see in front and around you when you are driving.

Filler cap
Provides access to the vehicle's fuel tank, for filling up with petrol or diesel.

Fog lights
Extra bright rear (and sometimes front) lights which may be switched on in conditions of very poor visibility.You must remember to switch them off when visibility improves, as they can dazzle and distract other drivers.

Ford
A place in a stream or river which is shallow enough to drive across with care.

Four-wheel drive (4WD)
On a conventional vehicle, steering and engine speed affect just two 'drive' wheels. On 4WD, they affect all four wheels, ensuring optimum grip on loose ground.

Frustration
Feeling annoyed because you cannot drive as fast as you want to because of other drivers or heavy traffic.

Fuel consumption
The amount of fuel (petrol or diesel) that your vehicle uses. Different vehicles have different rates of consumption. Increased fuel consumption means using more fuel. Decreased fuel consumption means using less fuel.

Fuel gauge
A display or dial on the instrument panel that tells you how much fuel (petrol or diesel) you have left.

Gantry
An overhead platform like a high narrow bridge that displays electric signs on a motorway.

Gears
Control the speed of the engine in relation to the vehicle's speed. May be hand operated (manual) or automatically controlled. In a low gear (such as first or second) the engine runs more slowly. In a high gear (such as fourth or fifth), it runs more quickly. Putting the car into a lower gear as you drive can create the effect of engine braking – forcing the engine to run more slowly.

Handling
How well your vehicle moves or responds when you steer or brake.

Harass
To drive in away that makes other road users afraid.

Hard shoulder
The single lane to the left of the inside lane on a motorway, which is for emergency use only. You should not drive on the hard shoulder except in an emergency, or when there are signs telling you to use the hard shoulder because of roadworks.

Harsh braking (or harsh acceleration)
Using the brake or accelerator too hard so as to cause wear on the engine.

Hazard warning lights
Flashing amber lights which you should use only when you have broken down. On a motorway you can use them to warn other drivers behind of a hazard ahead.

High-sided vehicle
A van or truck with tall sides, or a tall trailer such as a caravan or horse-box, that is at risk of being blown off-course in strong winds.

Impatient
Not wanting to wait for pedestrians and other road users.

Inflate
To blow up – to put air in your tyres until they are at the right pressures.

Instrument panel
The car's electrical controls and gauges, set behind the steering wheel. Also called the dashboard.

Intimidate
To make someone feel afraid.

Involved
Being part of something. For example, being one of the drivers in an accident.

Jump leads
A pair of thick electric cables with clips at either end. You use it to charge a flat battery by connecting it to the live battery in another vehicle.

Junction
A place where two or more roads join.

Liability
Being legally responsible.

Manoeuvre
Using the controls to make your car move in a particular direction. For example turning, reversing or parking.

Manual
By hand. In a car that is a 'manual' or has manual gears, you have to change the gears yourself.

Maximum
The largest possible; 'maximum speed' is the highest speed allowed.

Minimum
The smallest possible.

Mirrors
Modern cars have a minimum of three rear view mirrors: one in the centre of the windscreen, and one on each front door. Additional mirrors may be required on longer vehicles, or when towing a high trailer such as a caravan. Some mirrors may be curved (convex or concave) to increase the field of vision. The mirror on the windscreen can be turned to anti-dazzle position, if glare from headlights behind creates a distraction.

Mobility
The ability to move around easily.

Monotonous
Boring. For example, a long stretch of motorway with no variety and nothing interesting to see.

MOT

The test that proves your car is safe to drive. Your MOT certificate is one of the important documents for your vehicle.

Motorway

A fast road that has two or more lanes on each side and a hard shoulder. Drivers must join or leave it on the left, via a motorway junction. Many kinds of slower vehicles – such as bicycles – are not allowed on motorways.

Multiple-choice questions

Questions with several possible answers where you have to try to choose the right one.

Observation

The ability to notice important information, such as hazards developing ahead.

Obstruct

To get in the way of another road user.

Octagonal

Having eight sides.

Oil level

The amount of oil needed for the engine to run effectively.The oil level should be checked as part of your regular maintenance routine, and the oil replaced as necessary.

Pedestrian

A person walking.

Pegasus crossing

An unusual kind of crossing. It has a button high up for horse riders to push (Pegasus was a flying horse in Greek legend).

Pelican crossing

A crossing with traffic lights that pedestrians can use by pushing a button. Cars must give way to pedestrians on the crossing while the amber light is flashing. You must give pedestrians enough time to get to the other side of the road.

Perception

Seeing or noticing (as in Hazard Perception).

Peripheral vision

The area around the edges of your field of vision.

Positive attitude

Being sensible and obeying the law when you drive.

Priority

The vehicle or other road user that is allowed by law to go first is the one that has priority.

Provisional licence

A first driving licence. all learner drivers must get one before they start having lessons.

Puffin crossing

A type of pedestrian crossing that does not have a flashing amber light phase.

Reaction time

The amount of time it takes you to see a hazard and decide what to do about it.

Red route

You see these in London and some other cities. Double red lines at the edge of the road tell you that you must not stop or park there at any time. Single red lines have notices with times when you must not stop or park. Some red routes have marked bays for either parking or loading at certain times.

Red warning triangle

An item of safety equipment to carry in your car in case you break down. You can place the triangle 45m behind your car on the same side of the road. It warns traffic that your vehicle is causing an obstruction. (Do not use these on motorways.)

Residential areas

Areas of housing where people live. The speed limit is 30mph or sometimes 20mph.

Road hump

A low bump built across the road to slow vehicles down. Also called 'sleeping policemen'.

Rumble strips

Raised strips across the road near a roundabout or junction that change the sound the tyres make on the road surface, warning drivers to slow down. They are also used on motorways to separate the main carriageway from the hard shoulder.

Safety margin
The amount of space you need to leave between your vehicle and the one in front so that you are not in danger of crashing into it if the driver slows down suddenly or stops. Safety margins have to be longer in wet or icy conditions.

Separation distance
The amount of space you need to leave between your vehicle and the one in front so that you are not in danger of crashing into it if the driver slows down suddenly or stops. The separation distance must be longer in wet or icy conditions.

Security coded radio
To deter thieves, a radio or CD unit which requires a security code (or pin number) to operate it.

Single carriageway
Generally, a road with one lane in each direction.

Skid
When the tyres fail to grip the surface of the road, the subsequent loss of control of the vehicle's movement is called a skid. Usually caused by harsh or fierce braking, steering or acceleration.

Snaking
Moving from side to side. This sometimes happens with caravans or trailers when you drive too fast, or they are not properly loaded.

Staggered junction
Where you drive cross another road. Instead of going straight across, you have to go a bit to the right or left.

Steering
Control of the direction of the vehicle. May be affected by road surface conditions: when the steering wheel turns very easily, steering is 'light', and when you have to pull hard on the wheel it is described as 'heavy'.

Sterile
Clean and free from bacteria.

Stopping distance
The time it takes for you to stop your vehicle – made up of 'thinking distance' and 'braking distance'.

Supervisor
Someone who sits in the passenger seat with a learner driver. They must be over 21 and have held a full driving licence for at least three years.

Tailgating
Driving too closely behind another vehicle – either to harass the driver in front or to help you in thick fog.

Tax disc
The disc you display on your windscreen to show that you have taxed your car (see Vehicle Excise Duty, below).

Thinking distance
The time it takes you to notice something and take the right action. You need to add thinking distance to your braking distance to make up your total stopping distance.

Third party insurance
An insurance policy that insures you against any claim by passengers or other persons for damage or injury to their person or property.

Toucan crossing
A type of pedestrian crossing that does not have a flashing amber light phase, and cyclists are allowed to ride across.

Tow
To pull something behind your vehicle. It could be a caravan or trailer.

Traffic calming measures
Speed humps, chicanes and other devices placed in roads to slow traffic down.

Tram
A public transport vehicle which moves along the streets on fixed rails, usually electrically powered by overhead lines.

Tread depth
The depth of the grooves in a car's tyres that help them grip the road surface. The grooves must all be at least 1.6mm deep.

Turbulence
Strong movement of air. For example, when a large vehicle passes a much smaller one.

Two-second rule

In normal driving, the ideal minimum distance between you and the vehicle in front can be timed using the 'two-second' rule. As the vehicle in front passes a fixed object (such as a signpost), say to yourself 'Only a fool breaks the two second rule'. It takes two seconds to say it. If you have passed the same object before you finish, you are too close – pull back.

Tyre pressures

The amount of air which must be pumped into a tyre in order for it to be correctly blown up.

Vehicle Excise Duty

The tax you pay for your vehicle so that you may drive it on public roads.

Vehicle Registration Document

A record of details about a vehicle and its owner.

Vehicle watch scheme

A system for identifying vehicles that may have been stolen.

Vulnerable

At risk of harm or injury.

Waiting restrictions

Times when you may not park or load your vehicle in a particular area.

Wheel balancing

To ensure smooth rotation at all speeds, wheels need to be 'balanced' correctly. This is a procedure done at a garage or tyre centre, when each wheel is removed for testing. Balancing may involve minor adjustment with the addition of small weights, to avoid wheel wobble.

Wheel spin

When the vehicle's wheels spin round out of control with no grip on the road surface.

Zebra crossing

A pedestrian crossing without traffic lights. It has an orange light, and is marked by black and white stripes on the road. Drivers must stop for pedestrians to cross.

Part 6
The Answers to the Theory Test Questions

ALERTNESS – SECTION 1

1 C	2 BDF	3 C	4 D	5 C	6 C	7 C	8 C	9 B
10 D	11 AC	12 ABCD	13 AD	14 AB	15 AB	16 ABCD	17 C	18 B
19 D	20 B	21 C	22 B	23 B	24 ABE	25 C	26 B	27 B
28 D	29 C	30 C	31 C	32 A	33 D	34 D		

ATTITUDE – SECTION 2

35 D	36 A	37 C	38 B	39 C	40 D	41 D	42 B	43 B
44 BCD	45 ABE	46 A	47 D	48 B	49 A	50 A	51 B	52 A
53 A	54 C	55 A	56 B	57 D	58 D	59 D	60 A	61 A
62 B	63 C	64 A	65 C	66 A	67 C	68 B	69 C	70 DE
71 B	72 D	73 B	74 C	75 AB	76 D	77 C	78 A	79 A
80 B	81 A	82 D						

SAFETY AND YOUR VEHICLE – SECTION 3

83 B	84 AB	85 ABF	86 BEF	87 C	88 ACF	89 C	90 B	91 D
92 C	93 D	94 D	95 D	96 A	97 AE	98 D	99 B	100 D
101 D	102 A	103 B	104 BCDF	105 D	106 D	107 BC	108 BC	109 A
110 D	111 A	112 B	113 B	114 D	115 C	116 D	117 D	118 D
119 B	120 B	121 B	122 D	123 ABF	124 ABC	125 ABC	126 BDF	127 ADE
128 BD	129 B	130 CDE	131 B	132 B	133 C	134 B	135 DE	136 A
137 C	138 B	139 D	140 D	141 D	142 B	143 C	144 A	145 B
146 D	147 A	148 C	149 A	150 B	151 AB	152 A	153 D	154 B
155 BCD	156 C	157 CD	158 A	159 A	160 D	161 C	162 B	163 B
164 B	165 D	166 ABE	167 ADE	168 D	169 A	170 B	171 C	172 D
173 A	174 B	175 C	176 D	177 A	178 C	179 D	180 B	181 B
182 A	183 A							

SAFETY MARGINS – SECTION 4

184 D	185 D	186 BC	187 B	188 D	189 D	190 C	191 B	192 C
193 A	194 ACE	195 B	196 A	197 B	198 A	199 B	200 AE	201 C
202 B	203 C	204 BDEF	205 B	206 D	207 A	208 C	209 A	210 AD
211 C	212 B	213 B	214 B	215 C	216 C	217 B	218 B	219 BC
220 C	221 C	222 B	223 C	224 D	225 BC	226 B	227 ACE	228 D
229 D	230 D	231 A	232 D	233 BD	234 D	235 B	236 A	237 D
238 A	239 B	240 B						

Answers to Questions

HAZARD AWARENESS – SECTION 5

241 D	242 CD	243 B	244 C	245 A	246 D	247 ACE	248 D	249 C
250 A	251 C	252 C	253 D	254 B	255 B	256 A	257 A	258 A
259 C	260 C	261 CD	262 A	263 B	264 A	265 C	266 BF	267 B
268 AE	269 A	270 D	271 D	272 C	273 B	274 B	275 C	276 A
277 B	278 B	279 CD	280 B	281 D	282 B	283 A	284 A	285 D
286 A	287 B	288 AE	289 C	290 B	291 BC	292 D	293 B	294 B
295 C	296 D	297 C	298 CD	299 AC	300 AB	301 A	302 A	303 B
304 A	305 ABC	306 C	307 C	308 C	309 ABE	310 C	311 D	312 D
313 C	314 C	315 D	316 ABD	317 ABC	318 D	319 C	320 AB	321 B
322 B	323 CD	324 D	325 ACE	326 ABE	327 A	328 A	329 D	330 D
331 A	332 D	333 A	334 A	335 ACD	336 B			

VULNERABLE ROAD USERS – SECTION 6

337 D	338 D	339 C	340 C	341 B	342 D	343 D	344 AD	345 B
346 C	347 D	348 A	349 D	350 D	351 B	352 D	353 B	354 D
355 D	356 C	357 AC	358 C	359 C	360 A	361 D	362 C	363 D
364 ABC	365 C	366 B	367 B	368 AC	369 ABD	370 B	371 D	372 A
373 A	374 D	375 D	376 A	377 A	378 C	379 C	380 C	381 D
382 ACE	383 D	384 B	385 A	386 C	387 D	388 C	389 C	390 A
391 D	392 D	393 A	394 A	395 B	396 B	397 D	398 C	399 C
400 B	401 C	402 AE	403 D	404 C	405 C	406 B	407 B	408 D
409 D	410 A	411 C	412 C	413 D	414 D	415 B	416 A	417 D
418 B	419 B	420 C						

OTHER TYPES OF VEHICLE – SECTION 7

421 B	422 A	423 A	424 B	425 B	426 D	427 B	428 A	429 BC
430 B	431 D	432 A	433 A	434 C	435 B	436 D	437 D	438 D
439 B	440 B	441 B	442 AC	443 BD	444 B	445 D		

VEHICLE HANDLING – SECTION 8

446 ACE	447 A	448 CD	449 D	450 A	451 BDF	452 C	453 D	454 C
455 DE	456 D	457 B	458 C	459 C	460 D	461 D	462 D	463 C
464 C	465 BD	466 BD	467 D	468 B	469 C	470 CE	471 C	472 D
473 A	474 A	475 C	476 B	477 ABDF	478 A	479 D	480 B	481 B
482 AB	483 BD	484 A	485 ACD	486 B	487 A	488 C	489 B	490 A
491 A	492 C	493 C	494 A	495 B	496 C	497 D	498 B	499 D
500 ABD	501 D	502 C	503 C	504 C	505 D	506 D	507 A	

MOTORWAY RULES – SECTION 9

508 ADEF	509 ADEF	510 D	511 D	512 D	513 D	514 A	515 B	516 C
517 BE	518 C	519 A	520 C	521 A	522 D	523 A	524 C	525 C
526 C	527 C	528 C	529 C	530 B	531 C	532 B	533 B	534 A
535 B	536 B	537 D	538 CDF	539 C	540 D	541 C	542 D	543 A
544 B	545 B	546 D	547 C	548 A	549 B	550 D	551 A	552 D
553 D	554 A	555 C	556 B	557 B	558 C	559 A	560 A	561 B
562 D	563 D	564 B	565 D	566 D	567 B	568 C	569 D	570 D
571 C								

RULES OF THE ROAD – SECTION 10

572 C	573 B	574 D	575 B	576 A	577 C	578 D	579 ADF	580 AD
581 A	582 B	583 A	584 B	585 A	586 D	587 A	588 D	589 D
590 C	591 A	592 ACE	593 B	594 C	595 D	596 BD	597 B	598 A
599 D	600 C	601 A	602 B	603 CDE	604 B	605 AE	606 B	607 A
608 ABD	609 A	610 B	611 B	612 A	613 D	614 A	615 D	616 C
617 D	618 D	619 BEF	620 D	621 D	622 D	623 C	624 C	625 D
626 A	627 A	628 A	629 C	630 B	631 A	632 D	633 AB	634 A
635 D	636 D	637 A	638 D	639 B	640 ABC	641 D	642 A	643 D
644 A	645 A							

ROAD AND TRAFFIC SIGNS – SECTION 11

646 D	647 D	648 A	649 A	650 B	651 A	652 D	653 B	654 D
655 D	656 D	657 A	658 C	659 B	660 D	661 C	662 B	663 A
664 B	665 B	666 C	667 C	668 A	669 C	670 B	671 C	672 B
673 D	674 D	675 C	676 D	677 C	678 B	679 C	680 D	681 A
682 D	683 B	684 D	685 B	686 A	687 A	688 A	689 A	690 B
691 B	692 A	693 D	694 ACEF	695 C	696 A	697 A	698 C	699 D
700 B	701 C	702 B	703 B	704 B	705 B	706 D	707 A	708 C
709 A	710 C	711 D	712 A	713 C	714 B	715 D	716 A	717 B
718 B	719 C	720 C	721 A	722 A	723 C	724 C	725 B	726 D
727 C	728 B	729 A	730 C	731 D	732 C	733 B	734 A	735 A
736 C	737 BDF	738 A	739 C	740 C	741 B	742 B	743 A	744 C
745 A	746 B	747 A	748 B	749 D	750 D	751 B	752 A	753 A
754 D	755 C	756 D	757 C	758 B	759 C	760 C	761 A	762 B
763 D	764 B	765 B	766 A	767 D	768 A	769 B	770 B	771 D
772 C	773 B	774 A	775 B	776 A	777 C	778 A	779 B	780 A
781 A	782 C	783 C	784 A	785 B	786 C	787 B	788 A	789 C
790 ACE	791 A	792 A	793 C	794 C	795 B	796 B	797 B	798 A
799 B	800 B	801 A						

DOCUMENTS – SECTION 12

802 C	803 B	804 B	805 BE	806 C	807 C	808 B	809 D	810 AB
811 D	812 D	813 CDE	814 CD	815 B	816 B	817 C	818 ABF	819 BCE
820 ABE	821 BD	822 D	823 A	824 C	825 ABD	826 D	827 B	828 C
829 A	830 C	831 C	832 D	833 B	834 C	835 D		

ACCIDENTS – SECTION 13

836 A	837 BCDE	838 B	839 ABE	840 A	841 ACF	842 A	843 ABD	844 ACE
845 DEF	846 ABE	847 ACF	848 AE	849 ACDE	850 C	851 BC	852 A	853 B
854 B	855 BDE	856 B	857 C	858 D	859 CD	860 D	861 C	862 C
863 B	864 D	865 B	866 BDE	867 A	868 B	869 AB	870 A	871 A
872 B	873 B	874 D	875 C	876 C	877 B	878 D	879 C	880 ABD
881 A	882 CD	883 CE	884 C	885 DEF	886 B	887 C	888 A	889 A
890 BE	891 ABCE	892 ADE	893 A	894 D	895 B	896 C	897 D	898 A
899 D	900 B	901 A	902 BE					

VEHICLE LOADING – SECTION 14

903 AD	904 A	905 D	906 A	907 D	908 BD	909 D	910 B	911 A
912 D	913 BC	914 A	915 A	916 C				